HOW SETTLERS GET AWAY WITH MURDER

Courtesy of Vanessa Moody Hans

Gloria Levina "Lee" Moody with her children,
Vanessa Moody Hans and Daniel Moody, September 1969.

HOW SETTLERS GET AWAY WITH MURDER

THE KILLING OF INDIGENOUS WOMEN AND TWO-SPIRIT PEOPLE IN THE AMERICAS

LIZA BLACK

BEACON PRESS, BOSTON

BEACON PRESS
24 Farnsworth Street
Boston, Massachusetts
www.beacon.org

Beacon Press books
are published under the auspices of
the Unitarian Universalist Association of Congregations.

Printed in the United States of America

29 28 27 26   8 7 6 5 4 3 2 1

This book is printed on acid-free paper that meets the uncoated paper ANSI/NISO specifications for permanence as revised in 1992.

Text design and composition by Kim Arney

Versions of material in this book previously appeared as "Native Mother, Native Daughter, Native Granddaughter: The Murder of Savanna Greywind and the Abduction of Haisley Jo," in *Gender and the American West*, ed. Susan Bernardin (Routledge, 2022), and Harvard Kennedy School published Carr Center Discussion Paper 2025-02, "Savanna Greywind: Motherhood, Murder, and Settler Colonialism," March 2025, at https://www.hks.harvard.edu/centers/carr/publications/savanna-greywind-motherhood-murder-and-settler-colonialism.

Library of Congress Cataloging-in-Publication Data is available for this title.
ISBN: 978-0-8070-2477-5;
e-book: 978-0-8070-2478-2;
audiobook: 978-0-8070-2551-2

The authorized representative in the EU for product safety and compliance is Easy Access System Europe 16879218, Mustamäe tee 50, 10621 Tallinn, Estonia: https://beacon.org/eu-contact.

CONTENTS

AUTHOR'S NOTE

In 2017 I was teaching a Native history course. One student disrupted every lecture, enraged by critiques of assimilation policies and the Dakota Access Pipeline protests. When we read Sarah Deer's *The Beginning and End of Rape*, he unraveled. During his group's presentation on her statistics chapter, he called Deer a fraud, rejected her statistics from government agencies, and nearly brawled with non-white classmates. Later he made a website attacking me and Deer.

I wondered if I should stop teaching that content.

Instead, I added more, and from that decision, this book grew. In searching for materials to challenge that skepticism, I found something else: videos, blog posts, and social media announcements created by the families of victims. These heartfelt messages presented their grassroots research on the cases. Their posts often yielded fewer than fifty views, sometimes even fewer than ten. Their dedication inspired this book. They were doing the research.

Their quiet labor—posting those videos with a handful of views—poses a fundamental question: Why read a book about people whose names have gone unnoticed, whose stories have never or barely been told? What value does a meticulously researched timeline of their cases hold? For the families and activists, that full timeline represents a more complete narrative—a truth hard-won against the state's monopoly on the official record. The families possess knowledge but lack access to the levers of the legal system and the gates of the publishing industry. The state, for its part, seems to lack the will to disclose the full evidence. Thus, the evidence remains fragmented, hidden in plain sight.

This book, then, acts as a scholarly assemblage. By triangulating sources the state never meant to be parsed or read together—police reports, coroner's records, court documents, and oral histories—it offers readers, the families of victims, and their communities a fuller timeline. No other work has assembled these particular sources in this way to make these claims. This book does not merely represent past accounts. This book presents a reassemblage: read against the grain, parsed, dissected, and pulled apart to make claims that have never been made. As a work of history, the book offers something far different from the true-crime genre. The book avoids sensationalism, instead seeking to document.

This approach also speaks to a question within academia, an industry often focused on producing new scholarship from previous scholarship, keeping the conversation within known topics and authors. Within that expectation, what does this book contribute? The book answers a stark challenge: If those who care lack a platform, and those with platforms control the narrative, who else, if not someone with access to both academic training and publishing—will pursue and prepare the evidence? This book offers an answer.

Some notes on approach and terminology.

A word of caution: Please exercise care while reading. Some of the content may be disturbing, especially chapters 2, 4, and 5. The book refrains from unnecessarily graphic or gratuitous descriptions of violence but uses correct terminology to avoid sanitizing history. At times, the book provides some details to document patterns and similarities between killings. Chapters 2 and 4 deal with s--ual assault. Chapter 3 shows patterns in violence against Navajo people. Chapter 5 discusses violence against mothers.

All that follows is alleged.

Lastly, an explanation of terminology. The movement to end this violence uses a number of different acronyms for missing and murdered Indigenous people: MMIW for women, MMIWG to include girls, MMIWG2S to include Two-Spirit people, MMIWGT to include trans people, MMIP for people, and MMIR for relatives. Each acronym reflects a community's priorities. When the movement began, activists mostly used MMIW. Later, many began adding a *G* for girls and a *2S* for Two-Spirit people. Others prefer to think of the crisis with no reference to gender or sexuality, using MMIR or MMIP. This book includes chapters on Native and Indigenous women and Two-Spirit people. The book does not use any of these acronyms.

INTRODUCTION

A HISTORICAL INTERROGATION

Researching this book required a form of historical combat. Archives exist not as neutral repositories but rather battlegrounds where evidence can be buried alive. They act as the curated documents of the powerful, the meticulously kept logs of the state, records designed to show a world where violence never happened if it never appeared in writing. We live in a culture that asks perpetrators for their calendars, as if a man would notate his own crime; a culture that believes the carefully archived alibi of a Brett Kavanaugh over the memory of a Christine Blasey Ford, a disbelief so pervasive it becomes a national punchline on *Saturday Night Live*.

To excavate evidence, I became a forensic sapper, disinterring what bureaucrats planted deep. Every request for records turned into a request the state claimed was unclear and confusing, and I never knew whether the next page would detonate, arrive redacted, be "lost," or be handed over with corrupted files. Writing this book meant watching as new traps snapped shut behind me. The violence exists not just in the killings; violence surfaces in record making and keeping as well. The cases that follow have been excavated against this active resistance.

The story of the Americas tells not just of injustice; it constitutes a crime. The violence against Indigenous women and Two-Spirit people and the movement to end it represents no metaphor. The crisis represents an ongoing historical pattern. *How Settlers Get Away with Murder* explores not an idea; it investigates a crime scene that remains active. *How Settlers Get Away with Murder* examines crimes against Native women and Two Spirit people, guided by one central truth: The Americas have functioned as a crime scene. *How Settlers Get Away with Murder* begins with that truth. The Americas were built on theft and violence that continues today. From the first moments of colonization to today's courtroom rulings, the Americas have been shaped by violence, theft, and erasure. Native women and Two-Spirit people have been the most frequent targets of that violence, and their stories have been silenced or forgotten.

These cases exist not as isolated tragedies. They provide the foundation on which the Americas, including Canada, the United States, and Mexico, built themselves. The Americas did not coincidentally harm Native people; the nations within the Americas built themselves on that harm, and they continue to produce violence. *How Settlers Get Away with Murder* reexamines historic crimes against Native women and Two-Spirit people. My focus centers on the gendered and colonial nature of the violence, which disproportionately targets those perceived as feminine and Native or Indigenous.

The Americas maintain violence through narrative arbitrage. The word "arbitrage," in its original use in Europe, meant the resolution of legal disputes. Later, "arbitrage," referred to the financial exploitation of under- and over-valued markets for profit. Tech bros popularized the term narrative arbitrage in the first decades of the twenty-first century to describe assets that are mispriced based on their narrative, or perception. My book uses the term "narrative arbitrage" to think through the narrative gaps between the state's narrative, the victim's narrative, and the emergent narrative between the two. In *How Settlers Get Away with Murder*, the state exploits their control over the public narrative of the killings. The state engages in narrative warfare, ensuring that some narrative threads are pushed to the fore while others are silenced. My book provides a historical accounting, serving as the emergent narrative between the state and victims' narratives. The book refuses the state's economy of silence. It pursues a forensic history that considers all evidence, all possibilities, and especially Native voices, even and especially when they conflict with the state's narrative.

How Settlers Get Away with Murder merges academic critique and historical investigation into a forensic-historic hybrid that dismantles state narratives using state records and oral history. With meticulous rigor, the book reconstructs each case, dissecting files and challenging official narratives to expose how media and law conspire to protect settler killers. This approach traces patterns of state-enabled violence while centering what conventional true crime erases: the systems that disappear Native women and the families fighting for answers.

How Settlers Get Away with Murder refuses euphemisms. Like the activists in Winnipeg demanding that authorities "Search the Landfill" for missing and murdered Indigenous women, this book finds purpose not in dwelling on damage but in detailing the structures that produce it. Carefully studying these cases stands as an act of defiance: naming what was designed to operate in obscurity, and in doing so, reclaiming the narrative as both weapon and witness. As Unangax̂ scholar Eve Tuck reminds us, resistance research must center desire and decenter damage. This book answers that call by treating evidence as liberation rather than lament.[1]

With an ensemble of characters, including oil field workers, roofers, police officers, soldiers, attorneys, and judges, *How Settlers Get Away with Murder* tells histories of Native people and their deadly encounters with settlers. Instead of blaming Native victims, this book looks to the state as the key that unlocks the cases of missing and murdered Indigenous women and Two-Spirit people. These deaths have come to be seen through extensive and expensive studies conducted by the state. That conclusion comes close to blaming the victim by depicting Native history as a tragic story in which Native people were left damaged by colonialism and the state. This book challenges the idea that the crisis should be viewed only as tragic or sad. The book asks a harder question: How has the state made Native women and Two-Spirit people targets for violence? The book points to power. Power moves in silence and invisibility. This book reveals power's concealed actions. Writing *How Settlers Get Away with Murder* has often felt like walking through a crime scene, searching for what really happened and for the people only their families seem to remember. This book wades through the reverberations of crimes against Native women and Two-Spirit people to find the events at the heart of these murders and to trace all that unfolded after.[2]

Much of the conversation about the crisis in the United States centers on the jurisdictional quagmire among tribal, state, and federal authorities on reservations. This book argues otherwise: Settler jurisdiction cleared the path for violence. Across the Americas, every person exists under overlapping jurisdictions; police agencies routinely collaborate across borders to solve crimes—from Interpol operations to multistate task forces. The settler nation's claim to Native and Indigenous lands and its consequent claim of jurisdiction over said land fueled the crisis. This book argues that the US began making systematic efforts to prevent tribal nations and police officers from investigating, charging, or incarcerating settlers on tribal lands as early as 1885, if not earlier. Chapter 1 demonstrates this incursion of federal power into the Cherokee Reservation and stands as the only case in the book that took place on a reservation, reserve, or autonomous zone. The remaining chapters take place on land defined by the nation-state as that of the settler nation. On land controlled by the nation-state, including Canada and Mexico, Native women and Two-Spirit people moved fully into the jurisdiction of the state, where the same state that failed to prosecute settlers for violence against Indigenous people on their own territory claimed sole authority over their cases. Together, these cases reveal the pattern: When authorities identify the victim as Native and the perpetrator as a settler, jurisdiction becomes a weapon regardless of whether the victim was murdered on Native or Indigenous territory as perceived by the settler state. Over the long twentieth century, settler nations in the US, Canada, and Mexico have ensured that their governments controlled any cases involving settler perpetrators, regardless of where the murder occurred.

In choosing the five cases, I sought breadth geographically and temporally. As a historian, I wanted as much temporal span as I could achieve, seeking cases since 1492 with enough documentation that I could write an entire chapter. *How Settlers Get Away with Murder* exposes how the machinery of murder evolved within modern legal and bureaucratic systems; while the violence stretches back to first contact, the depth of evidence required for a microhistory often eludes us for earlier periods. Thus, my earliest microhistory begins in 1908. From there we jump forward to 1969, then 2001, 2007, and 2017. The book moves sequentially from chapter to chapter. Each chapter offers a brief history of the tribal nation.

The book includes one nonbinary Native person, as Two-Spirit people experience even higher rates of violence than cishet Native women. The book also reflects the age spectrum and includes an Indigenous elder. The book's structure uses one microhistory per chapter as a way into larger questions, with each chapter illustrating and illuminating one cause of the crisis, while centering the victim's story within their nation's tribal history. Some questions will have to go unanswered, but they must be asked. With great purpose and thought, I have chosen the victims' names as the chapter titles in an effort to place Native women and Two-Spirit people at the center of this history. By telling these stories of loss, I hope to replace silence with evidence, and evidence with conclusions.

Yet even as colonial systems perpetuate harm, Native women and their allies refuse to surrender. Across the Americas, Indigenous-led organizations are reclaiming power and rewriting narratives. Groups like the Native Women's Society of the Great Plains, under Amanda Takes War Bonnet's leadership, safeguard cultural sovereignty, while the Sovereign Bodies Institute exposes gendered violence and demands accountability. In New Mexico, Indigenous Women Rising champions reproductive justice, echoing the work of Katsi Cook, Mohawk midwife and founder of Canada's National Aboriginal Council of Midwives, which centers Indigenous health and bodily autonomy. From Mexico's Lucha Mixteca to Argentina's Coordinadora Nacional de Mujeres Indígenas and Peru's Organización Nacional de Mujeres Indígenas Andinas y Amazónicas del Perú, Indigenous women dismantle colonial legacies through advocacy, land defense, and community care. The Missing and Murdered Indigenous Women's Inquiry in Canada never would have happened without the organizing efforts of the National Women's Association of Canada. Their resistance matters. This book acts as a response to and documentation of the structures that protect settler violence against Indigenous women and Two-Spirit people. Through forensic attention to specific crimes and their perpetrators, this book exposes how settlers get away with murder and how the system continues to protect them.

Chapter 1 begins on the Cherokee Reservation in the 1880s, when Congress generated tribal rolls, allotted tribal lands, and seized the rest. The Major Crimes Act of 1885 plays a major role in this chapter, setting the stage for the hiding of the settler perpetrator's name. Looking at the life of a Cherokee woman immersed in her community and family, Lydia Kingfisher, this chapter explores the world of early twentieth-century eastern Oklahoma as a place where attorneys and settlers took advantage of Native women through American law. Chapter 2 moves to British Columbia in Canada. This murder took place far from the victim's traditional lands and explores the role of the state in the abduction and murder of a Nuxalk woman in 1969. Murdered far from her nation's territory, she visited the city that held full jurisdiction over her case. For nearly six decades, the state has concealed the names of the perpetrators. Chapter 3 addresses the case of a Two-Spirit Diné person who was murdered in 2001 in Cortez, Colorado, many miles outside of the boundaries of the Navajo Reservation. Although the case was closed with a conviction on record, chapter 3 reinvestigates all aspects of the case and gives new insights and evidence into the murder of the youngest LGBTQ+ victim of homicide as of 2001, documenting the investigation and court proceedings. Chapter 4 investigates the 2007 murder of an elderly Indigenous woman in the hills of Tetlatzinga in the state of Veracruz, Mexico. At the time, she lived in an Indigenous-majority territory with only partial Indigenous control, where the Mexican president held the power to position federal soldiers on what they see as Mexican, not Indigenous, land. The chapter explores the timeline of events after the attack, highlighting the contradictions and suggesting the culpability of the state in protecting the assailants of Ernestina Ascension. Chapter 5 takes the reader to 2017 and the murder of a pregnant Native woman and the abduction of her unborn child by her neighbors in a city many miles from her parents' reservations. Police and the state consider this a solved case with convictions. However, the book reexplores all aspects of the case, examining state interventions that served to re-abduct Savanna's baby and protect one of her killers. The only case in the book that takes places on a reservation, reserve, or autonomous Indigenous zone lies in the first chapter.

This book reopens cases to ask a question: What does the evidence reveal? The state acted and continues to act as an enemy of Native women. By "state," I mean the nation-states of Canada, the US, and Mexico, and their military, police, national and state bureaucrats and bureaucracies, government medical care, and government educational systems. But by "state," I also mean the citizens who pursue violence against Native women and Two-Spirit people. As Mohawk scholar Audra Simpson writes, "States do not always have to kill, its citizens can do that for it."[3] Thus, the state includes the nation, individual states and provinces, all aspects of their governments, and their citizens.[4]

In the Americas, Native communities exist both within and without the nation-state. Native communities operate outside the nation-state through a constant stance of refusal. Yet they exist within as the nation-state asserts nearly full legal and physical control over Native communities. Nation-states of the Americas did not just ignore Native people; they treated them like enemies through war and incarceration. For example, in the US, the original Bureau of Indian Affairs was housed in the Department of War. Canada formed the Royal Canadian Mounted Police for the purpose of defeating and subduing First Nations peoples. Native people continue to be seen as threats to the state today. The Zapatistas in southern Mexico were seen and treated as threats to the state. Activists at the Dakota Access Pipeline were seen and treated as threats to the state. Activists on Wet'suwet'en territory were seen and treated as threats to the state. Even those who search for the missing and murdered are seen as enemies of the state. Being surveilled, stalked, and harassed because of her relentless quest to find the dead and expose their assailants, Lissa Yellow Bird of Three Affiliated Tribes asserts: "I'm perceived as an enemy of the state. I'm a threat."[5]

In 2016 the National Institute of Justice in the US documented the alarming and often cited statistic: Four out of five Native women will experience violence in their lifetime. And Native women suffer the highest rate of sexual assault in the country. These staggering rates reflect a unique double burden: Native women face violence from within their communities and, with even greater impunity, from settler men with the privilege to target anyone and receive protection from consequences for that violence. This book zooms in on individual lives to show what these statistics mean at the micro level. This violence stretches across the US, Canada, and Mexico, tied together by the same state systems. Looking at these five cases helps us see how deeply violence is structured into the systems that govern Native life.[6]

How Settlers Get Away with Murder suggests that Native and Indigenous women face femicide because of ideas rooted in colonial culture, including laws and systems that protect assailants instead of victims, the dispossession of Native people, the stripping of tribal authority over tribal lands and peoples, the introduction of poverty into Native communities, the continued occupation of foreign police and military on tribal lands, and late-stage capitalism's grip on Native women who are swept into spaces outside their tribal communities where only settlers are meant to thrive and Native women are marked as those already discarded. Although Native communities in the Americas face serious crises—such as losses of treaty rights, water rights, land, culture, and language; forced relocation; human trafficking; environmental devastation; intergenerational trauma from prisons for children (aka boarding schools); lack of access to traditional foods and medical care; poverty and starvation—the crisis of missing and murdered Native and Indigenous women and Two-Spirit people must be seen as central to these devastating realities. This crisis does not represent another item on a list. The crisis connects to each loss Indigenous communities face today, from land to language to life itself. *How Settlers Get Away with Murder* looks to the state as a threat to Native women, not a hero or savior. As scholar Sherene Razack writes, "The fiction, therefore, that they [state professionals] cannot attend to the matter of 'who did it,' brackets the involvement of state professionals in acts of murder or neglect and keeps the discussion in the more abstract realm of devising better systems of care and vigilance over dysfunctional bodies and a dying race."[7]

How Settlers Get Away with Murder takes aim at the idea that the law embodies morality. Europeans colonized the Americas and used the law to pave their way into Indigenous homelands by enshrining private property and refusing Native jurisdiction. With the transition from colonies to nations, the former colonies held tribal nations back from exercising full control over their lands and peoples. Canadian, Mexican, and US laws function as legal fictions that justify and perpetuate Native dispossession and violence against Indigenous peoples.[8]

Systemic violence against Native women and Two-Spirit people began with the colonization of what Emil Keme, the K'iche' Maya scholar, suggests we call Abiayala, otherwise known as the Americas. Abiayala represents the ancestral name of the Western Hemisphere for the Indigenous Guna people in present-day Panama. Sarah Deer, a Muskogee scholar, points to Christopher Columbus to locate the first moments of violence by European men against Native women and girls. She highlights Michele de Cuneo's 1492 sexual assault of an unnamed Indigenous girl living as his captive, which he wrote of in a letter, to historicize the relationship between Native women's bodies and colonization. Deer continues this line of thinking to reinterpret historic battles and wars between tribal nations and European powers as having been caused by European men assaulting, disappearing, and killing the female relatives of Native men. European men viewed and used Native women's bodies as vehicles for violence from the inception of colonization. Many women's historians would agree with this in the broadest terms, and their writings show how Native women's status, positions, and opportunities declined in the crucible of colonization. Yet those same historians make much of Native women's roles in new, precapitalist economies of the Americas, finding themselves as valuable speakers of many languages, working as interpreters, processors of animal carcasses, and creators and sellers of their arts. These scholars point to Native women's skills to suggest that this positioned them such that European men needed them prior to the reign of capitalism, giving the women power and position to maintain value and importance in their interactions with European men.[9]

But even the most optimistic see a severe historic shift for Native women at the end of the nineteenth century, in the US especially, with the birth of boarding schools (a.k.a. prisons for children), a new form of land theft called "allotment," confinement on reservations, and widespread poverty on lands with a dominant population of Native people. This only worsened moving into the twentieth century as Native women additionally experienced forced sterilization, environmental extraction on their tribal homelands, and the US government's efforts to relocate them to cities far from their extended families and tribal communities. Where Native women possessed valuable skills in the seventeenth, eighteenth, and nineteenth centuries used by European traders and conquerors in what became the US, Canada, and Mexico, in the capitalist context of the twentieth century, Native women faced a predicament in finding economic paths to security and safety while navigating intergenerational trauma, anti-Native racism, and misogyny from settler cultures surrounding them. For some women, this meant limited opportunities in the tourist industry, often connected to sales of arts and crafts—whereas for others in cities, work opportunities could be found in service industries, such as clerk positions, cosmetology, and domestic work. Late-twentieth-century capitalism and governmental policies pushed Native women out of their communities and into cities where some thrived, but others faced a decidedly deadly environment. For Two-Spirit people, settlers rejected and sought to eliminate them from the beginning of contact. By the twentieth century, living openly as a Two-Spirit Native person, especially with feminine markers, meant a higher chance of violence or death.[10]

The crisis of missing and murdered Indigenous women and Two-Spirit people demonstrates the logic of occupation, the founding principal of settler colonialism. Built into the structures that govern Native people in the United States, Canada, and Mexico, the tenets of occupation include violence through law, policing, capitalism, and even discourse. Occupation functions by way of violence. This occupation extends itself into the everyday lives of Native people as they clean the trailers of the occupiers working on fracking wells or tend their sheep in the hills while soldiers watch nearby. Native people lack access to the self-defense, protection, and impunity enjoyed by settlers, which doubles the effects of settler power to control and direct Native land and life.

Transforming Indigenous spaces into settler space required eliminating Native people through war, murder, and incarceration. *How Settlers Get Away with Murder* shows how the state upholds violence against Native people. This book draws on the work of Chickasaw scholar Shannon Speed who sees the fusion of white supremacy and settler colonialism in violence against Indigenous women. Speed insists this fusion cannot protect Native women, and the settler-colonial state will continue to fail to protect and, thus, do harm to Native women. The settler state claimed, upon arrival, an intention to build a better society. But this better world excluded Native peoples, and women and Two-Spirit people most of all. As imperialism cast a wide net to enable financial gains, settler colonialism supported this system to ensure that economic relations were lopsided in favor of Europeans. Settler colonialism worked to control and extract submission from Indigenous peoples, without which imperialism and colonialism could not function. Some may question the book's inclusion of Mexico. But settler colonialism describes any project where outsiders come to stay, claim Indigenous land, and erase Indigenous governance. Mexico fits that frame.[11]

True crime generates billions of dollars annually, yet its profits are built on a selective gaze. Investors reap rewards from a genre that sidesteps the concept of structural violence—the very systems of imperialism, colonialism, and white supremacy that produce the violence it claims to merely document. To grasp the perverse economics of this consumption, consider that the true-crime industry, largely consumed by women, generates an estimated $5 billion annually. This vast figure is dwarfed by the profits of the sports industry in the Americas, a world of violence-themed entertainment largely consumed by men, which rakes in over $80 billion a year. This gender and genre-based disparity serves as a testament to what we value as a culture: We will fund empires of violence, but not justice for the murdered. True crime narrows its gaze relentlessly. It creates mostly white landscapes where white victims are martyrs and white murderers are villains. But true crime also applauds the state without question, rarely presenting evidence that contradicts the narrative presented by the state. Further, true crime's popularity hinges on simplistic narratives that focus on individual psychopathy. By centering white pain and obscuring structures of power, the genre indirectly tells its audience that only some lives and deaths deserve a story, while the murders of Native women and Two-Spirit people are deemed unprofitable.

The US media fails to tell the stories of those most impacted by violence. True-crime followers in the United States devour stories about missing white women and even injured or threatened white women, yet murder does not place in the top ten causes of death for white women in the US. Despite the disparity in statistics, the media covers the stories of white women far beyond those of women of color. Journalist Gwen Ifill called this "missing white woman syndrome" at a 2004 conference, and, decades later, this description continues to accurately describe the reality wherein those who experience violence the most are covered the least. Ifill diagnosed the crisis of racialized, gendered violence, observing that the cases involving white women and girls receive a disproportionate amount of media attention and compassion. This leads to law enforcement and the public focusing on those cases, resulting in leads, arrests, discovery of bodies, and convictions, helping to keep the numbers of white female victims of violence lower than for other women. Women of color and their families receive none of that attention and, thus, none of that resolution or prevention. This abundance of attention on missing white women fuels outrage and contributes to the activism around missing and murdered Indigenous women. Missing white woman syndrome disappears women of color twice: first in their criminal disappearance, and second in their disappearance from cultural representation and compassion.[12]

Many feel that true-crime movies, TV shows, podcasts, conventions, and books spectacularize violence for profit. Writing about missing and murdered Indigenous women can easily fall into this trap. Writing can harm families who have already been harmed by profound violence. How we tell the story matters. And justice does not look the same for everyone. For families who have lost a loved one, a conviction might not bring peace; it might reopen the wound. A courtroom win does not always feel like justice for many families. Victories can feel like another reminder that the system was never built for them. The 2016 Sepur Zarco case resulted in Guatemala convicting a general and a military commissioner for sex crimes against fifteen Q'eqchi' Maya women during Guatemala's US-backed civil war, but the women themselves may not view the convictions as just. Six years later, that same court sentenced five Guatemalan soldiers for raping thirty-six Achi Maya women during the same US-incited war. Perhaps the victims feel vindicated, but we need to ask: Does a conviction really bring justice? Some families of the missing and murdered feel traumatized by the legal processes, the bias toward perpetrators, and the leniency shown to killers—even when convicted. All the victims and their families would prefer that the violence had never happened and will never happen again.[13]

Although the true-crime genre tends to run the same program aiming for the same profit, some iconoclasts challenge the genre. Connie Walker, a Pulitzer Prize–winning Canadian Cree journalist, has generated incredible work in the true-crime genre using podcasts as her vehicle for telling the story of missing Native women. She does so with sensitivity, concern, and care. Walker produced podcasts on Alberta Williams, Cleopatra Nicotine Semaganis, Jermain Charlo, Ella Mae Begay, Kristina Carrillo, and survivors of St. Michael's Indian Residential School in British Columbia, including her father. But Walker's work pushes against the true-crime paradigm and earned her a 2023 Pulitzer Prize in Audio Reporting. *How Settlers Get Away with Murder* strives to emulate Walker's storytelling of missing and murdered Indigenous women and Two-Spirit people.[14]

Too many reports and articles place the blame on Native people and communities instead of the people causing harm. Especially in Canada, the many studies and reports can suggest that First Nations women go missing or are murdered because of the aftereffects of residential schools. They imply that First Nations women and men suffer from poverty and addiction, which causes vulnerability, and this vulnerability causes the crisis. Rarely do we see writing or documentaries blaming the assailants, except in the case of serial killers. Rarely are the assailants explicitly said to be male or white. Rarely are the killers discussed within a larger societal context. We almost never hear about the histories of settlers who hurt Native women or how they came to do it. Almost no one asks what role settler law plays in all this. But that silence speaks volumes. This book rejects victim blaming. Instead, it asks: What systems allowed the assailants to act with impunity?[15]

Law and law enforcement made residential schools in Canada and boarding schools in the United States possible. Both relied on settler police to restrain and abduct Native children to transfer them into the institutions, but also to locate those who ran away and bring them back into full compliance with the infrastructure of the state. Today Canadian and US police officers often ignore Native parents when they call to report their children missing. Police use the term "runaway" to label their disappearance as something other than a crime, requiring no investigation. "Runaway" can become a label applied excessively to Indigenous, Black, and Brown women.

This book centers Native women, guided by relationships, respect for tribal and Indigenous lands, and a commitment to showing how their stories are shaped by power and violence. Settler nations, including their states, provinces, municipalities, counties, and cities, have stolen the lands and sovereignty of Indigenous peoples. That theft explains why women are being killed at crisis levels. As individual agents of the state, assailants damage and destroy the bodies of Native women within the vacuum of juridical responsibility for Native women. These acts of femicide always take place on Native and Indigenous land, whether that land is recognized by the state as Native/Indigenous or not. Too often, research takes from Native communities without giving anything back. This book was written by building trust and listening, with care, not extraction. Those who have lost their loved ones bear an immeasurable burden. Those who carry that burden have often been harmed by the media and police. They may choose to protect themselves by not reaching out from under that load to engage with media, scholars, or police.[16]

The stories in this book were chosen with thought and intention, guided by values of accountability and community. I imagined how the family members would feel reading this book. My method meant standing with the families rather than doing a study on them. This book refuses to portray these women, Two-Spirit people, or their families, as defeated. *How Settlers Get Away with Murder* shows how much these families fight just to be heard, just to find answers. This book shows people who are not damaged but living in a world that seeks to damage them. The book puts the state at the center of these stories, showing the structures of violence in Native people's lives. By directly engaging with the state, especially through legal structures, this book exposes their actions, often for the first time.[17]

From the perspective of Indigenous people, the Americas continue to exist as a colonized space, and the nations of the Americas and its citizens continue to spit out an ongoing gendered and racialized violence. As forcefully articulated by scholar Sherene Razack, the tools of the carceral state are perverse, and settler law provides an opportunity to use those perverse tools. The lasting impact of my book will be in documenting the stories of Native women and Two-Spirit people. The book demonstrates that Native people are still here, still fighting for their lands, autonomy, and sovereignty.[18]

While all women in the Americas face gendered violence, especially from the men they love, Indigenous women and Two-Spirit people endure a unique double burden: targeted both by men within their communities and by settler men who render them disposable. This dual exposure fuels their staggering rates of disappearance and mortality; yet their struggle does not exist in isolation. Women are overwhelmingly harmed by men they know and love, but taboos silence them in racially stratified ways. White women are pressured to uphold the myth of white male benevolence; women of color risk state retaliation or communal betrayal if they speak in hostile spaces. Solidarity, then, requires more than amplifying Indigenous women's voices; it demands that white women, especially, break their silence about the violence committed by the men they know and love in their own communities. For women of color, it means being met with protection, not exploitation—support to confront harm from the men they know and love without inviting the intervention and further harm of the state. The path forward lies in naming the assailants, not promoting "stranger danger" but, in fact, the opposite: exposing familiar men who weaponize intimacy and the systems that reward them for it. *How Settlers Get Away with Murder* provides the archive and narratives that lead toward historic reckoning and accountability.

How Settlers Get Away with Murder argues that Indigenous women and Two-Spirit people were and are targeted for murder at an alarming rate because of ideas rooted in colonial culture, a legal structure that protects non-Native assailants, and the deep colonial hatred of Native women and Two-Spirit people. This book offers a way to understand why so many Native women are being targeted and why the violence has not stopped. A system designed to erase Native life does not produce anomalies. It produces this crisis. This historical understanding of Indigenous femicide in the Americas offers much-needed interventions in conversations about human rights, the law, settler colonialism, and genocide. From the first moments of colonization to today's courtrooms and police encounters, the Americas have functioned as a vast and ongoing crime scene. Rooted in the continued occupation of Indigenous communities and lands and in the false morality of settler law, the crisis relies on a legal and carceral system that shields non-Native assailants while incarcerating Black and Brown people across the hemisphere. Indigenous people sit at the center of the histories of the Americas, histories that expose the deep failures of modern justice and the limits of equality under occupation. This book uncovers the hidden architecture of settler violence and witnesses hidden evidence.

GUIDE TO KEY FIGURES IN CHAPTER 1

DAVID CORNSILK: Citizen of Cherokee Nation and United Keetoowah Band and active community member on the Cherokee Reservation.

REBECCA NAGLE: Cherokee Nation citizen, journalist, and host of the podcast *This Land.*

LYDIA KINGFISHER BLACKBIRD CUMMINGS: Cherokee woman, speaker, and mother. She is the woman in the story told on the *This Land* podcast, episode 5.

LOONEY RATTLING GOURD: Cherokee man, speaker, father, and Nighthawk. Accused of killing Sunday Christie. Jailed in 1903. Imprisoned in 1904. Released in 1910.

SUNDAY CHRISTIE: Cherokee man, speaker, and father who never took an allotment. Murdered in 1903. Cousin of Ned Christie.

NED CHRISTIE: A Cherokee man assassinated by federal marshals in 1892 and falsely accused of having killed US Deputy Marshal Daniel Maples. Cousin of Sunday Christie.

GEORGE WASHINGTON BENGE: Cherokee, but not a speaker of the language. Attorney. Cherokee delegate to the Dawes Commission. Lied to Dawes Commission that he was Looney Rattling Gourd's attorney. Took allotments in Rattling Gourd's name while he was incarcerated.

JULIA THORNE: Cherokee woman, speaker, and mother. Her allotment sat at the corner of Cedar and Downing where oral history places the attack on Lydia. Her allotment may have been stolen by Frank Griffin.

FRANK GRIFFIN: Settler. Justice of the peace for Grandview District in Tahlequah. Purchased Arch Christie's allotment through white banker Andrew Morton. Purchased Julia Thorne's Cherokee allotment by unknown means.

JOHN BLACKBIRD: Cherokee man, speaker, and father. Lydia's first husband. William Glory acted as his guardian. Attacked in 1934.

NIGHTHAWKS: Group of Cherokees who opposed enrollment, allotment, and assimilation. Supported Cherokee clans, Cherokee language, clan leadership, clan governance, and clan control of Cherokee lands.

SAMPSON CUMMINGS: Cherokee man, speaker, and father. Lydia's second husband.

ARCH CHRISTIE: Son of Sunday Christie. William Glory acted as his guardian after the murder. Allotment stolen by white banker Andrew Morton. Attacked in 1935.

WILLIAM GLORY: Cherokee, not a speaker. Part of the Treaty Party supporters who were overwhelmingly pro-assimilation. Took guardianships over several Cherokees, including John Blackbird and Arch Christie.

ANDREW DAVID MORTON: Settler. Banker at First National Bank of Tahlequah. Prairie Oil and Gas Company board member. Guardian of at least six other minors from 1904 to 1910. Sold Arch Christie's land.

ELLIS BLACKFOX: Cherokee man accused of harboring Looney Rattling Gourd.

JACK TEEKAHLANNEESKY (DOWNING): Cherokee man, Nighthawk. Arrested for murder in a case similar to Looney Rattling Gourd's in 1904. Imprisoned at Fort Leavenworth with Rattling Gourd, where he contracted tuberculosis.

KEETOOWAHS: Group of Cherokees who existed prior to Nighthawks and continue to exist. Obtained federal recognition as the United Keetoowah Band.

CHAPTER 1

LYDIA

DAVID CORNSILK: You know, one of the saddest situations that I've ever seen in the Cherokee Nation was the loss of land by Lydia Kingfisher.

REBECCA NAGLE: Lydia Kingfisher owned a clothes-washing business in the town of Tahlequah. She had two things that made her vulnerable: She was a full-blood, and she spoke Cherokee. Either could get her saddled with a guardian. One day, a grifter approached her and said he wanted to protect her from other white people who might steal her land. But Lydia declined his so-called help.

DAVID CORNSILK: And he became so angry that he poured a vat of boiling water into her lap and basically almost burned her to death, and she became disabled afterwards. Well, then he sued her in district court and the district court judge made him her guardian. And then he sold her land, and the judge purchased her land.

REBECCA NAGLE: The judge made her attacker her guardian so that he ultimately could take her land out from under her.

—*THIS LAND*

In July 2019 I listened to "The Land Grab," episode 5 of the podcast *This Land*, and found myself unable to stop thinking about Lydia Kingfisher and the horror she lived through: an attempted murder and the loss of her land. Determined to expose who attacked her and who stole her land, which occurred sometime after allotment closed in 1908, I continued to reflect on the systemic injustice that happened to Lydia. I thought about how many settlers stole the property of Native people after allotment, even killing them to take their land after the Allotment Act of 1887. I spoke with descendant communities and also with Cherokee Nation and United Keetoowah Band citizen David Cornsilk, a genealogist who works as an active community member on the Cherokee Reservation. I gathered hundreds of documents related to Lydia Kingfisher over several years. No one has ever written in English about Lydia or this incident.

When I listened to the podcast, I certainly imagined her attacker being a settler; however, I was unable to locate sale records connected to Lydia and thus found no name to confirm my suspicion. To determine whether a guardianship was ever imposed upon Lydia, one would need to petition a sitting judge to unseal records that may not even exist, a procedural reality confirmed by Cherokee County clerk Lesa Rousey-Daniels. Even if such a record lies in government storage, the court would likely deny access in the absence of clear proof of its existence. After encountering these obstacles, I learned her attacker may have been a fellow Cherokee, Looney Rattling Gourd. This shocked me, and I found it hard to believe. I hesitated to complete the research because of this revelation, wanting to avoid Native-on-Native crime which, just like Black-on-Black crime, can be used to support racist arguments.[1]

I have amassed a substantial archive looking for answers about the attack on Lydia. In my quest to contextualize Nagle's podcast episode with Cornsilk, I found corroborating settler archives to be both abundant yet elusive, obscuring the very truth they were meant to document, a hallmark of cover-up and corruption. Over multiple conversations about Rattling Gourd with his descendants, I learned he had been to prison. The prison records showed he may have murdered Sunday Christie, a fellow Cherokee, a claim for which I sought corroboration. But the prison records also opened a window into the deeply vexed world Rattling Gourd lived in as a result of allotment and showed the violent hand of the United States at work against this young Cherokee man.[2]

To find the name of her perpetrator, this chapter moves far beyond Lydia Kingfisher. The archives failed to name her attacker, failed to record her pain, and her land may have slipped into a judge's pocket like a stray coin. To tell her story, I dug through the dirt of settler paperwork to find the shape of her absence.

Before sharing the outline of the story and what I found, it's important for readers to understand that Congress claimed direct jurisdiction over Native people and Native lands in the 1880s, beginning with the Major Crimes Act of 1885. Congress then passed the Dawes Act in 1887 and created the Dawes Commission to fulfill the act. Through the Dawes Act, government workers empowered by Congress physically entered Native lands with ledgers, documenting each Native person—a process they called "enrollment"—and selecting a portion of land from communal, tribal lands formerly managed by tribal clans for each enrolled person, which they called "allotment." On the Cherokee Reservation, some Cherokee men volunteered to serve as Cherokee delegates to the Dawes Commission in an act of support and solidarity with Congress. But many Cherokees resisted the Dawes Act by refusing to enroll or choose an allotment. In return for their defiance, they faced a campaign of targeted violence and coercion.

A number of figures emerged simultaneously during my research process of interviewing descendants and visiting settler archives. Lydia led me to Rattling Gourd who led me to George Washington Benge. As a Cherokee delegate to the Dawes Commission, Benge committed crimes against Rattling Gourd immediately after Rattling Gourd's arrest, revealing what may have been his intentions all along. Benge used his position on the Dawes Commission to select Rattling Gourd's allotments while Rattling Gourd sat in jail and then federal prison for criminal actions that suggest his incarceration may have been fabricated for that very purpose. Oral history and archival records suggest it is more likely that either Benge or a settler killed Sunday Christie, a Cherokee man who was murdered in 1903.

This chapter reconstructs what Rattling Gourd learned while in prison: He had been robbed through the Dawes Commission, not in the way all Cherokees were robbed but in an even more sinister and underhanded manner. When Cornsilk told me about the exact location in Tahlequah, the capital of Cherokee Nation, where Lydia was attacked, I looked into the Cherokee County records and found Cherokee allottee Julia Thorne possessed that property, which may have been later stolen by local judge Frank Griffin.[3]

The account ahead follows the many threads, forces, and players around Lydia Kingfisher, which led to the attack. Those who surrounded her left many traces in settler archives. Lydia did not. This chapter shares the information that was painstakingly unearthed, as this creates an archive for the descendants.

Only one thing seems certain after six years of research: Someone attacked Lydia, likely in 1937. The attacker may not have been Looney Rattling Gourd; Looney Rattling Gourd may not have become her guardian. The state incarcerated Rattling Gourd for killing Sunday Christie, but the state provided no evidence of a trial or proof that he killed him. Clearly, someone murdered Christie, but that person may have been a settler. Records also show that Benge and the Dawes Commission likely defrauded Rattling Gourd.

Lydia Kingfisher (Blackbird Cummings), a Cherokee grandmother who spoke no English for much of her life, raised eight children through the Great Depression, and survived and endured an attempted murder. The Major Crimes Act and the Dawes Act made that violence possible. Because of those congressional policies, Native women like Lydia—monolingual Cherokee speakers in a land flooded with English-speaking settlers—became easy targets for guardianship scams, fraud, and violence. Settlers swarmed into the area, courts colluded, and collective Native control of land vanished. By the time Oklahoma became a state in 1907, Congress had rigged the system in favor of settlers.

Lydia only spoke Cherokee for much of her life. Now her fluency would make her a Cherokee National Treasure, perhaps even a Cherokee language instructor at Yale. She would live as one of only a few hundred Cherokee speakers alive today. But in the early twentieth century, settlers terrorized and hunted Cherokee-speaking Cherokees who dared to say no to the settler state. Lydia came of age in the shadow of two fires: the systematic slaughter of the Osage for their oil wealth, which peaked between 1921 and 1926, and the ashes of Greenwood's Black prosperity in Tulsa in 1921. The Osage Reign of Terror and the Tulsa massacre are both remembered as moments of massive, historic bloodshed that defines Oklahoma's past. Cherokees were burned, maimed, robbed, and incarcerated under the same settler hunger; their wounds buried in bureaucratic silence.

Then came the Great Depression as Oklahoma's white supremacist vortex tightened around Lydia, as it had around so many others. The settlers around her would have seen the conquest of Oklahoma as historically settled, a fait accompli, by the height of the Great Depression. Congress had forced allotment, and US judges, attorneys, and well-connected settlers had taken much of the privately held and allotted lands of tribal citizens by the 1930s. Those Cherokees who held on tight to their language, community, and land titles through the Great Depression became even more of a target. Powerful Oklahoma settlers viewed Native people, but especially Native women, as easy prey.

This chapter serves as a testament to the oral histories shared by Cherokee descendants, not as "sources" to be mined but as experts guiding me. When I consult settler archives, their records supplant Cherokee memory, which needs no validation, and exposes how bureaucracy weaponized paper and ink to disappear Cherokees from the history of Oklahoma. Where documents are silent, I listen to Cherokees, to those who remember.

Lydia Kingfisher was born April 16, 1907, in Indian Territory, the youngest of six children in a Cherokee-speaking family to John Whipporwill West and Cora Bugg Josie Kingfisher. Named after Whipporwill's mother, Lydia L. Sleeve, Lydia Kingfisher belonged to a web of kinship that allotment would soon try to crush. Before removal, Cherokee clans—not just women, but the entire kinship system—held collective power. Women like Nanyehi (Nancy Ward), a political leader of the Cherokees who lived from about 1738 to 1823, negotiated treaties as clan representatives, not as solitary leaders. By Lydia's era, the US had severed this: Matrilineal land rights were outlawed, women's agricultural authority was erased, and the US imposed property titles. The attack on Lydia did not arrive as simple violence. It followed a long assault on the entire Cherokee clan structure, reducing relational power to individual vulnerability, that began on Cherokee homelands in the Southeast.

History books memorialize Cherokee leaders, men who signed treaties, not women who washed laundry. Lydia's story survives in the stains they ignored. At eighteen, she married John Blackbird, a thirty-year-old Cherokee man and Cherokee speaker. Lydia bore her first five children with him in 1926, 1928, 1932, 1934, and 1936, and all their children would later be pulled into the storm of the aftermath of Lydia's attack in 1937. By 1939, after separating from Blackbird, Lydia married Sampson Cummings, also Cherokee and a Cherokee speaker. She bore four more children in 1940, 1943, 1945, and 1948. Lydia outlived both husbands, dying in 1979. Her long life testified to surviving an attack that laid bare the violence of settler law. Lydia had no way of knowing that the simple act of being a Cherokee-speaking woman married to a Cherokee-speaking man would leave her scarred, likely not by a Cherokee man but by the settler hands that had stolen Cherokee lands.

The attack on Lydia was said to have taken place at the corner of Cedar Avenue and East Downing Street in Tahlequah, Oklahoma, where the State Farm Agency building sits today. Dawes Commission records revealed the Cherokee allottee for that land as Julia Ann Terrell Thorne. Like Lydia, Thorne lived as a Cherokee woman and monolingual Cherokee speaker. She married Lucullus Vann "Cull" Thorne and bore eleven children. Someone tampered with the date of her allotment records, but the document remains otherwise legible. She took an allotment, or had one forced on her, in 1900, 1902, or 1903 in the Grandview District of Tahlequah. Someone with access to US government records repeatedly wrote several different numbers over the year of her allotment. The US government stipulates that changing government records constitutes a crime. Changing government records to benefit yourself in a scheme constitutes fraud. Changing dates on government documents could facilitate the theft of land title.[4]

The Grandview District of Cherokee County became a microcosm of the violent dispossession wrought by allotment, where the theft of Julia Thorne's land unfolded under the guise of legal paperwork. Thorne's allotment at the busy intersection in east Tahlequah may have caught the attention of Grandview District judge Frank Griffin and his wife, Lila. Through a series of potentially illegal actions that may have occurred around 1906, before Oklahoma existed as a state, Griffin took possession of Thorne's allotment. The Cherokee County clerk may have illegally transferred all ten acres of Thorne's allotment to a white woman without either of their signatures in February 1906, but through legal means. In January 1907, Cherokee County moved the stolen land into Griffin's hands. Again, there were no signatures. In 1913, the Cherokee County clerk quite belatedly recorded Thorne's original allotment, a bureaucratic slip as they had already given it away to someone named Katie and then Griffin. In 1926, Griffin granted the state of Oklahoma an easement on what had been Thorne's allotment. In 1933, Griffin sold five acres of what had been Thorne's ten-acre allotment to Mittie Mae Cooper Shaddox. In 1939, he sold two and a half acres of the five-acre remainder of Thorne's allotment to Harry Williams. In 1943, Frank Griffin died, and the following year his widow and son sold the last two and a half acres of Thorne's original ten-acre allotment to Alta Lee Justus.[5]

Julia Thorne's stolen allotment became a battleground, one Lydia inherited if she set up her wash tub at Cedar and Downing. Mapping Lydia's and Julia's lives reveals their possible intersections: Cherokee County took Thorne's land in 1906, two years before Lydia was born; Thorne's husband died in 1910 when Thorne was fifty-one and Lydia three; the Cherokee County clerk recorded Thorne's allotment in 1913, after giving it away; Lydia married John Blackbird in 1925; Thorne died in 1927, Lydia then twenty; the attack on Lydia likely occurred in 1937. Grandview District judge Frank Griffin and his wife, Lila, held title to Thorne's allotment from 1907 to 1944. Had Thorne known of the transfer and then accessed an attorney with connections and clout, she could have proven the 1906 transfer was fraudulent. But no such attorneys practiced on the Cherokee Reservation during this siege. If Lydia worked as a laundress on Thorne's former allotment, she did so on land that Frank Griffin would have believed his, because Cherokee County declared the taking legal, even as it may have violated US laws. The land may truly belong to Thorne, but Cherokee County would dispute such an assertion until proven in their courtrooms.

At the center of the clash between settlers and Cherokees stood the settler Frank Griffin and his wife, Lila. The city of Tahlequah made him justice of the peace of the Grandview District. Grandview remained Cherokee land at this time, home to Cherokee-speaking families like Lydia's and Cherokee Freedmen alike. Griffin embodied the collusion between law and dispossession: He occupied the contested intersection, parceled out Thorne's land to settlers, and as justice of the peace, adjudicated the lives of the traditional Cherokees and Cherokee Freedmen who had managed to keep their land and remain in Grandview. His presence marked not just theft but the calculated control of Cherokee people and Cherokee land.

Records leave no doubt. Frank Griffin lived at Cedar and Downing in the 1930s like a soldier living at a fort occupying Native land. He lived at House 704 in the Grandview District in 1930. Newspapers reported Griffin living on East Downing in 1932 and becoming justice of the peace in 1935.[6] If Lydia worked at Cedar and Downing as a laundress on Thorne's allotment, which seems unlikely, this would have created a tremendous conflict with Frank Griffin who saw himself as protecting settler turf. But perhaps Lydia rented the space for her laundry business from Griffin. Perhaps Griffin wanted her removed. Thorne may have promised Lydia the land. Lydia may have valued Cherokee traditions of verbal agreements and refused to leave because Thorne passed the land to her without settler approval. The details of Lydia's connection to Thorne's allotment remain unclear.

Thorne's land clearly sits as an embattled space, and I continued to search for a connection between Lydia and this corner to find the name of her attacker. The question of whether and where Lydia owned land remains unanswered. This lack of evidence suggests she may have never owned property or lived at the corner of Cedar and Downing or even in Tahlequah. If she owned or used Thorne's allotment at Cedar and Downing, the settler records have disappeared, or she and Thorne held a verbal agreement. Possibly because of her April 1907 birthday after the end of allotment, no allotment records exist for Lydia. But the standard settler scam of assigning an allotment to a Cherokee, then simply forging papers at the Cherokee County clerk's office and seizing the land could still have been a possibility in her case. This either did not happen to Lydia, or it did and someone made the evidence vanish.

Nor did Lydia Kingfisher (Blackbird Cummings) come to hold land near Cedar and Downing through inheritance. Her family members never took allotments or purchases in east Tahlequah, but they did hold title to lands elsewhere in Cherokee County and other counties. Allotments were assigned to her parents, John and Cora, in 1903, and her father also purchased land for $100 from J. M. Warwick in the western district of Indian Territory. John also possessed lands in Muskogee and Delaware Counties. John, or someone representing him, removed restrictions on his Delaware County land and sold it in 1909. Lydia's sister Ida held title to surplus land in Delaware and Cherokee Counties (not in Tahlequah) worth $205 and to homestead land in Delaware County worth $120. Lydia's father passed away in 1918. The Department of the Interior filed his proof of heirship, which listed his wife and children but omitted ten-year-old Lydia, an odd oversight.[7] Lydia's sister Ida died in March 1927, but she passed that land onto her children, and in 1931, the children still held title. Her husband, Chu-nee-qua-lee-skee Drywater, and their children, Mary and Youngdeer Drywater, were each allocated a third of Ida's land. Other possibilities of inheritance include Lydia's brother Willis who held several parcels of land in Delaware and Sequoyah Counties as of June 14, 1929, and perhaps this became hers after his death, but this existed outside of Cherokee County. Lydia's mother, Cora, held three parcels—all in Delaware County as of May 18, 1929. Her oldest sister, Fannie, held title to six parcels of land in McIntosh and Delaware Counties as of May 15, 1929. Lydia was born into a family in which everyone seems to have had land except her, and none of that land was in Tahlequah. There are no known records of her obtaining an allotment or inheriting land. No one in her immediate family obtained an allotment at or near that intersection, but allotment records show that Julia Thorne did.[8]

Knowing where Lydia lived as a child and young adult could help show how she may have been attacked at the corner of Cedar and Downing in Tahlequah in the 1930s. At three years old, Lydia lived with her parents and siblings in Township 1 in Delaware County, just north of Cherokee County. At age thirteen, Lydia lived with her mother and siblings in the small town of Moodys on the Cherokee Reservation where she spent much of her life after the death of her father; her older sister Susie identified herself as the head of their household. According to settler records, Lydia did not live in Tahlequah.[9]

Nor did she have a connection to Tahlequah through her first husband. Lydia married John Blackbird in 1925. His allotments had not been in Tahlequah, and they continued to live in Moodys, on the Cherokee Reservation, near her kin while they raised their children. In 1930, Blackbird was working for a timber company, and they rented a home in Moodys. She possibly made the sixteen-mile round trip daily to work as a laundress in Tahlequah in the 1930s, but it seems unlikely, especially with small children.

But Blackbird's personal history may hold the key to understanding the attack on Lydia. John Blackbird entered the world in 1887, soon to become a target for Oklahomans. By 1900, he inhabited the defiant identity of an unenrolled Cherokee minor living with his aunt Peggy Sunday's family, all of whom had refused Dawes allotments, making them prey for land-hungry settlers. The Dawes Commission enrolled Blackbird by force in 1906, and Samuel C. Pitts (a name you will see again) signed his allotment over to guardian William Glory, a man who made at least part of his living stealing from Cherokee children.[10]

William Glory, a permanent member of the Executive Council of the Emigrant Cherokee Movement, a group opposed to Cherokee national leadership and the Nighthawk resistance, also took guardianships of Sunday Christie's wife and children after Christie's murder. That fall, he enrolled nineteen-year-old Blackbird into the Cherokee Male Seminary as a fourth grader, where he may have been made to sing colonial hymns alongside Felix Ross, another young Cherokee man trapped in the allotment machine. Blackbird fled the school.[11]

World War I took Blackbird to the trenches, far from William Glory and the settlers surrounding Cherokee-speaking Cherokees on the reservation. But when he returned, the 1920s brought more theft of Blackbird's land, followed by his 1925 marriage to Lydia. Sometime in the 1920s or early 1930s, the Department of the Interior lifted restrictions on Blackbird's remaining land at Glory's urging, to force a sale. But Blackbird refused to sign despite not reading or writing English, blocking the paperwork and clinging to what survived.

Then came 1934, when an ax nearly severed Blackbird's foot. The doctor predicted amputation, but Blackbird kept his leg. The timing forms a pattern: a serious accident at work during what may have been Glory's pressure campaign to sign the paperwork to sell. The freak accident read as a warning. The message was repeated more clearly the following August when a man with a knife ambushed Arch Christie from behind a tree. Christie, like Blackbird, remained a ward of William Glory. Two attacks, two survivors, one guardian. The system of dispossession may have escalated from paperwork and pressure to outright physical violence against those who refused to let go of their land.[12]

Then, in 1937, came Blackbird's defiant crescendo: election to the Five Tribes Council at Rocky Ford on the Cherokee Reservation, where he used his voice and respect from the Cherokee community to challenge the settler system devouring Cherokee land. That same year, he drove to Tulsa with Lydia, possibly on a mission, perhaps to consult an attorney or maybe to visit with Native activists, for one last stand to protect his acreage at Section 13, Township 20, Range 19.[13]

Then someone may have attacked Lydia, likely in 1937. The timing signaled no coincidence, a boiling warning to silence them both.

By 1942, Blackbird had completed a first-aid course, as if preparing for more violence. That same year, a Department of the Interior letter arrived like a hard-won trophy confirming his ownership of his acreage with a handwritten message by authorities showing their surprise: "Had conditional removal but did not sell." Blackbird had dared to keep his land. The bureaucrat's scribble marked Blackbird's victory, proof he had outmaneuvered Glory's theft machine.

The government document survived as a relic of his quiet war: Restrictions lifted. The land still his. Blackbird had won.

Like Blackbird, Lydia lived an active and busy life in the 1930s, seemingly unafraid to travel, committed to her kin, and bearing children with Blackbird. The newspapers noted a number of her updates: her mother's visit to her home in February 1934; her niece Nancy Russel's visit along with grandnephew Joseph Russel in March 1934; the birth of Lydia's baby in June 1934; and the visits she made with her children to see her sister, Fannie, in December 1934, August 1935, and September 1936. The paper also announced the probably fateful drive she made with Blackbird to Tulsa in 1937, a big trip even today for many Cherokees living on the Cherokee Reservation. In an era when settlers wanted Cherokees silent, stationary, and "vanishing," Lydia and Blackbird moved on their own terms. A car ride to Tulsa meant more than logistics; it staked a claim to space, an assertion of agency. The couple seemed to shout: "We belong everywhere." The drive refused their dispossession. Their trip also signaled to Blackbird's predators that he intended to fight for his land. In 1937, Lydia entered her handmade housedress in the Women's Club and 4-H Club Fair of Tahlequah, winning third place. She may have sewn to make a living, but pride in her handiwork seems equally possible. Fair entries demand effort: filling out forms, depositing creations with fair organizers, waiting for results, asking relatives and friends to view your display at the fair, and retrieving your display once the fair ends. With her dress, Lydia declared to the world, including the settler world: "Look at what I made." There can be no doubt that Lydia took pride in the satiny third-place ribbon pinned to her dress and kept it as a memento.

But then may have come the attack.

The attack may have happened between the birth of her child in 1936 and her marriage to Sampson in 1939. They'd fought as a team: John Blackbird in the council chambers, Lydia in her home and community, and the system tried to strike them down.

The Tahlequah Citizen had space to publish articles about hog killings and housedresses, but not for the crime committed against the woman who sewed them. Papers like *The Tahlequah Citizen* covered just about everything in the 1930s, including "Rocky Ford People Are Killing Hogs." The paper carried no notice of the attack on Lydia. That absence is telling. Oklahoma's message seemed to say: You can be in the paper for your dress, but not for your scars. You can go to Tulsa, but someone might pour boiling water on you for it. But perhaps instead of being astonished that the newspapers did not alert the community to a vicious attack on a Cherokee woman, we need to reflect on the complete unwillingness of Oklahoma newspapers to openly acknowledge the painful and violent realities of Oklahoma for Native people, an unwillingness that goes back to the time of allotment.

After 1937, the papers forgot Lydia, and she just dropped away from public record, like a stone into dark water. No more dresses at the fair. No more drives. No more family visits. The attack had carved a lesson into Lydia's and John Blackbird's bones: The settler world would notice them only if they played its game, and even then, only until it turned on them. So, they kept quiet publicly but carried on privately.

Lydia remained in the Cherokee community and bore four children with Sampson. She married Sampson in 1939, had her first child with him in 1940, and they didn't appear in the paper until 1967 when *The Pictorial Press* noted her leaving the Public Health Service Indian Hospital. Then came the ten-word announcement of her death in *Tulsa World* in 1979.

Her granddaughter remembers her salt-and-pepper hair, sometimes pulled back in a bun, and the way her hands were always curled around her cane. She recalls visits to Lydia's home in Oaks with Sampson, many years after the time she spent with John Blackbird in Rocky Ford. Although both Oaks and Rocky Ford sit inside the Cherokee Reservation, these places function as different Cherokee communities with unique histories and kin groupings. Her granddaughter believes her grandma Lydia might have quilted. She remembers with certainty that Lydia poured herself into the grandchildren she helped raise. Even at the end, in that mutual-help home for Cherokees, she was still holding her grandchildren close. Several of her descendants chuckled about knowing that she had a favorite among her children, clearly a poorly kept secret.[14]

This chapter demonstrates the unlikelihood that Looney Rattling Gourd threw a vat of boiling water on Lydia Kingfisher. Secondary sources provide no recordings of boiling water as a weapon in Cherokee law, history, language, or warfare. Rattling Gourd spoke and wrote Cherokee and lived in a deeply Cherokee world of Nighthawks and Keetoowahs. In traditional Cherokee society—and particularly within the Nighthawk Keetoowah and other anti-assimilation factions—disciplinary actions resulted not from personal vendettas but from collective decisions made in accordance with their own legal and spiritual codes. In traditional Cherokee justice, the focus fell on restoration, using restitution or ceremonial reconciliation. Additionally, Looney Rattling Gourd moved through a world of Cherokee speakers who had access to their clans and clan leadership for disagreements. While possible that he completely rejected Cherokee culture and teachings and everyone he knew and loved, it seems unlikely.[15]

By the 1930s, European settlers had a long and documented history of using torture. The historic precedent of scalding humans with boiling water goes back to slaveholders who used it as a punishment for enslaved Africans. The United States military used water to simulate drowning on Filipinos during the Philippine-American War. Scalding and near drowning made it easy for perpetrators to dismiss their violence. Burns disable slowly, prolonging suffering.[16]

A settler may have attacked Lydia in 1937. Blackbird's injury may not have been an accident in 1934. If both were deliberately attacked in 1934 and 1937, they might be connected. Rattling Gourd may not have harmed Lydia. He lacked the cultural or social background to do so, and his motive remains unclear.

US V. RATTLING GOURD

The story now turns to Looney Rattling Gourd, the young Cherokee and Cherokee speaker caught in the web of allotment and the violence it unleashed. His story and the story of the men connected to him takes up the majority of the chapter in an effort to determine whether he attacked Lydia. Lydia survived the attempted murder but was temporarily disabled because of the attack. Cornsilk was told that a judge granted Rattling Gourd guardianship over Lydia, and that, just as swiftly, he sold Lydia's land to the handler or a judge. In Cornsilk's oral history, the handler gained valuable land in Tahlequah, and Looney Rattling Gourd earned a reputation for harming a vulnerable Cherokee woman. Such an attack would have left Lydia physically disabled and mentally suffering from post-traumatic stress disorder.

Assimilation promised survival but delivered erasure, and men like Benge and William Glory became its bounty hunters. Guardianship papers acted as shackles. Forged deeds cut like knives. Every *X* pressed onto a land record hammered like a nail into the coffin of Cherokee sovereignty. These men acted as auxiliaries in the settler war against Cherokees, paid in stolen acreage and status. Lydia Kingfisher's burns and Looney Rattling Gourd's prison time act as the receipts.

As a monolingual Cherokee speaker who could write in Cherokee, Rattling Gourd likely knew or knew of Lydia. Born on December 26, 1882, just five years before the passage of the Dawes Act, he spent his entire life in the shadow of Congress's intention to overtake Indian Territory. By the time Looney Rattling Gourd sat inside a US federal penitentiary, he would have felt cornered by fraud and corruption.[17]

Because Rattling Gourd reached adulthood much earlier than Lydia, his young adulthood unfolded in the shadow of the Dawes Commission and the Nighthawks' fight against it, whereas Lydia's young adulthood occurred against the backdrop of the crimes against the Osages and the burning of the Greenwood District. Rattling Gourd's father, Jack Rattling Gourd, introduced him to the world of the Nighthawk Society, a society of Cherokees who stood firmly and deeply opposed to the Dawes Commission and any tribal cooperation with it. The United States passed law after law to force every last Cherokee, especially resisters, into the system of enrollment and allotment. This included Looney Rattling Gourd's parents who had enrollment forced upon them while their son languished in prison in 1905, which happened to other Nighthawk Cherokees as well.[18]

US authorities sentenced Rattling Gourd to prison for the murder of fellow Cherokee Sunday Christie in 1903, and that murder connects in numerous ways to the attacks on Lydia and John Blackbird. The granular attention to Rattling Gourd's imprisonment and the killing of Christie provides the central understanding of the attack on Lydia. Sunday Christie experienced a phantom murder. That is, the press buried his death until it became politically useful. When he died in May 1903, the newspapers said nothing. Not a single outlet—neither Cherokee nor settler—reported his killing until a suspect was conveniently produced by US authorities in late July. The absence of any contemporary report in May confirms the killing of Christie as no ordinary crime. If Christie had been murdered by a Cherokee in May, the pro-settler papers surely would have screamed about Native violence. If killed by a settler, the papers would have buried it—and they did. But the evidence of his killing endures in stone: Christie's kin memorialized the killing on his grave marker. His marker reads: "Sunday Christy was born [?] day of March [?] killed on Tuesday morning [?] o'clock [?] day of May 190[?] his age was 5[?] years and 6[?] days when he was the age of 16 he entered the army in the year of 186[?] the father of William Christie Richard." Today, his descendants carry two truths: that he was killed, as memorialized on the gravestone, and that a white man killed him, a truth only written in oral history—facts too dangerous for Cherokees to publish in 1903 when US newspapers existed to promote the settler takeover of Oklahoma, not expose settler crimes against Native people.

Like his cousin Ned Christie, the Cherokee man who was famously murdered by US marshals in 1892 for a murder he did not commit, Sunday Christie was targeted for his resistance. But where the US government demonized Ned as an outlaw to justify assassinating him, his corpse displayed as a trophy for the world to see, Christie was quietly killed. No display, no manhunt, no sensational headlines, just a silent killing. Then federal agents handed a Cherokee man, Looney Rattling Gourd, to the federal court as a sacrificial prisoner. The playbook remained unchanged: Eliminate two Nighthawk resisters, manufacture a "guilty" Cherokee, and legitimize the theft that followed. Only the paperwork differed.

The Muskogee Evening Times broke the story on the last day of July 1903 with glaring omissions. They named no witnesses, described no murder weapon, provided no motive, and cited no evidence beyond the arrest itself. Most damningly, they casually revealed Christie had been dead for months without explaining the paper's own silence. The paper did not investigate. They laundered a federal marshal's press release as news, dramatizing the arrest of Looney Rattling Gourd by claiming they found him sleeping at his hideout with fellow Cherokee Ellis Blackfox. When had the manhunt begun? Why had there been no postings about a search for Looney Rattling Gourd? When the papers announced Rattling Gourd's arrest, the public heard for the first time about a reward posted by a prominent resident of Peggs, a town on the Cherokee reservation. Rewards exist to solicit information. What, then, does it mean to offer a reward after an arrest? The reverse order of the reward notice and the arrest notification serve as the ultimate proof that the legal process worked as a cover.

The following conclusions seem obvious: A settler killed Sunday Christie. The Cherokee Nation and community, who knew the Major Crimes Act had stripped all tribal jurisdiction over major crimes, kept quiet about it. US prosecutors now held all the power, and they wielded it selectively, swiftly targeting Cherokees like Looney Rattling Gourd and remaining silent on settler violence against Natives. The cruelty of the Major Crimes Act functions as the point, then and now. Christie's death only became news when US marshals decided to weaponize his death against a Cherokee.

Deputy US Marshal Long performed the abduction of Rattling Gourd with Jessie Wofford. Wofford supported Marshal Long with no legal authority, just as a volunteer. This federal agent and his volunteer sidekick, with every reason to frame a Nighthawk resister, served as the only sources for the story that made its way into newspapers.

The sudden August 1903 frenzy of news coverage reeked of coordination. The record preserves no wanted posters, no newspaper alerts, no reward announcements. Accused of harboring Rattling Gourd, Ellis Blackfox and his Cherokee relatives never testified or faced charges. The first newspaper to report the arrest framed Looney Rattling Gourd as having been "caught in bed," "on the scout" (meaning on the run), and unaware of Deputy Long until he "felt the binding."

Deputy Long, or an ally, fed three lies to the press: that Rattling Gourd was sleeping (to suggest he was living with Blackfox), that he went "on the scout" (to imply guilt), and that Ellis's house served as a hideout (to implicate both men). Neither written archive nor oral history provides any proof of Rattling Gourd at Ellis's home. The "caught in bed" story reads as nothing more than cover for a kidnapping.

The submerged narrative seems clear: Rattling Gourd did not kill Sunday Christie. Oklahoma authorities never announced they were seeking him, and that omission signals intent. Rattling Gourd likely sat at his home, not Blackfox's, when federal agents took him into custody.

Cherokees who refused American systems of governance lived as targets. Rattling Gourd, his parents, and his siblings refused the 1900 census. Ellis Blackfox refused as well. Their census refusal and enrollment and allotment refusal confirm resistance to all things related to the federal government. By 1903, the Rattling Gourds had vanished from settler paperwork entirely. For federal workers in Indian Territory, this posed an outrage: Cherokee men with no paper trail, no fixed address, and no way to be tracked. When Deputy Long needed a scapegoat for Christie's murder, Rattling Gourd's invisibility to the federal takeover of the Cherokee Reservation made him the perfect target. The same system that weaponized ink and deeds against Lydia could not tolerate men who left no paper trail that would allow the settler government to locate and control them.

Arresting Rattling Gourd served two purposes: It manufactured a Cherokee scapegoat, and it guaranteed the real killer, likely a settler, would never face consequences. This arithmetic and the Dawes Commission's brutal work ended one Cherokee life (Sunday Christie's), shackled another (Rattling Gourd's), and diverted most eyes away from settler violence.

Federal agents likely kidnapped Looney Rattling Gourd from his own home. Speaking no English, he would have only understood that US agents had seized him—likely to his death. By keeping silent in the newspapers, the US authorities ensured Rattling Gourd would not know he needed to go into hiding.

Christie's death was conveniently resurrected to end Rattling Gourd's resistance to enrollment and allotment. Rattling Gourd's arrest flaunted federal power on Cherokee lands via the Major Crimes Act. The story that likely occurred but never got printed probably went like this: Christie refused to enroll and take an allotment. Someone murdered him in retaliation. The killer walked free because the settler government refused to punish, and Cherokees lived in fear of speaking the killer's name. Three months later, settlers pointed their fingers at another Cherokee resister: Rattling Gourd. They convicted him in a US federal court in a trial that was neither recorded nor archived and possibly never held.[19]

Rattling Gourd spent six years in prison for the murder of Christie. His descendants speak of his time there with pride, recounting how he bragged about having survived. Christie's descendants know their ancestor was murdered. But they doubt the convicted killer fits the story. Relatives always told them a white man killed Christie. The author of Sunday's epitaph wanted the Cherokee community to know Christie had been "killed" without naming his killer, and this memory lives on in his descendants.[20]

The written archive holds only one record of the alleged motive of Rattling Gourd. After years of George Washington Benge, a Cherokee delegate to the Dawes Commission, harassing Looney Rattling Gourd to sign land documents, he signed a "trusty prisoner" agreement, exchanging a confession for early release. In it, he allegedly wrote: "I got into a quarrel with Sunday Chisty [*sic*] about some land at Gideon Olka., [*sic*] who threatened to stab me[,] and to protect my self I got him[,] was arrested and plead guilty." This documentation held by the federal prison contradicts the record. Neither man held allotments at the time. The land dispute seems fabricated. Additionally, newspapers claimed Sunday Christie was "shot in a field," yet Looney Rattling Gourd, a twenty-one-year-old, claimed he had acted in self-defense against a fifty-seven-year-old with a knife. If true, why not flee if he stood in a field in fear for his life, with no barriers cornering him in? Finally, Rattling Gourd's phrasing ("got him") uses vague words, suggesting he did not know how Christie had been killed. Most damningly, as a monolingual Cherokee, Rattling Gourd could not read English, and he would not have known what articles in the papers said about the murder. He was guessing. Rattling Gourd's coerced confession does not align with the accounts in the papers. He confessed to get released. He very likely did not kill Sunday Christie.

George Washington Benge, who lied about being Rattling Gourd's attorney, undoubtedly had something to do with the murder of Sunday Christie. Benge—a Cherokee attorney, a delegate to the Dawes Commission, and the archnemesis of Rattling Gourd—targeted him when he reached a mere twenty-one years old. But Benge hardly functioned as a mastermind. He operated as a tool of settler colonialism, working within a preexisting system of theft. The real architect, the US government, created the conditions for men like Benge to thrive.

Rattling Gourd's encounters with Benge from 1903 to 1910 left him deeply distrustful. Benge used his position as a Cherokee delegate to the Dawes Commission to extract Rattling Gourd's wealth. Within one week of his arrest on July 30, 1903, Benge committed fraud by taking an allotment on Rattling Gourd's behalf, falsely presenting himself as Rattling Gourd's attorney; he repeated the action in September 1903. In November, Benge went even further. He signed a fifteen-year lease between Looney Rattling Gourd and Prairie Oil for land that had not yet been allotted to Rattling Gourd, a clear sign that Benge had already located land with oil and intended to profit from it.

The Dawes Commission did not stop Benge. Prairie Oil did not stop Benge. The Tulsa County clerk did not stop him either. The Tulsa County clerk even allowed delegate George Washington Benge to file his November 1903 contract in May 1906. With Rattling Gourd confined in jail and then prison, Benge could easily keep him in the dark about his crimes while Benge made money from his incarceration, a sign this originated with Benge all along.[21]

The 1903 murder of Sunday Christie is tied to the attack on Lydia in 1937 because both involve the plundering of Native people by guardians and attorneys, and both were allegedly carried out by Rattling Gourd. But the subterfuge of the settlers surrounding the attacks, especially after the killing of Christie and the imprisonment of Rattling Gourd, proves that Sunday Christie and Looney Rattling Gourd were targeted for failing to comply with the United States and were set up to be punished and looted. While the narrative may seem complicated, it is necessary to share additional details to adequately explain what happened next and why it connects to the attack on Lydia. First, the state of Oklahoma assigned guardian Curtis E. Holderman to the deceased Sunday Christie, and the Dawes Commission allowed Holderman to take allotments using Christie's name. He plundered Christie's land, then extended his reach into Christie's kin network. Andrew David Morton—a banker at First National Bank of Tahlequah, a Prairie Oil and Gas Company board member, and the guardian of at least six other minors from 1904 to 1910—selected allotments for Sunday Christie's minor children in 1904. Sometime between 1904 and 1908, William Glory became guardian to Christie's children—Daniel, Annie, Sallie, and Arch—and was selling their land by 1908 to settlers. Andrew David Morton sold Arch's allotment to Frank Griffin, the man who came to own Julia Thorne's allotment.[22]

The guardians and attorneys stole from the Rattling Gourd and Christie families and then began fighting each other over their stolen Cherokee goods immediately after Sunday Christie's murder. Samuel C. Pitts, a former clerk to the Dawes Commission and thus an insider, contested the allotment of Christie's son, Daniel, on behalf of Rattling Gourd's father, Jack, and succeeded in reverting control of Daniel's land to Jack. Samuel Pitts likely forged the signature of Sunday Christie's widow, Jennie. Jennie petitioned to recover her and her son's allotments. As a monolingual Cherokee speaker, she would have had to rely on others to assist her.[23] The allotment obtained by Benge one week after Rattling Gourd's arrest overlapped with the allotment assigned to his father in 1905. Pitts jumped on this opportunity as well and filed a contest on behalf of Jack Rattling Gourd, winning a confession of judgment signed by Benge.[24] In other words, the murder of Sunday Christie triggered a predatory scramble among guardians and attorneys, who then turned on each other to claim stolen

Cherokee lands. Not content with what they themselves had stolen, they even fought other settlers for what they had stolen. In the ensuing chaos, insiders like Samuel Pitts and George Benge fraudulently seized and even contested overlapping allotments, exploiting legal loopholes and forging documents to steal from both the Christie and Rattling Gourd families, another sign that both Cherokee men were harmed for just this purpose.

Congress, attorneys, clerks, guardians, oil company representatives, and commissioners bear the blame for the attack on Lydia, but judges acting on behalf of Congress must be included as well. Federal agents dragged Looney Rattling Gourd to federal court in Vinita, Oklahoma. US District Attorney Pliny Leland Soper brought the case forward. Yet the archives hold no record of a trial in *US v. Rattling Gourd*, not even a line item in the bench docket. Joseph A. Gill incarcerated Rattling Gourd over three hundred miles away from his tribe's relocated homelands, imposing a fine of $1,000 on him. Judge Gill acted as a legal weapon of Congress, riding a cascade of theft in Indian Territory on the Cherokee Reservation, and he, too, participated in the guardianship racket.[25] A contemporaneous book praised Judge Gill for never sending Native men to federal prison, knowing they died there from tuberculosis. Yet the very thing the book claimed the judge refused to do, he did. Perhaps the plan meant death for Rattling Gourd in prison due to tuberculosis.[26]

Much of the information about Looney Rattling Gourd comes from his prison records. Some of his descendants saw a photo of him for the first time when I sent them Rattling Gourd's mugshot from the prison archive. Major Robert Wilson McClaughry—a Civil War veteran, head of the Chicago Police Department from 1891 to 1893, and a Republican—had complete control over Rattling Gourd for the six years he was incarcerated. Looney Rattling Gourd entered prison on March 29, 1904, at twenty-one years old. The prison extensively documented the young Cherokee man's moles, calm demeanor, height and weight, pulse, and habits. However, they failed to mention his hormonal acne, an indication of his youth.[27]

The state documented Rattling Gourd's alleged act of violence while failing to record the violence against Lydia. The United States documented his moles but not her burns. The only public photo of him exists in the prison archive. You can see the sacred rage in Rattling Gourd's mugshot. You can see the pain and the anger. Prison workers pointed the camera at this twenty-one-year-old Cherokee, and he looked straight into the future. They wanted a record of a "criminal," but the lens caught something else. His eyes hold a century of grief, his jaw set against the lie of his guilt. The photo flashes like a war banner. You cannot look away because his face will not let you.

While Rattling Gourd fought his own battles in prison, Lydia may have scrubbed laundry, unaware that the same system stealing his land would soon boil her skin. Under the warden, Fort Leavenworth kept careful records of Rattling Gourd's letter-writing campaign. Rattling Gourd sent forty-eight letters to US marshals, senators, agents, attorneys, and the Dawes Commission during his prison sentence, likely assisted by a bilingual Cherokee speaker also facing incarceration. Many of his correspondents must have shared his concerns with others because he received almost twice as many letters as he sent, including many from individuals he never wrote. In prison, Rattling Gourd sought to document and expose the men stealing from him. Through incarceration, the state kept him isolated from relatives and community, limiting his access and movement. But Rattling Gourd could write Cherokee speakers on the outside using the Cherokee syllabary and used his time to learn of the dealings of the Dawes Commission, Indian agents, and corrupt attorneys such as Benge. He would not give up.[28]

Yet Rattling Gourd suffered this fate alongside another Cherokee man from the Cherokee Reservation in Indian Territory. In October 1904, the United States arrested Jack Teekahlanneesky (Downing) for the same crime as Rattling Gourd—allegedly killing another Cherokee over land. Yet neither Cherokee man held an allotment, a sure sign this cover story matched the one used to break Cherokee resistance with Christie and Rattling Gourd. Even Judge Gill admitted that two Cherokee men had been imprisoned and refused allotment, counseling all Cherokees to surrender to the allotment process. Teekahlanneesky, a Nighthawk, was sentenced in a US federal court and sent to Fort Leavenworth. As with Rattling Gourd, his trial records do not exist, likely because the United States never held a trial. Like Rattling Gourd, Teekahlanneesky only spoke Cherokee. Once there, Teekahlanneesky contracted tuberculosis and remained ill throughout his imprisonment. Rattling Gourd and Teekahlanneesky lived under a double confinement: first, to the stone walls of a US fort, a place built to subdue Native nations, and second, to an isolating silence with one man in the hospital ward and one in the prison yard. They could have built a small nation, a shared world through the Cherokee language, but the system ensured their separation even in shared captivity.[29]

The brutal isolation of this system was captured years later, in 1916, when Tom Roach, a Cherokee speaker and "chief of the Indian police in eastern Oklahoma," visited Teekahlanneesky. The newspaper reported that Teekahlanneesky, who had not spoken to anyone for three years, was "as tickled as a child" to finally have someone he could speak with. He hovered near Roach throughout their visit, eager to converse as much as possible. When Roach left, Teekahlanneesky "cried like a child." The reality of incarceration emerged stark as a wound: a grown man, sick with tuberculosis, broken by years of triple confinement—prison, disease, a world that would not speak Cherokee—weeping for the fleeting comfort of a single conversation in the language of his home.[30]

The legal farce surrounding both Rattling Gourd and Teekahlanneesky is confirmed by their complete absence from the legal paper trail. A search of the records of the US District Court in the Northern District of Indian Territory found no trace of Rattling Gourd or Teekahlanneesky. Their names are missing from the comprehensive Name Index of 4,496 Criminal Case Files (1894–1907). They are also absent from the court's bench dockets and its judgments and sentences ledgers. For men serving federal prison sentences, this complete lack of a judicial paper trail seems more than an oversight. It serves as evidence of incarceration processed through extra-legal means, bypassing the documented court system entirely.[31]

Looney Rattling Gourd likely entered prison completely befuddled as to the truth about Benge, his land, the guardians, the attorneys, and the judges in his midst. It took him six years to figure out how Benge had betrayed him. Rattling Gourd spent his first year in prison writing only to his Cherokee relatives in the Cherokee syllabary. His letters to friends and family likewise show his savvy in seeking knowledge from Native people to uncover the truth behind the US government's fraudulent actions. All of this knowledge was gained through his parents having taught him the syllabary, which allowed him to stay in communication with them, even from three hundred miles away.

His Cherokee relatives may have pieced together some of the fraud committed against Rattling Gourd because, in 1905, he pivoted to Benge, Indian agents, and the Dawes Commission, demanding answers about his land. When Rattling Gourd began sending these letters in English, he must have paid a translator in crumpled prison wages, the same coins Lydia might have earned scrubbing stains from settler collars. But letters written in English, like the laws they invoked, circulated as part of a rigged game. Every English word bent his Cherokee truth into shapes the federal prison could file away. The lists bear witness to Rattling Gourd's persistence in recording the names of those who had taken authority over Cherokee people and Cherokee lands. The ledgers of his letters demonstrate his intense focus to grasp the US bureaucracy, as he meticulously gathered names and addresses of those who held control over his nation's homelands.[32]

THOSE WHO RATTLING GOURD WROTE TO:		THOSE WHO WROTE TO RATTLING GOURD:	
George W. Benge	attorney	W. W. Hastings	Natl Atty Cher. Nation
Dana H. Kelsey	Indian agent	George W. Benge	attorney
Dawes Commission	federal agency	Dana H. Kelsey	Indian agent
Curtis E. Holderman	guardian	Curtis E. Holderman	attorney
James H. Huckleberry	attorney	Dept. of Interior	federal agency
Francis E. Leupp	Indian agent	Indian agency	federal agency
Guion Miller	Indian Comm.	US Court of Claims	federal agency
George N. Wise	Dept. of Interior	Deuven McDonald	attorney
J. George Wright	Indian Comm.	Dept. of Interior	federal agency

THOSE WHO RATTLING GOURD WROTE TO:		THOSE WHO WROTE TO RATTLING GOURD:	
William M. Craven	attorney	William M. Craven	attorney
Horace Gray	US marshal	J. George Wright	Indian inspector
Robert Owen	US senator	Lee Bond	attorney
H. N. Morgan	attorney	Charles Mercer	attorney
James Finch	attorney	Bingo Oil Co.	US company
W. W. Bennett	attorney	Robert Owen	US senator
		G. F. Hawke	Dept. of Interior
		Thomas Ryan	Dept. of Interior
		George N. Wise	Dept. of Interior
		J. George Wright	Dept. of Interior
		Guion Miller	Dept. of Interior

What remains in the prison archive holds a tiny fraction of what Rattling Gourd received. It includes letters about him received by the warden, as some refused to reply directly to Looney. The letters bear witness to an unhinged Benge, frantic about the oil lease he signed before even securing the allotment. In fact, Benge spent years beseeching and demanding Rattling Gourd to sign land documents—offering money, making promises, and proposing to get him a pardon. Rattling Gourd refused to sign. George Washington Benge was so crazed in some letters that he revealed his own lies, claiming to be Rattling Looney's attorney at the trial yet not knowing his sentence or basic information such as how long he had been in prison. Rattling Gourd demanded that Benge provide the full written record of his allotments, leases, and proof of employment to prove Benge was lying.[33]

George Washington Benge never provided proof that Rattling Gourd had hired him. His four-page handwritten letter to the warden sits in the archive today, reeking of lies and manipulation. He claimed Looney and his father hired him for the murder trial and offered their allotments, in lieu of payment, to explain why he took allotments on Rattling Gourd's behalf while confined in jail, then prison. Benge denied knowing that Looney's third allotment had oil deposits despite signing a contract with Prairie Oil five days before he took the allotment. Benge demanded payment from Rattling Gourd for legal fees and his signature on the oil lease documents, promising to hold his oil money for him until his release from Fort Leavenworth.[34] Rattling Gourd made Benge an offer: He would sign the vouchers if his "funds can be left in the hands of the Indian Agent and disbursed" to him upon his release. He also let Benge know he wanted nothing to do with him.[35]

Imagine Rattling Gourd's fury on learning that, while he sat incarcerated, Benge stole allotments in his name, dragged him into a US federal process he opposed, then denied him access to his own records. Imagine the nation-state occupying his tribal lands and telling him these transactions passed as legal, that Benge merely acted as his attorney. From their standpoint, no thief existed. Only a legitimate attorney serving his client. The contest became Rattling Gourd's word against Benge's, and how could Rattling Gourd prove he had never hired Benge? Without proof, the script flipped: Rattling Gourd became a liar, Benge a competent attorney. Benge framed and blamed the victim, but so too did the federal government, which held Cherokee resisters in the lowest possible regard.

Rattling Gourd turned to the very sources of the bureaucratic violence that dispossessed him: US federal agencies. The Dawes Commission held his records. Benge would never turn them over. Even as Cherokees in the Keetoowah Nighthawk Society refused allotment, the US value-based system foisted it upon them, nonetheless. Rattling Gourd held title to land he never requested and possessed no physical proof. Nor could he easily access that title from a federal prison. Yet he worked urgently to uncover what Benge had taken and where those allotments lay, information dispossessed from him even as he himself was dispossessed. Between 1905 and 1910, he corresponded thirty-nine times with Dana H. Kelsey, a Department of the Interior agent at Muskogee. Agent Kelsey also corresponded with the warden, who intervened on Rattling Gourd's behalf, requesting his land records.[36]

In the years leading up to Rattling Gourd's release, even more players entered the scene. In 1908, attorney William M. Craven promised Rattling Gourd money but never sent it. Two parties terminated their oil leases with Looney in the following months, and the Department of the Interior signed yet another allotment deed for land Benge had already leased. In 1909, the warden confessed that Rattling Gourd felt "helpless" and predicted that he would lose his title without US intervention.[37]

Even as Rattling Gourd worked assiduously to catch Benge in his crimes, Benge was committing additional ones by forging Rattling Gourd's signature in English. Benge dragged the pen across the paper like the slow sear of boiling water, another mark of ownership to which neither Rattling Gourd nor Lydia consented. The oil and gas lease frenzy began while Rattling Gourd suffered incarceration in jail in Vinita in 1903 and continued into 1909 when he faced time in prison.[38] The 1909 Eastern Oil lease seems connected to Rattling Gourd's sudden release in 1910. In the summer of 1910, Looney signed the land documents Benge had been sending him for several years, and in November 1910, he walked out of prison a free man but a former felon. Confessing to murder and signing Benge's land documents resulted in his release from prison.[39]

Rattling Gourd left prison after six years, but they stole his paper trail of resistance. The prison took his personal items for inspection on the day of his release. He requested they be returned before he left, but prison personnel said they had vanished. Within hours of Rattling Gourd's departure for the Cherokee Reservation in Oklahoma on the same day of his release, the prison staff miraculously found some of his records, as noted in the warden's letter to Looney. But he only enclosed two of the dozens of letters that had been sent to him. The prison kept his other papers, and they only kept a handful of them in his prison file. The prison's denial of possessing Rattling Gourd's letters effectively erased the very correspondence that Rattling Gourd had fought and struggled to obtain in order to document the theft of his land. Without the dozens of letters held by Fort Leavenworth Prison, Rattling Gourd had little on which to base a legal battle against the state of Oklahoma.[40]

Rattling Gourd's freedom was restored as he returned to the Cherokee Reservation, even though his prison records were "lost." The warden's belated letter, a fraction of his letters, arrived too late.

Looney settled into marriage and family life after prison. In 1912, he married Lucinda Ketcher who gave birth to seven children from 1913 to 1927. She passed away suddenly in 1933, at the age of thirty, leaving six children behind.[41] After prison, Rattling Gourd had many land transactions, including with oil and gas companies. His 1909 oil lease with Eastern Oil Company ended in 1923, relinquished by the company's vice president, Edward Wheeler. Rattling Gourd's new leases in 1909 and 1923 received only an $18 advance and a $180 bonus, while 12.5 percent of the proceeds went to the US government to be held in trust. In 1931, Eastern Oil Company paid one dollar to cancel the 1923 lease, but the unsigned document was not filed with Cherokee authorities as required by law. By 1929, Rattling Gourd held five parcels of land in Tulsa, Washington, and Delaware Counties. In 1932, he sold a highway right-of-way to Tulsa County for $77.50, with a clause for land reversion if unused. The document was poorly notarized.[42]

Near the time of Rattling Gourd's death in 1950, the acting general superintendent at the Department of the Interior Five Civilized Tribes Agency secured tax-exempt status for Rattling Gourd's lands—a small victory. But Rattling Gourd's oil-rich properties in Washington County were entangled in exploitative deals, passing through lawyers, corporations, and courts. Even after his death, his children fought to reclaim what was stolen, suing Washington County in 1967. His legacy became one of relentless resistance, with his family inheriting both the land and his unfinished fight for justice.[43]

Rattling Gourd's nephew spoke of his uncle's alleged crimes as if he knew they were false. He remembered Looney carried a large gun with him at all times after he left prison. According to his nephew, rumors circulated that Looney killed multiple people. Rattling Gourd may have allowed the community to believe he killed Sunday Christie. Rattling Gourd may have confessed in prison to secure his release and never spoke of his innocence in order to stay safe, a bitter irony. The gun both protected and performed—signaling him as a "bad" man to shield him from future attacks. This left Rattling Gourd open to more accusations, possibly even the story that he harmed Lydia.

But such an accusation may have served as protection for himself and for the Cherokee community he loved. Had Lydia named a settler as her attacker, she and her children might have faced more violence. Looney's silence in the face of being labeled a violent man, like his gun, acted as a weapon of last resort.[44]

He lies in rest in the same cemetery as Sunday Christie, another indication the community knows Rattling Gourd did not kill Christie.

Lydia never testified about the 1937 attack. No court recorded her screams. But on the Cherokee Reservation, the pavement still ends where Julia Thorne's allotment began, and if you press your ear to the ground, you can hear the echo of boiling water hitting dirt. The attack on Lydia, her husband's ax wound, the knife attack on Arch Christie, Ned and Sunday Christie's murders, and the incarceration of Rattling Gourd and Teekahlanneesky represent not isolated tragedies but verses in the same hymn of settler violence. Each began with a Cherokee body broken: Lydia's skin seared, Blackbird's foot split like firewood, Arch Christie running from his would-be assassin, and Sunday Christie's blood soaking into the dirt. Each was followed by the hush of vanished records: no headlines for Lydia's screams, no investigation into John Blackbird's "accident," no manhunt for Sunday Christie's real killer. And each, in time, left land stripped from Cherokee hands: Julia Thorne's acreage pocketed by a judge, Blackbird forced into allotment and a guardianship, Sunday Christie's children's parcels signed away by men like banker Andrew David Morton.

The Cherokee community knew these stories wove together as threads in the same noose. They spoke of Christie's murder in lowered voices, not to hide the truth but to starve the lie. To name Lydia's attacker outright would have painted targets on her children and grandchildren; to demand justice for John Blackbird might have cost his remaining acres. Silence became a kind of suture, holding the wound closed against the infection of settler law. Looney Rattling Gourd had learned this the hard way: His prison letters, those paper arrows of truth, vanished into the prison abyss.

When Looney walked free in 1910, he carried this knowing in his bones. The gun he gripped served as more than just a weapon. His gun spoke the only language settlers understood.

ALLOTMENT MONSTER

Lydia Kingfisher's boiled flesh and Looney Rattling Gourd's stolen land represent two sides of the same coin. The violence took different forms—one brutal, one bureaucratic—but served the same purpose: to replace Cherokee control of their own homeland with settler control. What the Trail of Tears did not kill, allotment did, not with bayonets and forced marches but with deeds and fractions, ink and silence. The language was stripped, the land grid-carved, and kinship unraveled into "heirs" and "competency." The violence of removal did not end once in Indian Territory. Allotment arrived, and the 1887 law generated more than policy. The new violence of allotment performed a calculated undoing, unraveling centuries of Cherokee land relationships into fragments that could be burned, bought, or buried. The system spoke courtroom English while swallowing Cherokee futures through legal documents many Cherokees could not read, growing fat on the gap between what was the law and what was recorded.

Today, Amah Mutsun chairman Val Lopez in California voices the quiet catastrophe of this history for tribal nations beyond Cherokees in Oklahoma: "I can't afford to live in our territory." His words capture the cruel genius of allotment. Allotment did not just take Native lands. Allotment made Indigenous people strangers on their own ground, pricing them out of their homelands through the very system that claimed to protect their interests. This outcome happened by design. As Heidi Kiiwetinepinesiik Stark, Turtle Mountain Ojibwe scholar, reveals, framing Indigenous people as criminals or incompetents served to "avert attention from their own illegality." The Dawes Commission claimed to bring order. But instead it brought chaos, ignoring existing Cherokee settlements to impose a foreign grid of property lines that turned homes into legal abstractions: section numbers, township coordinates, fractions of fractions.[45]

The language of allotment never meant to communicate, only to exclude. "Warranty deed," "SE ¼ of SE ¼," "Book 12, Page 377," land drawn into squares, and titles and phrases impossible to translate into Cherokee. This syntax baffled and controlled even for English speakers, let alone Cherokee speakers. The system still runs on this calculus: coordinates instead of creek bends, subpoenas instead of stories. To demand your own land records in Cherokee County today means to face a gauntlet of clerks armed with plat maps and contempt, their jargon a weapon. The true violence of allotment lay in its forced migration, not just of bodies from land, but of minds from one world to another, where the rules were written in ciphers controlled by settlers.

The late nineteenth century saw the US perfect its machinery of dispossession. After using the Civil War to consolidate federal power, Congress passed the 1885 Major Crimes Act just two years before the Dawes Act. The 1885 act asserted jurisdiction over Native-on-Native crimes for the first time, a direct attack on tribal sovereignty. Boarding schools like Carlisle tore children from families while the "Civilization Regulations" outlawed Native ceremonies, creating what Luana Ross, Confederated Salish and Kootenai scholar, calls "the social construction of Native criminality." As Lakota scholar Vine Deloria Jr. famously countered: "To imply Indians were given land completely reverses the facts of history." The Dawes Act feigned to embody generosity. Theft wrapped in paperwork, what scholar Robert Nichols calls "recursive dispossession" operated as a form of "property-generating theft."[46]

By the time of Lydia's birth, in 1907, Oklahoma's county courthouses had become engines of erasure. Men like Judge Frank Griffin, who may have stolen Julia Thorne's Tahlequah allotment through forged deeds, acted as the system's operators. As scholar Shiri Pasternak writes, settler colonialism "organizes and manages authority" through jurisdiction. Griffin did not just take land; he became justice of the peace, weaponizing the law itself. The results devastated Cherokee communities in what became Oklahoma: Cherokee women like Lydia suddenly held individual deeds instead of clan-protected land rights, becoming sitting ducks for guardianship scams and violence. Scholar Jasbir Puar would suggest their bodies became sites of "value extraction, maimed to make them 'disposable.'"[47]

Yet Lydia's story goes beyond mere loss. Her survival, sewing prize-winning dresses while raising eight children through the Depression, mirrors what scholar Rose Stremlau identifies as Cherokee "strategies for physical survival [that] enabled cultural survival."

Even as allotment fractured families, Cherokees adapted: Looney Rattling Gourd, imprisoned on false murder charges, fought Benge's land theft by writing letters from prison to people who might help him. Their resistance matters today when 87 percent of Oklahoma's original allotments are owned by non-Natives.[48]

The paper trail reveals the human cost. Zitkála-Ša's 1924 investigation exposed how Oklahoma county courts treated "Indian estates as legitimate game." The Yankton Dakota writer documented the collusion between attorneys, judges, bankers, and undertakers in *Oklahoma's Poor Rich Indians*. But archives cannot capture Lydia's third-place ribbon at the 1937 fair—the way she may have pinned that satiny prize to her handmade dress, asserting her worth in a world that wanted her silent. Indigenous Australian scholar Aileen Moreton-Robinson reframes allotment not as "assimilation" but as property warfare: "From the 16th century, race and gender divided humans into owning property, becoming propertyless, and being property."[49] Lydia lived all three at once.

Her attacker used boiling water because burns leave no bullet holes, just like allotment left no visible scars on the land. But walk Tahlequah's streets today, past the State Farm building on Julia Thorne's stolen acreage, and you are walking through an open wound. But the monster did not win. The Cherokee Reservation is still there, as are Cherokees. Looney Rattling Gourd's granddaughter lived the rest of her life on her great-grandfather's allotment, not as a relic of loss, but as a testament to the quiet persistence of Cherokee kinship. Like Lydia's stitches holding fabric together, these unbroken ties defy the gridlines of allotment.[50]

Today, Sequoyah's Cherokee syllabary is celebrated on street signs and syllabary charts, with Downing Street in Tahlequah being a prominent example of this—ironically the same name as the man who languished in prison with tuberculosis—but true Cherokee language justice demands more. Cherokee language revitalization programs are vital, yet the contradictions of allotment remain. The syllabary is not a museum piece. The Cherokee language forms a weapon of survival. The Cherokee language presents an altogether different world. It deserves space to be, to breathe, to exist, to be heard, to be learned.

The monster of allotment left its marks: Rattling Gourd's prison file, Julia Thorne's forged deeds, Lydia's melted skin, Blackbird's scarred foot, Christie's chilling grave marker. But this story shows more than just scars. Lydia lingers in the way her descendants remember her love: fierce as her silence about the boiling water.

Allotment sought to replace clan-held land with a settler regime: governments who claimed jurisdiction, judges who stole, attorneys who forged, and agents who enforced the theft. Their power took tangible form; it lived in the hands of settlers like Frank Griffin, bankers like Andrew Morton, and government workers who were devoted to the Dawes Commission and who turned land into fractions and people into prey. In Canada, another woman's body would become the next battlefield in this war of dispossession. Her family called her Gloria Levina "Lee" Moody.

In the next chapter, "Levina," we move to Canada in 1969 to consider another arm of settler law: settler assailants on land fully controlled by settlers, the transition complete. The law acts through judges and courtrooms, but their actions rely on the police patrolling the spaces outside their courthouses, operating as collectors and speakers of truth. Settler law acted as an instrument to move ownership of Indigenous lands into the hands of settlers and their governments. The law in both the United States and Canada serve the interests of the nation. Their earliest function, protecting the property interests of owners, cast them in settler colonialism as support and protection, no matter the cost. In the case of Levina, we see how the infrastructure of settler colonialism via roads, towns, and Canadian police into British Columbia put her in the direct path of Canadian settlers and the legal system that shielded them from consequences.

GUIDE TO KEY FIGURES IN CHAPTER 2

GLORIA LEVINA MOODY: Nuxalk woman, speaker, and mother. Went by Levina or "Lee." One of eight siblings. Her family pronounces Levina as *luh-vine-uh*. Murdered in 1969.

VANESSA MOODY HANS: Levina's daughter.

DAISY MOODY: Levina's mother.

DAVE MOODY: Brother of Levina. Present with Levina on the trip to Williams Lake.

DANIEL MOODY: Levina's son.

DAVID MOODY: Levina's father. Died in 1972.

RON MOODY: Oldest brother of Levina Moody. Tried to discover who killed his sister. Hit-and-run victim. Murder victim.

KAREN ANDERSON: Nuxalk elder, matriarch, and Nuxalk speaker and teacher. Levina's cousin. Remembers Levina as brave.

DEAN MOODY: Younger brother of Levina. Creator of the Moody family photo collages spanning half a century.

LESTER EVANS BLAKE: A mechanic who worked for the City of Williams Lake. He was the passenger in Eugene Johnson's truck when they discovered Levina's body. He testified at the inquest.

EUGENE JOHNSON: Drove his truck into the area where he and Blake found Levina's body. He called the police from the two-way radio in his truck.

SIDNEY SAMUEL LEITH: Coroner and judge at Williams Lake in 1969. Ran inquest and selected jurors.

DR. HAN CHOO LEE: Doctor who performed the autopsy of Moody.

CORPORAL DONALD CHARLES MCDONALD: Present at autopsy. Testified to driving body parts to Vancouver.

FRED NAUNDORF: Jury member of inquest. Brother-in-law of suspect Darold Weir.

E-PANA: Group of Royal Canadian Mounted Police (RCMP) officers who reworked cases in the 2010s.

ALBERT WILLIAM BLOHM: One of the suspects named by the RCMP. Died in 1972 two weeks after a gunshot wound to the abdomen. Ex-husband of Georgia Toni Brecknock. His name was first published in Angela Sterritt's book, *Unbroken* (2023).

GEORGIA TONI BRECKNOCK: Sister of John Brecknock. Ex-wife of suspect Albert Blohm. Possibly worked for RCMP at Williams Lake in 1969. Went by her middle name, Toni.

MARTIN (SLIM) BRECKNOCK: John Brecknock's brother, who ran the Frontier Inn at Anahim Lake and hired brother-in-law Albert Blohm as a bartender.

DARLYNE BRECKNOCK: Wife of Martin "Slim" Brecknock, who co-ran the Frontier Inn.

HAROLD WYLIE: Coroner at Cranbrook who signed off on Albert Blohm's death certificate.

DAROLD EDWARD WEIR: One of the suspects named by the RCMP. Died at age thirty-one in 1973.

JUDY ELIZABETH NAUNDORF WEIR: Darold Weir's wife.

BUD WEIR: Darold's brother. Signed death certificate.

MORRIS WYNRIB: Doctor who signed Weir's death certificate. Later named in a case that went to the Supreme Court of Canada for having sexually assaulted a patient.

RONALD ALEXANDER MCMILLAN: One of the suspects named by the RCMP. Died in 1980.

SUSAN BULLER: Stepdaughter of Ronald McMillan. Completed and signed death certificate.

SHIRLEY JEAN DOYLE MCMILLAN: Ronald McMillan's wife.

JOHN ROBERTS: Australian veterinarian and coroner who signed McMillan's death certificate.

LYNN STATTON: Pictured with Ronald McMillan in 1976.

JOHN DOUGLAS BRECKNOCK: Retired RCMP officer. Albert Blohm was married to his sister, Georgia Toni Brecknock. Police source for the 1998 newspaper announcement naming three suspects.

GEORGE S. BRECKNOCK: Father of John Brecknock. Hired by RCMP at Alexis Creek after his retirement. Died in 1983.

ANNE BRECKNOCK: Mother of John Brecknock. Died in 1997.

SUSAN BRECKNOCK: Sister of John Brecknock. RCMP worker.

TERRY BRECKNOCK: John Brecknock's wife.

ANGIE MINDUS: Staff writer at *The Tribune* at Williams Lake.

DOUG NORBERG: Owner of Norberg Motors. The car found at the murder scene was registered to his dealership. Later married Judy Brecknock, sister of John.

SAM MOODY: Brother of Levina Moody.

MEL MCINTOSH: RCMP corporal at Williams Lake. His 1989 flight to investigate a lead on Levina's case crashed during takeoff. Later claimed that Officer Murray Neufeld told him the case was solved in 1994 following a deathbed confession from a suspect.

JOHN PILSZEK: The RCMP officer whose name was first published in 1998, stating Levina's case was solved.

MURRAY NEUFELD: RCMP corporal at Williams Lake. His 1989 flight to investigate a lead on Levina's case crashed during takeoff. Later claimed that Officer Murray Neufeld told him the case was closed in 1994 following a deathbed confession from a suspect.

EMMA HEWETT/"PHIL, THE TRUCKER": Person who contacted Vanessa Moody Hans through Facebook and phone calls using a false identity. Claimed to have information about Levina's murder.

CHAPTER 2

LEVINA

Along with her children, Levina visited a portrait studio the month before she passed. The photo saved from that studio session graces the front cover of this book. Her family's joy, so very palpable in the portrait, demands more than a footnote. Levina's daughter, Vanessa, had just turned four years old, and her little brother, Dan, had turned three, when someone murdered their mother, Gloria Levina "Lee" Moody. Fifty years later, the grief still clawed at Vanessa. Levina's mother, Daisy, raised Levina's children as her own. When Vanessa and Dan learned Daisy was not their biological mother, she asked them if they had memories of their biological mother. They did not.

In 1999, Daisy arranged a second memorial for Vanessa and Dan, who were now struggling to understand she was not their biological mother. Although holding a second memorial is unheard of in the Nuxalk Nation, Daisy wanted to create space for memories and healing for the whole Moody family—Levina's siblings, aunts and uncles, and children. "You bring the ancestors in our ceremonies," Vanessa explained to me during one of our conversations. "When my mom's spirit came in, I heard a scream. I realized it was me. I fell to the floor." In Nuxalk ceremonies, the ancestors enter not as silent guests. They arrive with the weight of history. That night, when her mother's spirit stepped into the room, Vanessa's scream sounded like a wound ripped open, one that Canada had bandaged with lies for decades.

Vanessa's mother is buried with other members of the Moody family in the graveyard at Bella Coola, British Columbia. Vanessa avoids taking the most direct route from her home to avoid the cemetery that also holds the grave of her only biological brother, Daniel. She knows he died as a result of the massive trauma everyone in their family endured as a result of their mother's murder. Dan used to introduce himself by saying, "Hi, my name is Dan, and I'm damaged goods." The 1969 murder of Levina, almost six decades ago, broke Levina's father as well. Vanessa remembers, "He locked himself in Levina's room and lay there without eating or sleeping. When he emerged, his hair had turned pure white." He too died an early death, in 1972, a man consumed by loss.[1]

Ron Moody also died an early death as a result of the 1969 murder of his sister. Ron, Levina's eldest brother, always had a strong, fiery personality, according to his siblings. Years after the murder, Ron relocated to Williams Lake from Bella Coola to investigate his sister's murder and find answers. He studied the Shuswap language (Secwepemctsín), a language completely different than Nuxalk, to be able to speak to Secwépemc people around Williams Lake who may have heard something about the murder. While there, he felt he had "come very close to the truth but intimidation and fear kept the facts from coming out." During this brave solo journey far from home in enemy territory, Ron was struck by a hit-and-run driver, perhaps not accidentally. In the Williams Lake hospital for weeks, he nearly died from his injuries, which included the crushing of his throat. Medical staff barely saved his life and his ability to speak. He left Williams Lake feeling defeated, returning to Nuxalk Territory at Bella Coola. Back home, he turned to alcohol to cope with the outcome of his Williams Lake investigation. Today, his brother Dean remembers Ron having never shared details of the attack or what he learned about the murder of his sister. He was effectively silenced, the flame inside him snuffed out. He turned to alcohol to cope. In 1994, he was murdered.[2]

For Vanessa, who lives and works in Bella Coola as a Nuxalk language teacher today, the psychological toll of driving past the cemetery that houses so many relatives takes too much for daily encounters, which prompts her to seek different routes, but at great emotional cost she visits the family burial site on holidays and days of remembrance. Despite a devoted and loving biological grandmother who raised Vanessa as if she were her biological mother—teaching Vanessa the Nuxalk language and surrounding her with a large network of relatives of her mother—Vanessa had to navigate coming of age along with realizing the woman she knew as her mother was her biological grandmother. Coupled with visits from RCMP officers inflicting further trauma as she grew from a child into a woman, Vanessa has carried the heavy, nearly unbearable lifelong burden of searching for the names of the people who killed her mother. She has spent the last two decades researching and piecing together what may have happened to her biological mother, Gloria Levina Moody. Every visit to the cemetery and her mother's grave confronted her with excruciating and unanswered questions: Who killed her mother? And why had Canada looked away and betrayed her?[3]

Descended from two important chiefs of the Nuxalk, Levina lived a life steeped in Nuxalk language, tradition, and culture with her mother, Daisy, and father, David. Her parents loved her deeply; practiced potlatch, a gift-giving and ceremonial feast; spoke Nuxalk fluently and primarily; and kept their children out of the hands of the Canadian government.

Levina's favorite flower was the purple aster. Her brother Sam remembered her as "a very loving person, very considerate of others. Her children were the world to her."[4] Her cousin, Karen, remembers Levina as always brave, even as a teenager. When they once rode their bikes too far, Levina was the one to ask someone for help. Levina filled the role of big sister in every way, being very protective of her youngest brother, Dave, always looking out for him. The Moody family is known for their generosity as Karen's parents took in individuals in need and made them kin. Levina's daughter, Vanessa, did the same decades later. The Moody family treasures their kin. Levina's younger brother, Dean, began building collages of family photos decades ago. When I met him, he held three massive poster boards covered with images of the entire extended Moody family spanning at least half a century.[5]

Dave—family members call him Al—traveled to Williams Lake with his parents and sister that weekend in 1969. In response to questions about that fateful night, Dave repeated the same intention: "I've tried so hard to forget."[6] We had been speaking for quite some time and looking at files, but when I pulled up a new record, I suddenly saw an ocean of pain moving through him. Something in him changed. Dean, his brother, did not see it because he was looking at the record. Vanessa was on the phone with her daughter and did not see it. But I saw and felt the change in Dave. When I stopped to ask if he was OK, he indicated he was, but I knew he wasn't and said so. Then Dave began sharing how much he loved Levina's children, how devastated he was by the loss of his big sister, and how much he wants peace.[7]

Despite the love, protection, and strength of her parents and extended family prior to 1969, a mere seventy-two-hour venture into the interior of British Columbia, to a town with a deeply violent residential school mission, placed Levina and her family at the epicenter of Indigenous trauma. The 1969 murder of Levina inexorably altered her parents, siblings, and community.

As Kahnawà:ke Mohawk professor Audra Simpson explains, no Indigenous woman remains immune from the crisis of settler violence, as evidenced by the murder of Loretta Saunders, an Inuk woman and student, in 2014:

> Her death demonstrates that no one is safe. . . . This structure, this assemblage, those people that articulate themselves through and for it, will find you, and subject you, it can kill you. You too can be emptied of your familial relations, your relationship to land, your signifying possibility as the ongoing project of empire transits . . . or plows through you. One's life, one's land, sovereignty, one's body, emptied out, in order for other things to pass through. . . . This is because if you are an indigenous woman your flesh is received differently. You have been subjected differently than others. Your life choices have been circumscribed in certain ways. And the violence, it seems, will find you, and choke you, and beat you, and possibly kill you.[8]

What happened to Levina Moody acts not as a random tragedy but proves Simpson's warning: The state will hunt down every last

Indigenous woman, even those who defy its narratives of brokenness, and will never admit to its own crimes against Indigenous people.

The cover-up of Levina's murder relied on more than a matter of lost paperwork. The cover-up proved an active, multigenerational operation. It involved coroners who made bizarre claims, doctors who defiled, and police who refused to disclose. It extended from the autopsy table to the courtroom, from the dusty backroads of Williams Lake to the Supreme Court of Canada. It ensured that those who killed Levina would never face justice in a Canadian courtroom, while those who sought justice were instructed to be silent. The system protected the suspected killers, especially their names, and suppressed evidence.

On Thursday, October 23, 1969, in Bella Coola, Levina left unceded Nuxalk territory with her parents and younger brother, Dave. She jumped in the car to head east toward Williams Lake on Highway 20. At twenty-six years old, she was a striking young Nuxalk mother, and she enjoyed the scenic trek. The family stopped at the Frontier Inn at Anahim Lake where they played shuffleboard. A white man stared so intensely at Levina that Dave, her younger brother, confronted him. The man defended himself saying he found Levina to be a beautiful woman. Family members later suspected this man tracked Levina to Williams Lake and acted as one of her killers.

Levina vanished from Williams Lake that Saturday night on October 25, 1969. Only the assailants and, perhaps, witnesses, know exactly how and when she disappeared. While we do not know what transpired, we do know that Levina's parents were deeply alarmed that their daughter was missing and informed the RCMP that night. The radio station also put an announcement on the radio the next morning about Levina being missing at the request of her parents. Levina's family suspects that when her parents quickly activated their network—contacting everyone imaginable—that this created a fear among the killers of being caught. The killers and police did not anticipate how intensely her parents would work to find Levina, between making the announcement and contacting Indigenous communities, friends, and relatives all over Williams Lake and British Columbia. In short, the Indigenous network of British Columbia was activated that very day to look for Levina.[9]

While her parents frantically took steps to locate their daughter, two white men found her around 10:30 a.m., but, tragically, she had perished. That Sunday morning, on October 26, Lester Evans Blake, a mechanic from Williams Lake, rode in Eugene Johnson's truck along an old cattle trail off Chilcotin Road, about seven miles west of town. That trail led to a small, unnamed body of water. Near a grove of poplar trees, they found her body. Two men stumbling into this extremely isolated area where Levina's body had been discarded seems potentially intentional. Blake and Johnson had no explanation for discovering the site of the murder. Though Johnson was the one driving the truck, only Blake testified at the inquest, held December 9 of that year. Johnson's truck brought the two men to the scene of the crime, and Johnson called police from his truck's two-way radio. The location was so remote and difficult to describe and find that Blake and Johnson returned to Chilcotin Road, waited for the police, and then drove back to the scene with the police following them.[10]

In his inquest testimony, Blake left open the possibility that their gruesome discovery was no accident. He testified: "We drove in there and we were looking." Blake and Johnson never explained why they drove on an old cattle trail or how they arrived at that exact location. Blake used the word "looking" to describe his actions, which is a telling turn of phrase. The police never investigated their possible connections to the suspects, the timing of the radio announcement, and the discovery of Levina's body.

The Vancouver Sun covered for the two men, claiming they were out hunting, but the two men were never quoted as having said this to reporters, nor did they testify to such in the inquest. During the inquest, when Corporal Voynovich asked Blake why he was in the isolated area with Johnson on a Sunday morning, Blake never answered the question. The corporal did not repeat the question or acknowledge Blake's refusal to answer. Johnson, the driver, was not questioned at the inquest.

Murdered late Saturday night or early Sunday morning, Levina was photographed by police from 11 a.m. to noon before they quickly transported her body to Cariboo Memorial Hospital in Williams Lake.[11] According to state records, some of the first people to arrive at the crime scene were coroner Sidney Samuel Leith, Dr. Han Choo Lee, Constable Maclean (no first name recorded), and Constable William Goughnour. Though among the first on the scene, Constables Maclean and Goughnour never testified at the inquest. As they drove her body to the hospital, the police knew the woman they found was Indigenous and that an Indigenous woman had been reported missing. They knew Levina's family was in town searching for her. They knew every Indigenous person in British Columbia had been alerted and was also looking for her.

Dr. Lee performed the autopsy at Cariboo Hospital the following day, Monday, October 27. According to Dr. Lee, both coroner Leith and Corporal McDonald were present during the autopsy.

Based on records released to me by the state, state employees may have committed crimes during the autopsy, according to federal Canadian and provincial laws. For instance, at the inquest, Dr. Lee testified to inserting as many fingers as possible into the vaginal canal of her corpse to measure the opening, in what can only be described as a postmortem sexual assault. No medical manual sanctions or recommends such an act, and it reveals nothing about cause of death. He recorded the removal for inspection of some of her organs but none from her reproductive system. Before the day ended, Dr. Lee confirmed on the record the cause of her death: "hypovolemic shock from the tear of the right uterine arteries."

The second potential crime by the state against Levina Moody occurred sometime between her autopsy and burial. At the December 9 inquest, which lasted a mere hour, an RCMP officer made a horrifying statement that begs investigation. Corporal McDonald testified to transporting "the female sex organs, parts of the uterus, etc." of Gloria Levina Moody on Wednesday, October 29, 1969, to the RCMP Crime Detection Laboratory in Vancouver for testing. Yet Dr. Lee did not document removal of those parts in his inquest testimony or in the autopsy report he authored. If Dr. Lee did not remove her organs, who did? Under Canadian criminal code, tampering with a corpse constitutes a serious crime.[12]

Corporal McDonald's inquest testimony about her body parts deployed a language of violence: "The female sex organs, parts of the uterus, etc." McDonald's words dehumanized Levina three times: The term "female sex organs" lacks medical precision; "parts of the uterus" obscured whether he took fragments or her entire organ; and the term "etc." shows indifference and reduced her to debris. He claimed to have received "some" of the test results by Wednesday evening, October 29. Although he received some test results that night, he only disclosed one test result at the December inquest, her alleged alcohol level. Additionally, Dr. Lee could have tested for alcohol levels in Williams Lake, but he did not.

Corporal McDonald further testified to returning to Williams Lake on Friday, October 31, without disclosing what had happened to the parts he drove to Vancouver. Her body lay in Bella Coola on October 31, and her family buried her that very day, never reunited with the body parts taken to Vancouver, never even knowing they had been removed. If the lab did not preserve her parts or the results, that removal would have destroyed evidence, including semen evidence. The autopsy and inquest as released to me failed to document obtaining bodily matter in Vancouver, conducting testing, or preserving the tissues or test results.[13]

With the inquest testimony of the potential dismemberment of Levina, we can ask questions. Given the long history of trafficking in Native body parts in the United States and Canada, we might wonder whether the possible removal of Levina's body parts echoes earlier practices of exploiting Native bodies. Chapter 5 explores this history in detail in the US, tracing grave robbing during the early Republic period into the nineteenth and twentieth centuries by medical schools, archaeologists, and anthropologists. We might also wonder about the similarities between what may have been done to Levina's body and what was done to Cindy Gladue's body. Gladue, a Bigstone Cree woman, was also murdered by sexual assault. The medical examiner removed the tear in her vaginal wall. In 2015, her flesh was brought into an Alberta courtroom to prove her injuries. In 2023, the court admitted to the Gladue family that they had "misplaced" her body part and their relative's full body could not be repatriated.[14]

Based on the historical context of grave robbing in Canada and the lack of confirmation of testing or preservation of tissue in the record, McDonald's testimony about Levina's body parts fails to demonstrate evidence testing or collection. If someone removed her body parts and McDonald drove them to Vancouver, those actions did not help to solve the crime. Serial killers and serial sexual offenders take trophies from their victims, a physical reminder they treasure. If someone removed her body parts, never took them to Vancouver, and never repatriated them to the family, someone may have trafficked her body parts, mirroring the killers' brutality by stealing her organs, particularly organs that symbolized Levina's womanhood and motherhood and also the crime against her. Where are her body parts?[15]

The state's records as released to me offered only one account of Levina's body between the early afternoon autopsy on October 27 in Williams Lake and October 31, when she was buried in Bella Coola. Corporal McDonald's testimony that he drove her "female sex organs, parts of the uterus, etc.," to Vancouver on October 29 and returned to Williams Lake on October 31. Dave Moody told me the family was informed that her body, not her body parts, was taken to Kamloops during those same days. McDonald's testimony about Vancouver and Dave's testimony about Kamloops could be about the same thing: the removal and transfer of her body parts. Telling the family that her body, in full, had to be sent to Kamloops could have been a story used to delay release of her body. Why did the state need to keep her body for three to four days in Williams Lake after the autopsy if they had already removed her body parts and never returned them to her body? The state records as released to me do not account for the removal, testing, or final destination of her body parts. The conflicting accounts of Levina's body parts in Vancouver and body in Kamloops mirror the conflicting accounts of how the RCMP obtained the suspects' names. In both cases, the state produced multiple stories that contradict each other.[16]

Coroner Sid Leith bore responsibility for choosing the jurors for Levina's inquest. He chose six men: Wayne Gardner, Fred Naundorf, Rene Johnson, Doug Pare, Robert Granberg, and Frank Armes. Fred Naundorf's sister was married to one of the suspects. Coroner Leith seems to have performed a similar role in the 1971 murder of Fred Quilt, a Tsilhqot'in man who died after being severely beaten, allegedly by RCMP officers, near Williams Lake at Alexis Creek. Leith stacked the inquest jury with an RCMP auxiliary officer who lived with two other RCMP officers. Despite witness testimony describing police brutality, Leith ruled the death as resulting from "natural causes," a decision that sparked public outrage and forced a reexamination of the case.[17]

Coroner Sidney Leith's silence during McDonald's testimony about Levina's organs suggested agreement. Leith's duty was to ensure that the autopsy and inquest adhered to Canadian and provincial laws, yet he let McDonald's account of trafficking organs go unchallenged. A juror who was the brother-in-law of a suspect, the absence of vaginal swabs, the possible removal of the victim's body parts—never reunited with her body or returned to the family—and phantom lab results together formed a protective ring around the killers of Levina.

Over the last five decades, the police have barely interacted with Levina's family. In the 1990s, when Levina's children were both in their twenties, the police brought them a box of extensive crime scene photos. The police counseled that they could look inside the box. Levina's son, Dan, opened it and viewed the entirety of its contents. Vanessa briefly saw one photo of her mom. She ran out of the station and fainted. Severely impacted by the many images he saw that day of his mother, Dan was traumatized, and he died an early death.[18]

In 1999, RCMP officers visited Levina's family again, claiming the case had been solved. The officers shared the names of three suspects, and assured the family that all three suspects were dead. They also informed the family they would not be releasing the names to the public. The message to Levina's family at the 1999 meeting seemed clear to them: You can have the names of the three dead suspects, but we are not going to investigate, and neither should you.[19]

In 2007, RCMP officer Pierre Lemaitre told the press that, contrary to earlier statements by other officers, the Moody case remained open. He also spoke out about violence against Indigenous women, particularly rape. He was harassed by fellow RCMP officers for years. In 2013, he took a medical leave and hanged himself. Not everyone believes he died by his own hand.[20]

Imagine the family's surprise when the police wanted to see them again and investigate the case in 2012. These RCMP officers worked as part of the E-Pana task force, established in 2005 and designed to investigate cases of missing and murdered Indigenous women. Seventy RCMP officers worked on eighteen cases over nine years, receiving approximately $25 million CAD for their work. Notably, E-Pana never made a single arrest.

E-Pana moved all case files to their headquarters in Surrey, near Vancouver, and invited Levina's family to their offices, some six hundred miles south of Bella Coola. At that meeting, E-Pana took DNA samples from the family without explaining why. At the 2012 meeting, E-Pana officials claimed to know nothing of the three suspect names given to the family in 1999. This constituted the last contact initiated by the RCMP with the Moody family.[21]

Since the murder in 1969, the suspected murderers of Levina Moody escaped justice, as they were never publicly named, arrested, or charged. Their names were buried under a half-century of narrative warfare, a strategy designed to protect the killers and present the case as closed. Even as the RCMP eventually produced three names, they offered conflicting accounts of how they obtained them, a shifting story that forms its own act of narrative warfare. This chapter first presents detailed sketches of the three white Canadian men named by the RCMP to Levina's family in 1999: Albert Blohm, Darold Weir, and Ronald McMillan. Then, it interrogates the narratives of how the police obtained these names. Since 1969, the nation-state of Canada and the province of British Columbia appear to have assaulted her corpse, potentially stolen body parts from her corpse, placed a suspect's relative on the inquest, and taken DNA from the Moody family without explanation. Additionally, based on oral history with Levina's family and state records, a clear pattern of suspicious deaths of suspects has emerged. The state labeled two suspects' deaths as suicides, despite evidence to the contrary, and the third suspect's death as a result of cirrhosis at just thirty-one years old.[22]

ALBERT WILLIAM BLOHM (1936–1972)

Albert Blohm died two years after the murder of Levina, the first of the suspects to die. Born in Kincaid, Saskatchewan, in 1936, Albert William Blohm was one of nine children of William and Emma Blohm. Blohm's father was born in North Dakota, and his mother immigrated from Dusseldorf, Germany. His family moved to British Columbia in 1951 when he was fifteen years old, living at 1322 Coghlan Road in Langley Township, now the Fraser Common Farm Co-Op. Known for being attractive and charming, Blohm committed crimes with ease, as people trusted him based on these superficial qualities. He married at age eighteen and had two sons, Steven and Leslie, with his first wife, Ann Elizabeth.

In 1955 at age nineteen, Blohm gang-raped a sixteen-year-old girl with William Edward Shore, age twenty-one, and Kenneth Leslie Shore, age sixteen, in Matsqui, British Columbia. A judge sentenced Blohm to three and half years in prison for the rape, adding that the details of the crime were "revolting and unspeakably bad." After prison, Blohm moved into an apartment on West Pender in Vancouver but moved out shortly before committing his next crime. At age twenty-two, he and Richard James Shellenberg committed armed robbery at the Aldergrove Hotel near Abbotsford. When caught, their female driver was found in possession of narcotics.[23]

After Blohm was sentenced to six years in federal prison, his wife, Ann Elizabeth, filed for divorce on May 11, 1959, and fled to England with the boys, wanting an ocean between her and her ex. Leaving prison for a second time, Blohm moved north to Williams Lake. He married Georgia Toni Brecknock around 1964. Toni gave birth to their first child in November 1965, very close to the time that Levina gave birth to her first child. Blohm obtained work as a bartender at the Frontier Inn from his wife's brother, Martin Brecknock, and Martin's wife, Darlyne. Levina's family wonders if Blohm was the man at the Frontier Inn who stared at Levina while she played shuffleboard and potentially followed her to Williams Lake with a plan to abduct and kill her.[24]

After Levina's murder in 1969, Blohm moved with his wife, Toni, many miles south to Cranbrook, British Columbia in 1970. When

Toni wanted out of her marriage, someone had two motives to help her: They could protect Toni and look like a hero, and they could prevent Blohm from being exposed as Levina's murderer and even, potentially, confessing. Blohm died in 1972. The death certificate lists a self-inflicted gunshot wound to the abdomen, an injury more commonly caused by another person. With the physical challenge of shooting oneself in the abdomen with a gun held backward, the death certificate makes little sense. Yet the death certificate records the death as suicide and indicates an autopsy was performed. No autopsy record exists. Harold Wylie, coroner for Cranbrook, British Columbia, signed the questionable document.[25]

Wylie also listed contradictory dates on Blohm's death certificate. He noted the date of injury as August 19 but noted that Blohm did not die until fifteen days later, on September 4—and not at a hospital. Wylie initially listed the date of death as August 19, then scratched it out and replaced it with September 4. Wylie's changes show potential confusion about the story they had potentially fabricated. He listed time of death as immediate, which would make it August 19, but he also said two weeks had elapsed between injury and death. The coroner allowed the victim's ex-wife, Toni, to sign the death certificate, but she wrote "no relation" on it and then ordered a rushed cremation. This official death certificate performed the charade of a death certificate. Could Blohm's death have been an execution wrapped in settler bureaucracy, designed to eliminate the weakest link? Did someone shoot Albert Blohm in the stomach in his apartment, leave him there for two weeks to die, and then call police to say they found a body?[26]

The death of Albert Blohm became the first building block in a narrative that would grow over the coming decades. In the telling of Blohm's death in the years since 1972, his end served as a kind of reckoning—karmic, inevitable, and the result of a guilty conscience finally catching up. In the narrative pushed by the RCMP and local newspapers, Blohm's "suicide" proved justice had been served. But Blohm's death, and those to come, was also used to assert there was nothing to investigate.[27]

DAROLD EDWARD WEIR (1941–1973)

In 1999, the RCMP also gave Levina's family the name of Darold Edward Weir. Weir died only five months after Albert Blohm. Weir was married to Judy Elizabeth Naundorf, whose brother, Fred, served as a juror at the inquest into Levina's death. Born on October 26, 1941, Weir was turning twenty-eight the weekend Levina vanished from the woods. He may have been out celebrating on Saturday night, October 25, when she disappeared from downtown Williams Lake.[28]

Originally from Elk Point, Alberta, Weir relocated to British Columbia as a teen. Like Blohm, Weir committed crimes at a young age. In 1960, at the age of eighteen, Penticton authorities charged him—along with Raymond Matkovich and Barry Ragget—for stealing from Canadian Canners Ltd. A few months later, he stole a car and drove it with a suspended license in Wells, getting him sent to Oakalla Prison in Vancouver.[29]

Weir's brothers lived north, in Williams Lake, and Weir relocated there after prison. Less than six months after Blohm's "suicide," a gunshot wound to the abdomen in 1972, Weir also died suddenly at only thirty-one years old, on February 12, 1973. The same hospital where Levina's body may have been ransacked for body parts produced Weir's death certificate. According to the RCMP's own later account, the third suspect, Ronald McMillan, was present at Weir's deathbed to ensure he made no deathbed confession.[30]

The paperwork for Weir's death presents irregularities that echo those of Blohm's. On the medical death certificate, Dr. Morris Wynrib indicated immediate cause of death to be acute hemorrhagic pancreatitis due to hepatitis. If true, the long-standing condition of hepatitis (inflamed liver) coincided with hemorrhagic pancreatitis, which can result from acute heavy alcohol use or trauma to the pancreas. But acute hemorrhagic pancreatitis plus hepatitis is a survivable condition if the patient receives proper medical treatment. Dr. Wynrib indicated that Weir had been in his care for forty-eight hours, raising the possibility that the hospital could have saved the relatively young man.[31]

Someone whose handwriting differed markedly from Dr. Wynrib's wrote in the margin of Weir's death certificate. The person added to the document the diagnosis "Laënnec's cirrhosis (alcoholic)." This addition shifted the focus away from the suddenness of the two diagnoses originally listed. But this addition in the margins only added more suspicion. The combination of Laënnec's cirrhosis and hepatitis, two conditions not noted together in the body of the document, would have made Weir stop working around 1969, the time of the murder, because of the debilitating nature of cirrhosis of the liver. Instead, he was doing physical labor, installing insulation, according to the death certificate. The person who added "Laënnec's cirrhosis (alcoholic)" to the medical death certificate may have falsified records to create a narrative of inevitable death. Yet most people who die from Laënnec's cirrhosis die in their fifties or later. At thirty-one, Weir would have been at least two decades away from death due to cirrhosis.[32]

Weir's death certificate holds still more anomalies: the incorrect spelling of his wife's name (correctly spelled *Naundorf* but with an *X* added over the *d*); Weir's last day of work being listed as six months after his date of death; the changed date at which the doctor had first seen Weir; the suspicious note in the death certificate's margin about Laënnec's cirrhosis; an indication that the autopsy was performed between the time of death on February 12 and the signing of the death certificate on February 13; no autopsy record in the BC Archives; the rushed burial on February 15; and Weir's brother, Bud, signing as informant instead of his wife. Surely his wife would have been present during his forty-eight-hour hospital stay. Dr. Wynrib may have produced a phantom hospitalization and autopsy. Canada may have crafted paperwork to cover up the suspicious death of the second suspect.[33]

Three more likely possibilities emerge, each more damning than the last. Weir may have died elsewhere, with hospital records fabricated postmortem; Weir may have been harmed and brought to the hospital moribund, then denied proper treatment to ensure his silence; or Weir may have already been dead when he arrived at the hospital, his certificate signed by Dr. Wynrib. The doctor later emerged as the villain in the 1992 Supreme Court of Canada case *Norberg v. Wynrib*. In that case, the court concluded that Dr. Wynrib had invoked an inherent power imbalance by obtaining sexual acts from Laura Norberg, a drug-dependent woman who received prescriptions from him in exchange for sex in Williams Lake. Laura Norberg was the daughter of Doug Norberg, who owned the car dealership where the vehicle used in Levina's abduction had been registered. But before Dr. Wynrib found himself at the Supreme Court of Canada, which ruled against Dr. Wynrib, none other than Justice Wally Oppal ruled at a lower level in favor of Dr. Wynrib, claiming that the forty-six sex acts with Laura Norberg in exchange for prescriptions were consensual. The Honorable Wally T. Oppal later authored the celebrated 2012 *Forsaken: The Report of the Missing Women Commission of Inquiry, Executive Summary.*[34] Dr. Wynrib acted within the nexus of settler-colonial privilege and crime by possibly falsifying a death certificate in 1973 and demanding sex for prescriptions in the 1980s. The same system that accepted Wynrib's potentially inaccurate death certificate later celebrated Oppal's report on missing women. Darold Weir's death certificate functions as a masterpiece of settler fiction, a medically implausible ending for a man who may have participated in the murder of Gloria Levina Moody on his twenty-eighth birthday.

RONALD ALEXANDER MCMILLAN (1925–1980)

The RCMP gave Levina's family the name of a third man in 1999: Ronald McMillan. In 1969, the year Levina was murdered, McMillan would have the oldest of the men at forty-four years old. Born on August 22, 1925, in Lethbridge, Alberta, McMillan died in 1980 of a rifle shot wound to the head at the age of fifty-four. His death followed the same pattern as Blohm's and Weir's: no obituary, no funeral, and no autopsy record, although the death certificate indicated an autopsy was performed.[35]

Albert Blohm and Darold Weir died violently within months of each other and just a few years after Levina's murder, under circumstances that hint at the potential of foul play. McMillan's 1980 death exhibits similar contradictions eleven years after the 1969 murder. On July 22, 1980, coroner John Roberts, a veterinarian from Australia, recorded McMillan shooting himself in the head with a rifle and

.22-caliber bullets on July 20 and dying on July 21. Holding a lengthy rifle to your own head is even odder than holding a gun to your own stomach. McMillan's death, like Blohm's, was rubber-stamped as a suicide. His body was cremated on July 23. Roberts noted an autopsy had already been held when he signed on July 22. Roberts created yet another impossible scenario on behalf of the state for the archive.

McMillan's stepdaughter, Susan Buller, signed the death certificate as informant on July 21. As a thirty-year-old wife and mother living in Horsefly some forty-two miles away from her stepfather in Williams Lake, she intervened much like the brother of Weir. McMillan's wife, Shirley Jean Doyle McMillan, did not sign, similar to Weir's wife. Buller's answers reeked of deception: She listed McMillan's father's last name as McLogan (not McMillan), omitted his father's first name and birthplace, and claimed no knowledge of his mother's name or birthplace. She noted his job as a bartender in Williams Lake. These inconsistencies mirror Blohm's potentially falsified death dates and Weir's potentially doctored cirrhosis diagnosis. All three suspects may not have died at their own hands. The state held no investigations into their deaths, although in each case, the coroner claimed an autopsy was performed. The archive suggests someone, with the help of doctors and coroners, may have actively buried evidence.[36]

The only available photo of McMillan comes from 1976. By then, Blohm and Weir were dead, and McMillan remained the only known suspect still living. It had been three years since the last "suicide." The Williams Lake newspaper ran a story entitled "Wolf gang," without capitalizing gang. The two men, McMillan and Lynn Statton, seemed to be openly marking themselves as a gang. The photo and caption took up the top half of the second page of the paper. *The Tribune* featured a large photo of the two men, both smirking, lit cigarettes dangling from their mouths, holding up a massive dead wolf found near Lake la Hache, south of Williams Lake. The photo was published without an attribution to a photographer, so was there a third member of the gang who took the photo? The headline and caption read like coded mockery. The caption's report of the men finding the wolf "still warm" reads like a celebration of the macabre. Why would the newspaper run the photo and caption in 1976, after two of the suspects were dead, and reprint it partially in 1996, sixteen years after the death of the third suspect? The photo and caption and its partial reprint seemed to send a coded message to the citizens of Williams Lake that only they could have fully deciphered. No bystander to brutality, years later, Lynn Statton shot and beat his own son while his house was on fire, trapping his granddaughter inside. She burned to death.[37]

By 1980, four state and medical workers had signed off on four related deaths: a doctor may have tampered with a corpse, a coroner scratched out dates, a physician later traded sex for prescriptions, a veterinarian from Australia produced a record that looked like suicide. Each produced paperwork that looked official. Each may have worked against the guidelines, rules, and laws of their province and nation

Levina's family members have come to believe that a fourth man was involved in some way. His name is John Douglas Brecknock. The night Levina died, he was a twenty-two-year-old RCMP officer. His brother-in-law was Albert Blohm. And when the RCMP finally produced the names of the three suspects in 1998, nearly two decades after all three were dead, it was Brecknock who presented himself to the press as the special investigator who had solved the case.

JOHN DOUGLAS BRECKNOCK (1947–)

When the RCMP gave the Moody family the three suspects' names in 1999, they never clearly explained how they obtained those names. For that, we have to look more closely at John Douglas Brecknock. Born on July 12, 1947, Brecknock, at twenty-two years old, would have been younger than three suspects in the 1969 murder.[38] Angela Sterritt became the first writer to publish his name in relation to the murder of Levina in her 2023 book, *Unbroken*.[39]

Born in Montreal, John was the fifth child of George S. Brecknock and Annie Harvey Brecknock. They married at St. Thomas Anglican Church in 1935 in Montreal where they later baptized their children. In Montreal, George worked in graphic arts—photoengraving and printing—and was a member of the Alpine Club of Verdun. John's mother, Annie, bore five children in total. George served as an instructor to the seventeenth Duke of York in the Royal Canadian Hussars during the war. He also rose to the level of sub-lieutenant in the Navy League of Canada. After these war duties, George returned, and the family then moved to the elite neighborhood of Beaurepaire, just outside of Montreal, in 1950. John's brother, Martin, also known as Slim, moved to Williams Lake in the 1950s. When the family visited Martin, the patriarch made the drastic decision in 1956 to move his large and privileged French-speaking family to Alexis Creek in British Columbia, not far from Williams Lake. Once in Alexis Creek, George opened the Hitching Post Motel and made his wife, Ann, the owner. He relocated without his family to Vancouver to work for Cleland Kent Western Ltd. as a graphic artist. Spending his teen years in Alexis Creek, by 1966, John Brecknock possessed avid hunting skills and knew the woods in the Chilcotin well enough to set and maintain trap lines.

John Brecknock became a police officer immediately after his high school graduation. Only nineteen years old when he was sworn into the RCMP, he was twenty when he went through the Pass Out ceremony. He appears to have left the province of British Columbia once he became an RCMP officer. Based on public records, it seems that since 1968, John Brecknock has been stationed and living in the province of Alberta east of the province of British Columbia (BC), while many of his relatives and friends remain in Williams Lake and Alexis Creek in BC. Brecknock's Facebook shows him stationed at Stony Plain in 1968 and at Derwent in 1971, both in the province of Alberta. In 1969, he appeared in the Edmonton, Alberta, paper helping sheriffs secure a scene. Shortly after Levina's murder, the RCMP station at Alexis Creek hired his retired father, George, with his 1960 drunk-driving charge on his record and a lifetime of office expertise. Two years after the murder, on October 9, 1971, Brecknock married his girlfriend, Terry. His brother-in-law, Albert Blohm, died in 1972 in British Columbia. In 1974, Brecknock was registered to vote in Edmonton, Alberta.[40] His wife bore their first child in 1977, then two more while Brecknock earned the rank of sergeant in the RCMP. In 1982 he traveled to Hawaii with his RCMP friend, Howie. His father, George, died in 1983. In March 1997, his mother died. In 1999, he retired.

Despite his long RCMP career in the province of Alberta, John Brecknock inexplicably and officially entered the investigation into the murder of Levina in 1998 despite it being centered in a different province. The Williams Lake newspaper suddenly claimed to have solved the murder of Levina that year. Reporter Angie Mindus wrote two articles only two days apart, one on December 22 and another on December 24. The December 24 article involved John Brecknock.[41]

The first article on December 22 cited RCMP officer John Pilszek who attributed the murder to three men, all of whose names would be protected. Mindus laid guilt on the hearts of the killers, noting that the first, presumably Blohm, died by suicide and the second, presumably Weir, "drank himself to death," and the third suspect, presumably McMillan, hovered "over the second man's deathbed in an effort to curtail any last-minute confession." Mindus attributed suicide to the third suspect as well, presumably McMillan, placing his death vaguely yet firmly in the 1980s.[42]

Only two days later, Mindus published on the murder of Levina again, but with entirely new content. Her second article, on December 24, cited a woman anonymized as "Georgia," who was, in fact, John Brecknock's sister, Toni, the former wife of Albert Blohm. Mindus suggested "Georgia" had suffered during her marriage to the unnamed suspect, moved to Cranbook with him in 1970, left him, then faced his 1972 "suicide." Mindus never named the suspect. Mindus wanted to know why "Georgia" came forward, and "Georgia" attributed it to a "personal situation" that arose in 1997, likely the death of her mother. While Mindus had relied on the authority of officer John Pilszek in the first article, in the second one, she turned to John Brecknock while hiding his relationship with "Georgia." Mindus wrote: "With Georgia's assistance, a special investigator on the case, Sgt. John Brecknock of Alberta, was able to gather enough corroborating statements to satisfy suspicions." In addition to hiding their relationship, "Georgia" appropriated the trauma suffered by Levina and her family by claiming that the murder of Levina created many victims, including herself and even the other killers who allegedly died by guilt-induced suicide. She also penned a poem about Levina that year in which she made the same assertion. Toni saw herself not as the widow of a killer but as a survivor who had done the right thing by coming forward. She crafted a story, and the newspaper repeated it, absolving her and everyone still living.[43]

Mindus's second 1998 article made Brecknock and "Georgia" look like heroes for solving the crime without revealing any of the suspects' names, not even the name of "Georgia's" dead husband. When "Georgia"—who was actually Toni—died in 2007, someone circulated a printout of the poem she had written about Levina in 1998, "On the Wings of an Eagle," along with a portrait of Levina at Toni's memorial in Williams Lake. Toni's words dedicated to Levina included: "Your eyes were emptied of her sight; Your hearts were heavy; I knew your plight; The Healing Ceremonies you did impart, to cleanse your souls and heal your hearts." Even at her memorial, someone in the family wanted others to see Toni as connected to Levina in a positive way. Although the pile of handouts vanished abruptly at the celebration of life for Toni, perhaps because someone did not want them distributed, Levina's daughter, Vanessa, was given one by a community member.[44]

The momentous meeting between the RCMP and Levina's family took place in 1999, not long after these 1998 articles appeared. At the 1999 meeting, the RCMP disclosed the names of the suspects to the family but not to the general public. The 1999 meeting and disclosure along with the 1998 articles made it seem as though Pilszek and Brecknock had obtained the names in 1998. But there were other versions offered by the police on how they found the names of the three suspects. One comes from Corporal Mel McIntosh.

In April 1988, RCMP Corporal Mel McIntosh joined the Williams Lake detachment and promptly began working on Levina's case. In 1989, he flew out of the province of British Columbia into the province of Alberta to pursue a lead on the investigation. More specifically, he flew to Hinton, Alberta, with two other officers. During takeoff out of Hinton, after tracking the lead, the RCMP plane "crashed and caught fire." The RCMP plane "had its right wing ripped off, windshield smashed, and a cabin door pop off on impact with the runway." Given the many other acts of violence since the 1969 murder, it remains a distinct possibility that someone deliberately caused these damages to the RCMP plane carrying McIntosh.[45]

Some five years after the 1989 plane crash, McIntosh learned that, in 1994, the Moody case was closed. A suspect on his deathbed had made a confession of the names of the men who murdered Levina to his brother and sister, but he had convinced them to wait to divulge the information until their parents had died. McIntosh claimed he got this information from RCMP officer Murray Neufeld. This constitutes the third (McIntosh) and fourth (Neufeld) versions of how the RCMP obtained the names of the suspects.[46]

The fifth police version of how the RCMP came to have the names of the suspects was revealed in 2019. Brecknock relayed that a witness from Alexis Creek, in British Columbia, called him in Edmonton, Alberta, in the fall of 1998 with information about the murder. Brecknock interviewed others and established the three names via the witness phone call and additional statements.[47]

These five stories from four officers do not line up. Pilszek said the killers had died by the 1980s. Brecknock claimed to be a special investigator who "gathered corroborating statements" sometime around 1998. Assigned to the case in 1988, McIntosh claimed to have learned of the closing of the case from another officer in 1994, despite Brecknock's claim that it happened in 1998. Neufeld pointed to a 1994 disclosure from siblings who held the story for an unknown number of years after learning it during a "deathbed confession." The December 24, 1998, article with Brecknock and his sister makes it clear that Al Blohm did not confess. And the December 22, 1998, article with Pilszek makes it clear that Weir did not confess, because McMillan was there to make sure he could not. That leaves McMillan, who died in 1980 from a rifle shot to the head. How does one make a deathbed confession during a suicide by rifle to the head? And why the 1994 and 1998 discrepancies?

These officers told stories that contradict each other and the record. These five versions of events from four RCMP officers suggest the possibility that they produced narratives to conceal how they obtained the confession. How exactly did the RCMP get the three suspects' names and when?[48]

The four earlier police versions from Pilszek, Brecknock, McIntosh, and Neufeld of how the suspects were identified all point toward the fifth: Brecknock's 2019 account of a witness calling him from Alexis Creek. The names Brecknock supplied to the Williams

Lake detachment in 1998 may well be accurate. But officers in Williams Lake never publicly stated that they verified the witness phone call and corroborating statements collected by Brecknock. If the officers in British Columbia accepted Brecknock's report from far-flung Alberta without vetting his sources, then the case closed on the word of an officer in another province whose brother-in-law was the prime suspect.

John Brecknock's involvement in the case in 1998 did not end there. In the summer of 2019, John Brecknock reached out, unsolicited, to Angela Sterritt as she was writing *Unbroken*. On July 23, they spoke by phone. He told Sterritt the story that led to his role in the 1998 article, disclosing that a witness had contacted him directly, and his interviews established the names of three suspects. The very day after Sterritt's interview with Brecknock, he messaged Levina's daughter, Vanessa, on Facebook Messenger. They had never had contact before this message. He sent her the first of the 1998 articles—not the one in which he and "Georgia" are cited. Sent without words—only photos—the message was clear: Here lies your closure. Vanessa did not reply. Brecknock sent the same photos again in January 2020, and she, again, did not reply.[49]

After John's 2019 and 2020 Facebook messages, Vanessa began encountering strangers on Facebook reaching out to her. In 2021, an individual named Emma Hewett began commenting on Vanessa's posts about the Nuxalk Nation language and culture—posts that had nothing to do with Levina—in an attempt to get her attention, claiming to have police contacts and information about Levina's murder. But when they spoke by phone, "Emma" became "Phil, the trucker," and could not explain the discrepancy. Vanessa came to believe the caller's true identity was John Brecknock, based on his bids for her attention via Facebook Messenger, the caller's repeated slips into first person, the caller's references to a "handsome cop" being present that night, and the caller's crude assertions about Vanessa's mother and the officer having sexual relations. Vanessa found the calls disturbing. The caller even asked Vanessa if the family ever found Levina's shoes. How would he have known to ask about her shoes? After that conversation, "Phil" called repeatedly, leaving four messages. In one of his messages, he referred to another number he had used to text Vanessa but explained that she should call him back at the original number. She also received two hang-up messages from unknown numbers in the same time period. Meanwhile, John Brecknock continued to message Vanessa as himself on Facebook Messenger. He messaged her in July 2021 offering help, but she did not reply. He messaged again in August 2021, giving many personal details and offering information. In April 2022, Vanessa responded, asking Brecknock why he was doing this. He instantly became defensive.[50]

On July 26, 2025, after six years of seeking contact with Vanessa, John blocked her from messaging him on Facebook in response to a question she posed. Vanessa had asked why he never disclosed to the RCMP his conflict of interest in investigating a case in which his brother-in-law, Albert Blohm, was the prime suspect. John did not answer her question. He instead repeated that she must accept that the deaths of the suspects equaled justice. He remains the only person known to be angry that the three suspects' deaths did not end the family's investigation.

Although Brecknock held a pivotal role in the investigation, many of his relatives also worked or currently work for the RCMP. RCMP officers told Levina's family that Toni—wife of Blohm and sister of John—worked for the RCMP at the Williams Lake detachment in 1969. Around 1970, they hired John's father, then Brecknock's sister, Susan, in 1975. John, John's father, and his two sisters may have participated in the investigation of Levina's murder. The RCMP file on the investigation contains a 1960s style checkout roster. With only two initials, and many not written carefully, it does nonetheless appear to contain three checkouts with a last name of B. One appears to be an HB; another could be JB (March 16, 1970); one is TG (November 6, 1970), potentially Toni Georgia; and another possibly JB (December 22, 1970).[51]

George, his son John, and his daughters Toni and Susan formed a sustained RCMP presence within the Brecknock family from the 1970s to 1990s. Even as they aged and passed away, the family's foothold in the RCMP did not diminish. John's niece—Kelly Brecknock, daughter of Martin "Slim" Brecknock (the man who ran Frontier

Inn and hired Blohm as a bartender)—secured RCMP work at Alexis Creek, the same station as her grandfather, George.[52]

John's daughter also obtained employment with the RCMP, working as an administrative assistant. She married RCMP Staff Sergeant Chris Smiley who went viral for defending protestors at an anti-racism rally in Red Deer on Twitter (now X). Although the anti-racism protesters were being assaulted, police stood by, arresting no one. When journalist Rachelle Elsiufi confronted Smiley, he smirked: "Are you suggesting one side's voice is more important? We let everybody speak." The counter-protesters cheered. In 2021, Smiley was in the news again for criticizing Black Lives Matter activists for failing to protest the murder of Chantelle Firingstoney, a First Nations mother.[53]

In sum, possibly hired by the RCMP right out of high school, John's sister, Toni, may have worked for the RCMP in 1969 while married to one of the suspects; his father began work at the RCMP around the age of sixty years; then other family members joined: his sister Susan; then his daughter, Carey; then his son-in-law Chris; and his niece Kelly. And perhaps there are more. The RCMP does not list their employees on their websites or release employee records.

The Brecknock family's connections reached beyond the RCMP and into the business infrastructure of Williams Lake. In 1968, Doug Norberg established Norberg Motors, a local car dealership and repair shop. The relatives of Levina Moody were told the police found the car used to abduct Levina, and the abandoned vehicle was registered to Norberg Motors. The men may have borrowed or stolen a car from the dealership to execute the murder. Both Blohm and Weir had experience with theft. Is it pure coincidence that John Brecknock's sister, Judy, married Doug Norberg in 1976? Or that Doug Norberg's daughter, Laura, was sexually abused by the same doctor who signed Weir's death certificate?

The Brecknocks and those close to them, deeply embedded in both the RCMP and Williams Lake, have repeatedly sought out Levina's family. Collectively, their message seems to be that the case is solved but also that the Brecknocks deserve some of the credit for this closure and resolution. Sam, Levina's brother, went to Deni House at Williams

Lake for medical care when he suffered a stroke in 2022. While there, John Brecknock's brother, Slim, and his wife, Darlyne (who were the in-laws of Blohm), sought out Sam. They were running the Frontier Inn when Levina encountered the man who ogled her. Slim and Darlyne let people know how urgently they needed to speak with Levina's brother, but they never connected. While we do not know their intentions, Levina's family had been pressured since 1999 to think of the case as resolved, and it's possible that they similarly wanted to pressure Sam to see the murder as a closed chapter safely in the past.[54]

Another attempt to communicate with Levina's family came decades after the murder. At the hospital at Williams Lake, a white man whispered to a relative of Levina: "They avenged her death. Don't worry about it." The man seemed to know the identities of those who killed Levina, but the core of the message was that others had resolved this, and Levina's family was being directed to find closure in their actions. This up-close whisper in the hospital may have exposed the "suicides" of Blohm and McMillan and the sudden pancreatitis of Weir as farces. This whisperer had transformed the "suicides" of Blohm, McMillan, and Weir into revenge killings. The whisperer reframed this as justice for Levina and a gift to the family, as though the people who may have killed her killers did it for a love of justice and for Levina. Levina's brother, Dean, somewhat agrees with this view. From his Nuxalk perspective, descending from an important lineage with great respect for his father, David, the killings could have been done on behalf of the Moody family. However, if someone had killed her assailants, benefited from those killings directly, concealed the names of the assailants, and convinced others to falsify state records to look like suicides, those acts failed to serve as true vengeance for Levina and her family done out of respect and deference.[55]

The system's logic seems to have snapped into focus once authorities in Williams Lake knew someone had murdered Levina: State and medical employees allowed astonishing discrepancies and potentially tampered with state records, while Levina's organs may have vanished into an RCMP cruiser. Justice has not failed in this case. Justice has operated exactly as designed in occupied territory.

HISTORIES OF NUXALK, BRITISH COLUMBIA, AND CANADA

The impunity of everyone involved in the murder of Levina figures less as an anomaly and more as a mirror of Canada's broader system: a colonial machine designed to protect settlers who commit violence against First Nations people. The murder of Levina Moody illustrates state indifference and systemic violence against Indigenous people, especially women. These patterns began centuries earlier, when the Crown first imposed its violence on Nuxalk lands. The murder of Levina took place as part of the colonial violence and the fight for Nuxalk sovereignty, potlatch bans, and Highway 20's forced construction into Nuxalk lands. The British Crown sent its agents, mapmakers, fur traders, and soldiers to carve up Nuxalk territory. George Vancouver and Alexander Mackenzie charted the land not to understand it but to own it, their surveys paving the way for forts like Victoria in 1843. What began as isolated outposts metastasized into full colonies, each a military occupation disguised as civilization.

The Nuxalk have always lived and will continue to live on the coastal terrain of what is now called British Columbia. Managing, maintaining, and thriving in the region, the Nuxalk never ceded an inch to the British Crown. For First Nations people of the British Columbia province, their colonial relationship continued with Britain, and Canada became a second foreign power with whom they had to contend. Nuxalk see themselves as having always been independent of both Britain and Canada.

Of course, settler attacks on Indigenous women did not begin in 1969. Although Nuxalk territory hugs the coastline, the people are deeply connected with the bands and nations in the Chilcotin region, further inland from their territory. At Quesnel in 1864, six First Nations men were executed by the colony. These men upheld their diplomatic protocols when settlers began building a road on their lands without their permission. Settlers retaliated against the Indigenous men with sexual violence against Indigenous women. Chief Joe Alphonse of the Tl'etinqox-t'in explained: "When they decided to take our women for entertainment, that was the final straw." The men revolted. The Nuxalk leaders were captured under pretense of negotiations, sentenced to death, imprisoned at Quesnel, and executed by hanging. The executions led to the Chilcotin War. Although these events occurred over a hundred years ago, they set the pattern of settlers seeing access to Indigenous lands and Native women's bodies as rights.[56]

Residential schools perfected the violence from settler wars. Canada mythologizes itself as benevolent, but that myth collapses under the weight of residential schools. The Indian Act of 1876 weaponized compulsory attendance, deliberately placing schools far from Indigenous communities to sever families. Children like author Bev Sellars were stripped of their names and reduced to numbers at St. Joseph's Mission in Williams Lake. Funded by the state and run by churches, these institutions starved, abused, and murdered children. When survivors like Sellars speak of settler violence, they name the blueprint: Residential schools taught settlers that Indigenous lives could be erased without consequence.[57]

The Indian Act of 1876 weaponized education but also religion, criminalizing potlatch, a ceremony that functioned as the heartbeat of Nuxalk governance and kinship. People like Levina's parents defied these laws. The state retaliated by stealing their sacred objects, masks, rattles, poles, and the very bones of their ancestors, locking them in museums under glass cases labeled "preservation." Elite institutions like the Royal British Columbia Museum (RBCM) clung to these trophies, delaying the return of a stolen totem pole for years despite public promises. In 2022, Nuxalk Chief Snuxyaltwa reminded the media that the RBCM publicly promised the return of their totem pole in 2019. Chief Snuxyaltwa filed a case with the Supreme Court of British Columbia against RBCM which eventually led to the pole's return in 2023.[58]

The attempted conquering of the Nuxalk continued into the twentieth century, as the province of British Columbia built Highway 20 into Nuxalk territory in 1953, without the band's consent, and named the village Bella Coola, also without Nuxalk consent. Despite Highway 20's 18 percent grade, steep turns, and three-hundred-mile route between Williams Lake and Bella Coola, white Canadians and world travelers happily make the trek to enjoy the beauty of the coast. Highway 20 became both a literal and symbolic path of destruction. The same road that brought tourists to "enjoy the breathtaking scenery" delivered Levina to her killers in Williams Lake.

Nuxalk have never surrendered and will never surrender. Today the Nuxalk maintain a closed border, with a clearly visible sign to visitors telling them they are barred from entering the unceded land of the Nuxalk Nation. Nuxalk Nation stands against the nation-state of Canada and the British monarchy, asserting their right to define and protect themselves, especially from Canada and Canadians.[59] Because Nuxalk never ceded an inch of their traditional territory or entered into agreements with Canada, Canada never created a Nuxalk reserve and has not recognized the Nuxalk as such. But Nuxalk do not acknowledge Canada as their overlord from whom they beg for rights. As the Nuxalk wrote in a 2021 eviction notice to the Juggernaut mining company: "At no time has the British Crown, Canada, or the province of British Columbia ever had jurisdiction over we, the People of Nuxalk."[60]

The settler violence that defined Nuxalk history, from massacres to highway incursions, persisted into the twentieth century, shielded by the RCMP's indifference. But it also defined settler and Indigenous life further east, in and around Williams Lake. When nineteen-year-old Secwépemc teen Rose Marie Roper was murdered in 1967 in Williams Lake, just two years before Levina, her killers flaunted her underwear as a trophy, and police indifference affirmed a long-standing truth: Indigenous lives were disposable to settlers, and the state would look away. Levina drove through this landscape of violence to Williams Lake in 1969 with her family.[61]

Roper's 1967 murder ties back to St. Joseph's Mission just a few miles outside of Williams Lake. In 1989, Roman Catholic priest Harold McIntee, who taught at St. Joseph's, pleaded guilty to seventeen counts of sexual assault against thirteen Indigenous boys, most aged ten to twelve. In 1996, another former St. Joseph's priest, Hubert O'Connor, was convicted of raping and indecently assaulting two Indigenous girls in the 1960s. Then, in 2024, more than half a century after Rose Roper's and Levina's murders, the world saw the full horror of Williams Lake. The documentary *Sugarcane*, co-directed by Julian Brave NoiseCat of the Canim Lake Band Tsq̓éscen̓, exposed the disappearances, the systematic torture, and the newborn babies of Indigenous girls assaulted by priests thrown into the incinerator at St. Joseph's Mission and Residential School. Williams Lake built itself upon violence against First Nations people.[62]

In 1990, Levina's cousin, Chief Jimmy Stillas of the Ulkatcho Band, died because local police refused to search for him. Instead, band members ran their own search party and made the terrible discovery themselves. Chief Stillas's death led to the Cariboo-Chilcotin Justice Inquiry, during which hundreds of Native people came forward to testify largely about the failure, abuse, and violence of the Canadian police.[63] When Chief Stillas's son, Kenny, was found frozen to death in 1995, many wondered if the police deliberately left him in the snow to die and also questioned the efficacy of the inquiry.[64]

Benign versions of Canadian history and culture work hand in hand with the vilification of Indigenous peoples of Canada. As scholar Sherene Razack writes, "When inquests and inquiries instruct us in the pathologies of Indigenous peoples, states provide themselves with alibis not only for inaction but also for crimes of overt violence." Canadian schoolchildren are taught to revere the state, and this reverence continues into adulthood and informs their identity. When settlers kill Indigenous people in Canada, the state tends to protect and defend the assailants, by ignoring and manipulating evidence to displace guilt onto the victims.[65] The blind worship of the state and the RCMP allows Canadians to remain indifferent to violence against Indigenous people of Canada. As the Stó:lō author Lee Maracle observed: "Nothing that happens to Indigenous people, no matter how unlawful, is of much consequence to many of the people occupying Indigenous territories."[66]

The media inadvertently supports killers by refusing to name and investigate the violence. As comparative literature professor Judith Butler writes: "In the silence of the newspaper, there was no event, no loss, and this failure of recognition is mandated through an identification with those who identify with the perpetrators of that violence." Although some killers of Indigenous women have been named in Canadian media, naming men as perpetrators remains extraordinary and unusual. When a memorial for murdered women was created in 1989, the words "murdered by men" became a battleground with media outlets and citizens fighting to prevent the use of those three words. The committee won, and the plaque at the memorial site reads: "For all women murdered by men."[67]

The murder of Levina Moody exists not as an isolated tragedy but as part of a system designed to erase Indigenous lives with impunity. From the Highway of Tears to serial killer Robert Pickton's farm where he fed the women he murdered to his pigs, from Judge David Ramsay's predation of Indigenous girls to the "starlight tours"—in which Saskatoon officers abandon Indigenous people in rural areas during winter to die—the pattern repeats: Settler violence gains institutional support as its perpetrators are protected. Even now, as Winnipeg landfills hold the remains of Indigenous women killed by white supremacist Jeremy Skibicki, the state's refusal to search for their remains echoes the state's indifference to Levina's death. The indifference represents not a failure of justice. The indifference operates as a central and deliberate function.[68]

Canadian discourse equates Indigenous women with sex. Wet'suwet'en youth victim advocate Lucy Glaim exposed this in 2006: "Aboriginal women are seen as prostitutes, as dispensable women by Caucasian Canadians." While a matter of perception, this equation functions as a policy that blames First Nations female victims of violence. University of Manitoba professor Adele Perry documents how settlers weaponized the lie that "Aboriginal women were, by definition, prostitutes," while University of Alberta professor Sarah Carter proves colonial officials actively portrayed them as "dissolute, dangerous, and sinister" to justify violence.[69]

The Canadian courtroom reveals settlers still act on this blueprint of equating Indigenous women with sex work. In 1995, two white male athletes beat Pamela George to death, then walked free after lawyers argued her Saulteaux identity made her murder a "job hazard." In 2011, Bradley Barton sexually mutilated Cindy Gladue, then claimed her Cree body was "rented property." As Sherene Razack writes: "Her activity was a crime . . . theirs was a contract." Stó:lō professor Lee Maracle named the pattern: "We have been the object of sexual release for white males. . . . For us, rape is not an oddity but commonplace." Canada never stopped waging war on First Nations women.[70]

As for who killed Levina Moody, the RCMP privately pointed to Albert Blohm, Darold Weir, and Ronald McMillan. But the RCMP did it. Fort Victoria did it. Vancouver and Mackenzie did it. The residential schools did it. The Royal British Columbia Museum did it. Smallpox did it. Every non-Native resident of Williams Lake who saw what happened did it. The complicity ripples out, and the silence on the matter echoes over the decades.

Today, white Canadians live in the possession of secrets about the murder of Gloria Levina Moody. Their refusal to speak protects the killers, even the ones who are dead. Levina's family and Nuxalk Nation deserve, at the very least, to know who took their relative. Many Canadians know some or all of what happened that night. Until someone speaks up, any words of consolation mean little. Dave told me he just wants peace. He has tried so hard to forget. His family has waited since 1969.

In the next chapter, we continue to think about how the state fails Indigenous victims. We return to the United States, moving forward to 2001, to another small town like Williams Lake, where the same narrative warfare worked to suppress certain narratives of what happened. In this town in the southwest corner of Colorado many miles off the reservation, a Navajo, nonbinary teenager became the object of an intense hate for decisions about their name, hair, shoes, and makeup. We will explore the world of Indigenous queer identity and the hate this generates within the settler-colonial dystopia, a reality that refuses to let the Indigenous queer exist.

GUIDE TO KEY FIGURES IN CHAPTER 3

FRED/FC/FREDRIKA/BEYONCÉ MARTINEZ: A sixteen-year-old Navajo (Diné) person who fluidly navigated gender expression. Murdered on June 16, 2001.

PAULINE CLY MARTINEZ DAUKEI MITCHELL: Fred/FC/Fredrika/Beyoncé Martinez's mother.

SHAUN DOUGLAS MURPHY: Convicted of second-degree murder for the murder of Martinez.

CLINT SANCHEZ: Murphy's friend with Murphy the night of the murder.

STEVE HARMON: Montezuma County sheriff's detective. The lead investigator and author of the key affidavit in the case.

BROOKS BENNETT: An agent for the Colorado Bureau of Investigation. One of the interviewers of Clint Sanchez on July 3 and one of the interviewers of Shaun Murphy on July 5.

JOEY CHAVEZ: Montezuma County sheriff's deputy.

ANN MILLER: A teacher at the Adult Education Center. May have known both Martinez and Murphy. Spoke at Martinez's funeral.

MELISSA GLOVER SCHARNHORST: A friend of Murphy and Sanchez. Allowed them to stay at her apartment the night of the murder.

ROBIN FLORES BILLINGS: A close friend of Martinez. Was with Martinez at the rodeo the night of the murder.

GAIL BINKLY: A Cortez journalist featured in the documentary *Two Spirits* on the murder of Martinez.

JOHN PETERS-CAMPBELL: A Cortez LGBTQ+ leader and spokesperson for the case.

DARREN RICHARD GOODRICH: An openly queer man in Cortez who was a few years older than Martinez. Allegedly at the party that Martinez attended after the rodeo.

MICHAEL GOODRICH: Cousin of Darren Goodrich. Hosted the party where Martinez was last seen alive.

ROBERT KURTZMAN: The forensic pathologist who performed the autopsy.

JOSEPH "JOE" OLT: The Montezuma County district attorney (DA). Previously represented Murphy. Downgraded charges, which led to a plea deal that avoided a trial.

JIM BOB WYNES: A Cortez Police Department detective who retrieved the bag left by Sanchez in the trash in Farmington, New Mexico, on July 3. Interviewed Murphy on July 5 with Brooks Bennett.

JUDGE TIM TUTHILL: Along with DA Olt, presided over a previous felony case against Shaun Murphy. Later suspended for drug possession and tampering with court documents.

WILLIAM FAUGHT: The Montezuma County coroner. Pronounced Martinez deceased.

KALVIN BOGGS: A sheriff's detective involved in the initial investigation. Claimed the body was "unidentified."

JIM SHETHAR: Detective sergeant. Murphy's mother lied to him when he sought Murphy's alibi

ANGEL MURPHY TACORONTE: Shaun Murphy's mother. Defended her son, lied to police, and threatened a witness in court.

MARY LOBATO: Ex-girlfriend of Shaun Murphy. Called as a witness who waited to testify behind the prosecution at a hearing. Angel Murphy Tacoronte threatened her inside the courtroom and was arrested. Stepsister of Melissa Glover Scharnhorst.

PAMELA BROWN: Shaun Murphy's public defender.

CATHY RENNA: A media representative from GLAAD, a nonprofit group focused on LGBTQ+ advocacy. Fought for accurate media coverage of the case as a hate crime.

JUDY SHEPARD: The mother of Matthew Shepard, a queer university student who was murdered in 1998. She became an activist and traveled to Cortez to support Martinez's mother.

ROY LANE: Chief of the Cortez City Police. Amplified the DA's pronouncement that the murder was not a hate crime.

ASPEN EMMETT: The primary reporter who covered the case for *The Cortez Journal.*

JUDGE SHARON LYONS HANSEN: The judge who replaced Judge Leroi. Presided over the hearings.

JUDGE CHRISTOPHER DANIEL LEROI: The initial judge on the case. Later suspended for misconduct unrelated to this case.

DENISE BALAZIC: The parole board member who approved Murphy's early release from prison in 2018.

JUDGE PLEWE: The judge who approved the motion to destroy exhibit 17 from Murphy's trial record in 2018.

CHAPTER 3

FRED/FC/FREDRIKA/BEYONCÉ

June 16, 2001. Saturday night. A clear night in the low 70s. Fred/FC/Fredrika/Beyoncé Martinez enjoyed the high of the biggest annual event in Cortez, Colorado. Bringing in Utes from the nearby Ute Reservation, whites throughout the Four Corners region, and professional rodeo riders from the national circuit, the Ute Mountain Roundup Rodeo promised to be the greatest one yet for the sixteen-year-old Diné, or Navajo. With their friends, they rode the carnival rides, enjoyed scrumptious offerings from the pop-up vendors, watched men hold onto bucking broncos, and listened to the best Cortez had to offer in live country music. That summer when they were sixteen, they must have felt exhilarated, like anything was possible, and imagined a bright future ahead, creating possibilities in their mind of what their life could be after finishing high school in Cortez. During their third night at the rodeo-carnival, they left their friend Robin Flores Billings to join a party. They had no idea that someone at that party would brutally murder them just a few hours later in a pitch-black canyon. Border towns function as death zones for Indigenous people, and especially for Two-Spirit people.[1]

Born to Diné, or Navajo, parents in 1985, Martinez entered the world inheriting the strength and the strife of their nation. Pauline Cly Martinez Daukei Mitchell, their mother, gave birth to them at the Tuba City hospital on the Navajo Nation Reservation. Then married to Fred Martinez, Pauline decided to name her new baby Fred, after her husband. Growing up in Monument Valley, they enjoyed their distinctively Diné childhood on the Navajo reservation where they felt the freedom of movement and expression living with their Diné parents and relatives. When Pauline divorced Fred Sr., she made the decision to leave the Navajo reservation for the border town of Cortez, Colorado. When she and her children arrived at their new home in a packed mobile home park on a tiny patch of land, Martinez immediately recoiled. They noticed how "nosey" the Cortez neighbors were. They did not like the feeling of constantly being watched if they chose to step outside the house, noticing the constant stares from settlers, something they had never experienced on the Navajo reservation.[2]

Shortly after moving to Cortez with their mom and siblings, Martinez began using their mom's purses, then her makeup. One of their older half brothers expressed concern about Cortez settlers in the border town and how they could impact their sibling, warning them to "be careful" when wearing purses, makeup, or scarves.[3]

The surveillance Martinez noticed upon moving into the Cortez mobile home park only increased as the years passed. Once in the local high school, administrators surveilled and punished Martinez for their gender nonconformity. They were sent home from school many times for wearing eyeliner and other physical markers of femininity. In 1980, two Parisian men created jelly shoes, and, in 1983, the shoes exploded in popularity all over the world. Fred/FC/Fredrika/Beyoncé managed to get themselves a pair in the small town, wearing them with pride to Montezuma-Cortez High School. Outraged, their teacher sent them to the principal's office for wearing the popular jellies. Martinez was sent home that day—and other days, too, for similar infractions. Martinez left Montezuma-Cortez High School before finishing their first year there and enrolled in the local Adult Education Center hoping to receive less exposure to homophobia, transphobia, and racism. But, according to their mom, they endured harassment there as well.[4]

Fred/FC/Fredrika/Beyoncé imagined their future before their life was stolen from them on June 16, 2001. They dreamed of lands beyond Cortez, Colorado—such as San Francisco or Los Angeles—and of working as a cosmetologist. In the months leading up to their murder, they confidently embraced their gender and sexual expression.

Martinez moved within identities as a queer teen who was male, but they also inhabited the Navajo world of the fluidity of being a feminine man, which can also include no longer being a man but being something else, something fluid and unique and not exactly male or female. Sometimes Fred/FC/Fredrika/Beyoncé wore bras using bandannas to push the cups out. Other times, they expressed a male identity, wearing sweatshirts or other male-presenting clothing, perhaps to conform and feel safer, but perhaps also because that choice felt true in that moment.

Martinez told their friends they wanted to be beautiful. They resisted the restrictions of Cortez and the US in the late 1990s and early 2000s that said only "gay" existed, but they saw few other possibilities in the larger culture around nonbinary identities, multiple pronouns, or gender fluidity. Less interested in the confining identity of "gay," Fred/FC/Fredrika/Beyoncé preferred to continuously ask themselves who they were at any given moment and to present that to the world. Even as they held a very nuanced understanding of who they were, many in Cortez simplified this complex expression. The residents of Cortez called them homophobic slurs.[5]

Although Martinez used he/him pronouns, as do those who have written about them, this chapter uses they/them pronouns. Had Martinez lived past 2001, they would have been exposed to more discourse and options around identity that emerged in the 2010s and 2020s. We will never know what identity would have felt right to them as an adult. The book uses they/them because they showed an interest in different gender expressions, depending on how they felt that day. They knew about Two-Spirit terminology and used it some. But they might have gravitated toward nonbinary expressions later in life. Even in 2001, they felt that being labeled queer or gay did not express their full identity.

Martinez fluidly navigated gender identities as Fred, FC, Fredrika, and Beyoncé in a Cortez dominated by white country music stars like Toby Keith. Without internet access, their embrace of the name of Destiny's Child's rising star Beyoncé in the late 1990s showed remarkable cultural foresight. While their rural community celebrated white artists, Martinez connected with Beyoncé's early work like "Say My Name" before her solo stardom. They never witnessed Beyoncé's 2003 breakthrough with "Dangerously in Love," but their identification with this Black star in the making revealed an intuitive understanding of cultural currents that defied their isolated, conservative environment. In choosing Beyoncé among their names, they asserted a visionary queer Indigenous identity that transcended their small town's limitations.

When the harassment continued even at the Adult Education Center, Martinez deliberately overdosed on Motrin. They told their mom they no longer wanted to live because of the hatred spewed upon them. After recovering, despite the surveillance and harassment, Martinez embraced their fullest self and lived life with joy and openness. With many friends such as Robin Flores Billings and a constantly ringing phone, Martinez spent most of their time out with friends.

As Martinez made their way through middle and high school in Cortez, so, too, did Shaun Douglas Murphy, the key figure in the 2001 murder. Born on March 14, 1983, Murphy moved through the same schools as Martinez but was two years ahead. He was expelled in sixth grade and convicted for stealing furniture from a Cortez home in ninth grade. At age fifteen in tenth grade, Murphy's mother drove her son to a Burger King, where he attacked another minor from behind, slamming his head into a wall by grabbing onto the hood of his jacket. When another minor stepped in to stop Murphy from beating his friend, Murphy's mother, who had been standing nearby, attacked the second minor.

For these convictions, Murphy was expelled from Montezuma-Cortez High School, then the Southwest Open program. He then entered the Adult Education Center in 1999 or 2000 to earn his GED around the same time when Martinez entered the program. Ann Miller, the teacher at the center, likely knew both Martinez and Murphy. Miller moved to Cortez in 1990 to work at Southwest Boards of Cooperative Educational Services (BOCES) directing the Adult Education Division. Murphy received his GED by studying with Miller at BOCES. Though the police and media insisted Murphy and Martinez had no previous interactions, they very likely met at the Adult Education Center. Miller may have felt sympathy with Martinez, prompting her to speak at Martinez's funeral.[6]

Public reports of the night that began with Martinez leaving home for the rodeo-carnival and ended with their death in a Cortez canyon generate more questions than answers. This lack of clarity emerges as the product of narrative arbitrage: Authorities produced certain narratives about Shaun Murphy, which the media and legal structure selectively amplified into an official narrative. But put together with community narratives and police records, the story of what happened that night seems far more tangled and messy than the state narrated. This chapter moves toward an emergent timeline taken from newspapers, documentaries, police and court records, and confidential informants. The party after the rodeo acts as the first casualty in the narrative warfare over what happened to Martinez on June 16, 2001. The party acted as the place where competing narratives began to fracture.[7]

THE RODEO-CARNIVAL

The summer they were heading into their junior year brought Martinez one step closer to adulthood and the possibility of moving away from Cortez, Colorado. As Martinez made plans to meet their friend, Robin Flores Billings, at the rodeo-carnival for the third night in a row, so, too, did Shaun Douglas Murphy and Clint Sanchez, both of whom use he/him pronouns. Sanchez and Murphy drove in from the border town of Farmington on the eastern side of the Navajo Reservation. Murphy broke his probation by leaving the county and state without notifying his probation officer.[8]

The only point of agreement in the narrative warfare stems from the night's beginning: Everyone could confirm Martinez, Murphy, and Sanchez attended the rodeo. This simple fact was later cemented into the official record by an affidavit notarized on July 4, 2001. The document stands as the bedrock upon which Montezuma County made their case, but it reads less like a legal document and more like a well-crafted public relations piece. Montezuma County Sheriff Steve Harmon wrote the affidavit for the issuance of an arrest warrant and offered a timeline spanning June 16 (when Martinez was murdered) to July 3, 2001 (when Murphy was arrested). Harmon admitted he wrote the affidavit with the assistance of many other officers and agencies. Harmon testified about his involvement in the case on at least three separate occasions, but he became confused each time. He was unable to articulate specifics.[9]

All sources agree that Martinez left their home for the rodeo-carnival on Saturday, June 16. They told their mom they were going to the rodeo, and Pauline heard them on the phone making plans. The documentary *Two Spirits* maintains they went to the rodeo with friends, stayed for some time, and left, but depicts them walking back toward Cortez alone. According to *Two Spirits*, as Shaun Murphy was driving, he saw Martinez on foot, offered them a ride, and they stopped at a convenience store. At that point Martinez left them, and Murphy and his friends went to their friend's apartment to sleep. Gail Binkly, a Cortez journalist, appeared frustrated in *Two Spirits* when she recounted the end of the simple story: Once Murphy arrived at the friend's apartment, he immediately left, killed Martinez, and then quickly returned. The narrative offered by Binkly weaves several versions together, leaves out the party, and also omits the name of the friend with the apartment: Melissa Glover Scharnhorst. But police always knew that Martinez attended the party. By June 28, they had interviewed the man who had hosted the party and confirmed that Martinez had been present.

THE PARTY

The police downplayed the party's importance to the press, and the district attorney seemed determined to expose nothing about the party as well. Taking their cue from the media and police narratives, *Two Spirits* leaves out the party from their narrative. Yet *The Cortez Journal* maintained that Murphy, Sanchez, and Martinez all attended the party, layering in the idea that they made a stop at a convenience store after the party. Writer Jeremy Quittner repeated the convenience store narrative in *The Advocate*, claiming his source to be the July 4 affidavit—but that was incorrect; the narrative was mentioned only in *The Cortez Journal*, not in the affidavit. *The Cortez Journal* got the story from the police who began interviewing partygoers as early as June 26.[10]

The *Two Spirits* documentary could have included the party in its narrative, as it featured John Peters-Campbell extensively in the film. When I asked John Peters-Campbell, the Cortez LGBTQ+ leader and spokesperson for the case, about the party, he did not deny it and even offered its location as having taken place north of the old high school and south of Main Street. He recalled the party having been at the home of the cousin of Darren Richard Goodrich, a man named Michael Goodrich. According to John, Darren was ten years older than Martinez, and both attended the party. Darren went through the Cortez public schools a few years before Martinez as an openly queer person who sometimes dressed in women's clothing, according to John. The 2023 documentary *Evil Lives Here* maintains Martinez lied to their friend, Robin Flores Billings, at the rodeo-carnival, saying they were sick and had to leave, but they, in fact, had made plans to go to the party.[11]

Media reports of the party began circulating on July 4, 2001, the same time the affidavit was released to the public and the day after police interviewed Clint Sanchez and Shaun Murphy. The Cortez sheriff's affidavit referred to the party and explained that Murphy, Sanchez, and Martinez attended. Harmon noted he "interviewed people" who had called "law enforcement" to share details about the party. The police never denied the party but certainly downplayed its importance. Harmon never told the public who hosted the party, where it occurred, who attended, what happened there, or when Martinez left or with whom.

The lack of details about the last known location of Martinez after the rodeo-carnival signaled no accident or oversight. Not a single partygoer gave testimony that was repeated by a reporter. However, a rumor circulated then and circulates even now that Murphy and Martinez kissed at the party. When Murphy learned Martinez's gender expression and sexual identity after the kiss, Murphy became enraged. According to the story, this rage motivated the killing. By 2001, many films had run similar storylines about trans people, but most likely to have been viewed by teens in Cortez in the 1990s would undoubtedly have been *Ace Ventura: Pet Detective* (1994). When Ace discovers Lieutenant Einhorn, his love interest, was assigned male at birth, he compulsively brushes his teeth, burns his clothes, and pukes, even using a plunger on his mouth to purge himself of sexual contact with transness. This unverified rumor, whatever its truth, echoes a familiar transphobic trope from popular culture, a narrative script that can surface in a community's attempts to explain violence against Two-Spirit people by pathologizing the victim rather than the killer. Sanchez, one of the suspects, invoked the *Ace Ventura* narrative in the 2023 *Evil Lives Here* documentary when he narrated that night, including many details about Martinez and Murphy having flirted with each other.

The *Ace Ventura* version of Martinez and Murphy at the party fails because the two likely knew each other from the Adult Education Center. In all likelihood, Murphy was aware that Martinez was assigned male at birth. If they kissed at the party, Murphy's prior knowledge could have caused that kiss to turn into a death sentence—either for Martinez or Murphy or both. In other words, if other men knew that Murphy kissed a person he knew was assigned male at birth, the men might have threatened both with violence. Alternatively, if Murphy pretended not to know Martinez was assigned male at birth, he might have participated in the killing of Martinez to prove his heterosexuality and transphobia. The *Ace Ventura* version of events might have been rolled out by Murphy to protect himself from his heterosexual male peers, but it also may have never happened.

The Denver Post first wrote about the party, publishing a piece on July 6. The newspaper named Martinez's friends Sammy Benally and Gabriel Gallegos, neither of whom attended the party. They saw Martinez at the rodeo, and Martinez told them they were going to a party "with some older kids, including 'some old brawlers' called the 'G's." Gallegos noted his confusion at why Martinez would go to a party with people who were not from their "usual crowd," specifically people much older than them.

Six days later, *The Cortez Journal* undid the progress made by *The Denver Post*, relying on the police version of the party. The police avoided the question of whether Murphy interacted with Martinez at the party, only admitting—based on Sanchez's account—that Sanchez and Murphy encountered Martinez on the street after the party. By July 26, the media directly inquired about what the investigation of the party revealed. The police flatly announced they had learned "nothing earth-shattering" about the party.[12]

The police suppressed any narrative that underscored the party. Along with Murphy and Sanchez, police also suppressed any narrative that proposed Murphy or Sanchez lured or forced Martinez to the canyon. Instead, the police pushed Sanchez to implicate Murphy. Sanchez may have understood what the police were suggesting and named him. The police may have hoped that pinning the murder on Murphy would stop the public from wondering what brought a sixteen-year-old with a terrible fear of the dark into an isolated canyon where they were murdered.

THE CANYON

Police discovered Martinez's body on June 21 in a canyon on the southeast edge of town, only dozens of feet east of a trailer park and across the street, to the south, from the apartment complex where Murphy and Sanchez had overnighted. The coroner documented Martinez's appearance at death. They were 5 feet 11 inches tall and weighed 163 pounds. Their hair was still tied back in a ponytail. Their mirror etched with their birth name lay nearby. Their backpack was still on, and their identification was inside. Hidden between two knots in the earth, their body could not be seen from the dirt road running from the trailer park to the sewer station. They lay on their back with their hands cradling their stomach, which had been slashed. Their blood lay in a thirty-foot path along the embankment. Several rocks with blood on them lay near their body. The back of their wrists bore imprints of force or restraint. News reports used the word "bludgeoning" to describe how Martinez had been killed, citing "preliminary autopsy results." Yet "bludgeoning" was never officially confirmed.[13]

The police told the press the body was an "unidentified man," yet police saw their name on their mirror and their ID inside their backpack. While police waited for dental records to formally confirm the identity, a standard procedure, they launched what some see as the vilification of the victim's mother. Police informed the press they could not identify the victim because Martinez's mother did not notify the police, an assertion she strongly denied. Additionally, the police held the victim's engraved mirror and ID once their body was found.

From Saturday, June 16, the day of Martinez's disappearance, through Wednesday, June 20, 2001, the day before police received the report of a body, confidential sources claim Cortez teens knew that Martinez's body lay in the canyon and made repeat visits to look at their corpse. According to Detective Steve Harmon, the body was found by Eric Sample and Andrew Gallegos, both aged ten, on June 21. Eric told his brother, Kevin, about the body, and Kevin drove to the scene and saw the corpse around 3 p.m. Kevin Sample notified police sometime after 3 p.m. and before midnight. William Faught, the Montezuma County coroner, pronounced Martinez dead at 11:50 p.m. on June 21. According to Officer Kalvin Boggs, the body was hidden, even from drivers on the road winding through the canyon. That two children would stumble upon the hidden crime scene seems unlikely and seems to confirm that many knew their body lay in the canyon. When Sanchez later told the police the exact location of Martinez's corpse, he said he knew because he had watched police discover the body from inside a car, protected by darkness above the canyon.[14]

According to the records, Martinez's mother did not know her child had been found before the autopsy was performed. Coroner Faught held access to the body on Friday, June 22, 2001, after Detective Steve Harmon, author of the July 4 affidavit, drove the body to Grand Junction Community Hospital in Grand Junction, some four hours and 223 miles away. Community Hospital received the body at 4:35 p.m., and Robert Kurtzman began the autopsy at 5 p.m., failing to note the backpack the police had reported. In the report Kurtzman signed almost a month later, he declared Martinez had suffered a fracture and abdominal injury, with no reference to bludgeoning.

Kurtzman minimized the fracture by reporting an event that the medical literature cannot explain. Kurtzman documented a "nondisplaced fracture line" of the inner table of the skull but distinguished this from the outer table, which was "scored superficially." Medical literature has documented only three cases in which a superficial injury to the outer skull resulted in an internal fracture. Scientifically, Kurtzman's report strains belief. One would have to sustain a considerable injury to the thick and strong outer table to fracture the thin and fragile inner table. Kurtzman's choice of words minimized the violence done to Martinez.

Although Kurtzman performed an autopsy in Grand Junction on June 22, he did not sign the report until July 17. In addition to pages of written descriptions, Kurtzman provided a preformatted drawing of a body to visually describe injuries. Kurtzman carefully noted the red toenail polish but failed to disclose the skull fracture on the diagram. He also called the stomach injury a "defect" instead of a cut, gash, or slash. Kurtzman's report made it clear that Martinez suffered a blow to the back of the head, albeit buried in medical jargon, a fact that no one in law enforcement, court, or the media noted or emphasized, which would make clear that Martinez's attacker did not face them. Martinez was attacked from behind.[15]

While Kurtzman performed the autopsy, *The Cortez Journal* released its first article about the murder, repeating Officer Boggs's claims that the body was not connected to a missing person. Boggs suggested a Cortez minor had gone missing, and the minor's family had not bothered to call police. The victim's mother, Pauline, learned of the murder that day in the paper. She called the police again, and they told her the body was unidentified—despite the personalized mirror and school identification. The police also informed the media that June 23 was the first time Pauline ever called and only in response to the newspaper article. The police maintained the story that they still had not identified the body until Monday, June 25, when Detective Harmon met with Pauline.

Working as a housekeeper at the Dolores Mountain Inn, thirty-five miles from Cortez in Dolores, Colorado, Pauline spoke with Sheriff Harmon and victim's advocate Martha Robinson. Sheriff Harmon told Pauline the body could be her child's based on the mirror and ID. Pauline visited the crime scene, feeling frustrated that many items that could have been documented and used in the investigation were left behind. She remembers the police showing her the body inside a body bag and the crime scene photos.[16]

THE INVESTIGATION

From June 26 to July 2, police interviewed many leads, one of those being Shaun Murphy. On June 26, police caught Murphy and his mother in their first deception. Detective Sergeant Jim Shethar called Murphy's home and spoke to his mother, Angel Murphy Tacoronte. She insisted he had been in Aztec, New Mexico, on the night of the murder, working at Aztec Well Service. After she handed her son the phone, Murphy repeated the story he had just heard his mother give police. Detective Harmon phoned Aztec Well Service and discovered Murphy had quit in May. With a documented fabrication, police continued to consider Murphy a suspect.

While police kept the investigation details vague for the press, they pathologized the victim's mother. By June 28, police claimed to have three suspects but did not give out their names. *The Cortez Journal* ran another article, quoting Martinez's friends Mandy Rollman and Jessica Wilson, referring to the cause of death as bludgeoning, and supporting the police narrative that Martinez's mother did not report them missing until after the body was discovered. *The Cortez Journal* quoted Sheriff Chavez: "Evidently, they [Martinez's mother] didn't report him right away because he frequently left and wouldn't come back for days." Chavez portrayed their mother as not only derelict for failing to call police but also derelict for allowing her child not to return home. After repeatedly representing her negatively, police distributed her home address three separate times to the media. Publishing the home address of a single Diné woman whose child identified as Two-Spirit and had just been found dead put her in the crosshairs of anyone who wanted to harm her.

In the narrative warfare run by the police, they insisted on a story in which no one had a motive to murder Martinez, that the murder was committed by a complete stranger. Police announced that Martinez had just finished their freshman year at Montezuma-Cortez High

School when they had, in fact, been attending the Adult Education Center, likely along with Shaun Murphy. The police and media never admitted Murphy and Martinez may have attended the same small GED program. Nor did police admit Martinez and Murphy may have interacted at the GED program.[17]

By July 3, police knew Murphy lied about his alibi, informants placed him at the party in Cortez, and they received an anonymous 911 call in which the informant claimed Murphy and Sanchez killed Martinez together. Police began an interagency surveillance of Murphy's mother's apartment where Murphy and Sanchez lived in Farmington, New Mexico, on July 3. This coordinated surveillance included Farmington city police, Cortez City police, Montezuma County sheriff's deputies, and state agents from the Colorado Bureau of Investigation (CBI).

Clint Sanchez, the man with Shaun Murphy the night of the murder, emerged from Murphy's mother's Farmington apartment the very moment the police surveillance began. Sanchez drove to a gas station, dumped a trash bag, and left. The timing was either impeccable, coincidental, or tragic. Detective Wynes grabbed Sanchez's bag out of the dumpster, followed Sanchez back to the apartment, approached him, found he had a concealed weapon without a permit, and took him into custody at the Farmington Police Department.

Police took Murphy into custody as well, taking him to the San Juan County Detention Facility in Aztec, New Mexico (demolished and rebuilt in Farmington in 2005). Sanchez sat in custody under city jurisdiction, while Murphy went to a county facility.[18]

Police examined the contents of the bag Sanchez left in the gas station dumpster: a pair of bloodied shoes, two belts, and a white T-shirt. Their interview with Sanchez that day centered on the bag and its contents.

Colorado Bureau of Investigation agents Frank Benecheck and Brooks Bennett conducted the July 3 interview with Sanchez. The agents interrogated Sanchez for hours, late at night, even after he admitted to having been on meth for a week but stating he was able to be interrogated. The agents wanted to know about the bag and bloodied shoes. The agents repeatedly suggested that the shoes might not have been Sanchez's, that Sanchez might not have been involved in the murder, that he might have placed someone else's shoes in the trash. They even suggested that someone may have been Murphy. Sanchez eventually relented to the many prompts by the agents, stating that the shoes were Murphy's, not his.[19]

Sanchez additionally admitted Fred/FC/Fredrika/Beyoncé was in the car with Murphy and himself after the party. Sanchez confessed to using a "queer voice" and asking Martinez about their "exotic name" during the ride, claiming to drop Martinez off near Sanchez's destination at the apartment complex where his friend Melissa Glover Scharnhorst lived. Sanchez claimed Murphy immediately left after arriving at the apartment to buy marijuana. He returned twenty minutes later covered in blood, telling Sanchez he "bug smashed a *joto*" (a Spanish-language slur for a queer man). Sanchez alleged Murphy changed out of his bloody clothes and left the apartment for Farmington with a duffel bag, suggesting the bloody clothing was inside. Sanchez further alleged that Murphy asked him to get rid of the bag between June 16 and July 3, a span of seventeen days, while the two lived in Farmington at Murphy's mother's apartment. Sanchez alleged when he failed to get rid of the bag, Murphy reminded him, but Sanchez still did not get rid of the bag. He could not explain why he got rid of the bag when police surveillance began. The agents asked Sanchez what size shoes he wore, a telling detail that indicates they wanted additional proof the shoes did not belong to him. Those shoes and other items were sent to the Colorado Bureau of Investigation and were never admitted into evidence at Montezuma County Court. Nor were the lab results from the shoes, shirt, or belts ever admitted into evidence.

With Sanchez's accusation of Murphy in hand, agent Bennett and Detective Wynes questioned Murphy two days later, feeding him information from Sanchez's July 3 interview. Murphy claimed he had been walking after the party and gotten jumped. Bennett and Wynes rejected that story. In response, Murphy revised his timeline: He was no longer on foot; instead, he claimed he drove from the party with Sanchez, that Martinez got into the car at some point, that he didn't know where Martinez was going, that one of them told Martinez to "get the fuck out," and that Martinez was angry. Bennett and Wynes pressed for more details. Murphy made it abundantly clear he refused to implicate Sanchez. He said so ten times before demanding that the agent and detective turn off the recorder. They complied. Only the three of them know what was said off the record.

Once back on the record, Murphy again emphasized he would be leaving Sanchez out of his narrative. Murphy's account changed slightly: Martinez got in Sanchez's car. Sanchez spoke to Martinez, but Murphy didn't talk. The three went to Handy Mart, or "Tweaker" Mart, for pizza. Sanchez asked Martinez if they had weed, and they didn't. Murphy did not know where Martinez wanted to be dropped off and told them to get out when they arrived at Handy Mart. Murphy and Sanchez returned to Melissa's apartment. They ate pizza inside her apartment. Murphy then went outside where he happened upon Martinez and a white man with marijuana. The three walked down to the canyon to smoke. Murphy insulted the white man's marijuana, and the white man and Fred/FC/Fredrika/Beyoncé attacked Murphy. Police begged Murphy to admit there was no white male attacker. Murphy claimed the white man and Martinez attacked him first, but police counseled Murphy, who was five feet ten, that his claim of self-defense could work even if he admitted there was no white man there because Martinez was larger than Murphy. Murphy would not comply. The agent and detective asked Murphy why he lied in previous versions. He replied: "I was trying to keep my cousin [Sanchez] out of the picture." The agent and detective never asked Murphy about the shoes, belts, and shirt placed in the trash by Sanchez.[20]

The police interviews initiated a number of legal actions. With Sanchez's July 3 accusation of Murphy and Murphy's partial confession of July 5 designed to protect Sanchez, Sheriff Harmon wrote an affidavit of arrest and had it signed and sealed by Judge Christopher Daniel Leroi, all on the same day. After Murphy was extradited on July 6, Montezuma County Court allowed him to use a post office box located 323 miles from Farmington on his court paperwork. This protected his privacy, a far cry from the treatment of Martinez's mother. While the court sealed all court records for the case on July 5, the Cortez community held a massive funeral for Martinez at Ertel Funeral Home on Main Street that same day.

Together, the narratives produced by police, the legal system, and media showed indifference and even disdain for the victim's mother, Pauline, and trust and sympathy for Murphy's mother. No one informed Pauline of Murphy's extradition or arrest. The Associated Press quoted Murphy's mother, Angel Murphy Tacoronte, on July 7. She praised her son for not challenging the extradition and downplayed the murder as the result of mere "fighting." On Saturday, *The Cortez Journal* and *Farmington Daily Times* published the first pictures of Murphy looking angry in his inmate uniform. Even as these two outlets published unflattering photos, the *Arizona Republic* and *Farmington Daily Times* emphasized the lack of evidence for a hate crime. Meanwhile, *The Denver Post* interviewed several of Martinez's friends, trying to get to a clear picture of what might have happened that night.[21]

The judicial proceedings continued to showcase a system more invested in protecting Murphy and its own image than in presenting evidence or serving justice for Martinez with a courthouse stocked with judges who later earned criminal charges. Sheriff deputies and volunteers began searching Mancos Valley on Sunday, July 8, 2001, north and south of Highway 160 along Mud Creek. Sheriff Joey Chavez claimed to be unable to speak due to a gag order, when the truth was the court sealed court records only, no gag order. Murphy's arraignment was held the next day at the Montezuma Courthouse, but Pauline was not present. When she called the district attorney's office to ascertain the time of the arraignment, she was told they did not know. Yet Murphy's mother, grandmother, girlfriend, and daughter arrived as a united front at the courthouse, having been notified, and his mother continued her multiday press tour defending her son, claiming Murphy was neither racist nor homophobic. DA Olt represented Murphy in 1998 when he was charged with a felony for beating another minor. That case had been heard by Judge Tim Tuthill, who was later suspended. *The Cortez Journal* represented the arraignment with a favoritism for Murphy and humanized him as a father. They noted that Murphy's child called out "Daddy!" and Murphy had smiled. Judge Christopher Daniel Leroi announced the charge of second-degree murder and reminded the defendant of the possibility of four to forty-eight years in prison and $1 million in fines. In 2012, Judge Leroi violated the Code of Judicial Conduct when he asked a court clerk to move his upcoming DUI hearing to a court and judge who would be lenient with him.[22]

Following the arraignment, the local authorities' campaign to deny the hate crime nature of the murder was challenged by a powerful outside advocate: Cathy Renna from the Gay and Lesbian Alliance Against Defamation (GLAAD). She flew in from New York City and met with DA Olt the afternoon of her arrival on Tuesday, July 10. As a media representative for GLAAD, Renna came to support the Martinez family but also to pressure the media to be accurate in their representations. Sheriff Joey Chavez had already refused to use the term "hate crime." Shaun Murphy's mother had been repeatedly quoted denouncing that characterization. *The Farmington Daily Times* ran the rejection of the killing as a hate crime on its front page well before Renna's arrival. Renna came to challenge these representations.

In a critical tactical error, the police and DA's attempt to shut down the hate crime narrative instead provided activists with the very evidence they needed to prove it. At the meeting between Renna and Olt, the DA quipped, "Well, all crimes are hate crimes, right?" Outraged, Renna told Olt she would "eat him for breakfast." She immediately reached out to her media contacts, and the media coverage increased and expanded. Police held a press conference on July 11, the day after her arrival, continuing to advance their "this was not a hate crime" narrative. Cortez City police chief Roy Lane amplified Olt's pronouncement at the press conference: "I've never seen a homicide yet that wasn't a hate crime."[23] Yet the police released their July 4 affidavit at the press conference, which provided the first documentation of the "bug smashed a *joto*" language. The police and DA spoke as though the offensive phrase meant nothing. Interpretations of "bug smashed a *joto*" created a divide between those who believed the murder was a hate crime, including LGBTQIA+ activists and allies, and those who believed it was not—namely, the police, media, and the district attorney. Releasing the "bug smashed a *joto*" language meant that GLAAD could more easily get media engagement from outside Cortez. The attention and sympathy toward

Martinez's sexual and gender identity challenged the narrative put forward by local police and DA Olt.[24]

The local media, epitomized by *The Cortez Journal* via their reporter Aspen Emmett, affirmed the police's narrative. Renna had zero sway over *The Cortez Journal*, which had the biggest influence in town and the greatest access to the police and the courts. The newspaper provided the most coverage, and all articles on Martinez were written by Aspen Emmett. She reportedly felt some pressure to write about Martinez without alienating the police, her main source of information. From an upper-class family in Colorado, Emmett referred to Martinez as "openly gay" in her July 12 article. Emmett echoed the police by refraining from using the term "hate crime" about the murder of Martinez, but she also did not openly reject the term. With a long history in equestrian riding, Emmett was chosen as Miss Rodeo Colorado in 1998, when she got to meet and be photographed with country music star Toby Keith.[25]

The question of how Murphy and Martinez ended up alone in that dark canyon represented the case's central mystery, one the legal system could have solved at trial. But the investigation evaded the question, securing an arrest without ever explaining the event's core context. The events of June 16 can be seen more clearly in the subsequent actions of the Montezuma County authorities as they may have taken actions to avoid a trial.

THE TRIAL THAT NEVER HAPPENED

The leadup to the trial that never happened began with the victim's mother, Pauline, issuing a media statement—with help from Renna and Matthew Shepard's mother, Judy Shepard—contesting police and media representations of her. But Colorado media outlets ignored Pauline's statement. Instead, they asked the police for an official statement on Pauline's statement.

DA Olt, the police, and the media used the autopsy final report in their narrative arbitrage. The autopsy final report gave them the ammunition they needed to dismiss the severe nature of the violence done to Martinez. Kurtzman's office sent the autopsy report to multiple agencies, and the sheriff's office released it to the media on July 26. Once again, Pauline read of her child's murder in the paper, with no warning of the autopsy results from state authorities. The autopsy report listed cause of death as "undetermined."

The media, especially Renna's contacts, sought confirmation of the deadliness of the attack, but the autopsy results allowed police to backpedal. With the report's finding of "undetermined," the police refused to confirm that the bloody rock was used to injure Martinez. Additionally, DA Olt seemed uncommitted to the case. He took frequent vacations from June 2001 to June 2002. When his office received the autopsy results on July 23, 2001, Olt was out of the office on vacation. Even when he returned to the office and reviewed the autopsy report, he failed to amplify or even articulate that the victim had been attacked from behind or that the attack had been vicious. But the autopsy report itself, as written, created that possibility.[26]

DA Olt may have undermined the case against Murphy through questionable decision-making and frequent delays. He initially charged Murphy with second-degree murder. He did not bump up the charges to first degree until August 13, at the peak of community outrage over Martinez's death. Many gathered for a vigil in honor of Martinez at Parque de Vida that same day. One of the speakers included Judy Shepard, along with many others who spoke and read poetry, followed by a march to the Montezuma County Detention Center where Murphy was incarcerated. The Native American choir from Fort Lewis College sang as the collective moved across the park to the detention center. Olt asked once again for a hearing delay and was approved, moving the hearing from August 13 to September 7. Public defender Pamela Brown motioned to have Olt removed from the case because of previous representation but was denied. Olt belatedly filed notice of his previous representation of the defendant on August 10, only after Brown exposed the conflict. In preparation for the newly scheduled September 7 preliminary hearing, First Assistant State Attorney General Paul Wolff was sworn in as special deputy district attorney, perhaps indicating a state desire to control the narrative. Judge Sharon Lyons Hansen replaced Judge Leroi, who was later convicted of a crime. In 2008, someone lit Hansen's car on fire. Government authorities never disclosed a motive on the record.[27]

Under Judge Hansen, the September 7 hearing devolved into a circus, orchestrated by Murphy's relatives. Sheriff Steve Harmon took the stand and relayed witness reports. Harmon told the court that Shaun Murphy returned to Melissa Scharnhorst's apartment covered in blood and breathing heavily. Upon entering, he announced he had "bug smashed a *joto*." Sheriff Harmon did not expose Scharnhorst's address as he had on more than one occasion with the victim's mother. Harmon emphasized that Murphy had no injuries and referenced incriminating remarks he made leading Harmon to believe he had killed Martinez.

While Harmon implicated Murphy, a group of his female relatives exited and entered the courtroom so frequently that Judge Hansen created a special rule about how often they could do so. Mary Lobato, only eighteen years old, sat behind the prosecution waiting to testify against Murphy. Murphy's mother threatened her inside the courtroom, where everyone heard her utter: "Trick whore, wait till we get outside the courtroom." Police arrested Murphy's mother, and she received felony charges for harassing Lobato. She and her son sat in the same jail for a period of time, but the charges were dropped, and she was quickly released. Although Judge Hansen permitted Murphy to wear street clothes, he left the courtroom in handcuffs. Nothing was said about Martinez's gender expression or sexual identity at the preliminary hearing. Neither side seemed to want it included in the proceedings.

The state's case relied on the interview with Clint Sanchez and the personal items he deposited in the trash. Colorado state investigator Kelly Eliassen also testified to witness testimonies. Like Harmon, he introduced hearsay evidence from Clint Sanchez and Melissa Scharnhorst, both of whom admitted to being with Murphy after the murder. Neither Sanchez nor Scharnhorst was charged, and Harmon did not reveal exactly when he had interviewed them. Public defender Brown questioned the value and integrity of Sanchez's statements, given his desire to avoid charges. She wondered whether he gave statements in exchange for not being charged. Judge Hansen ruled the hearsay based on Sanchez's interview was sufficient to sustain the first- and second-degree charges. She set Murphy's trial for February 20 to March 6 and revoked bond.[28]

At his arraignment in October 2001, Murphy was willing to go to trial on the first-degree charges but pled not guilty. At that arraignment, public defender Brown complained, as she frequently had before, about DA Olt's unwillingness to provide discovery—a significant tell, as Olt never provided discovery to the defense. DA Olt asked for a trial delay and received one, moving the trial from February 20 to March 4, with an omnibus, or pretrial, hearing set for December 5 to hammer out issues around discovery. On October 26, DA Olt asked for a delay on the omnibus hearing, and Judge Hansen shifted the date from December 5 to January 10 to accommodate him.

As the March 2002 trial date approached, Olt behaved erratically. He seemed to protect Murphy when he announced he would not seek the death penalty, although he could have. Murphy's attorney, Pamela Brown, was confident she could win a not-guilty verdict on first-degree charges as the autopsy did not indicate a time or cause of death. In court on October 26, Brown made clear she would use the autopsy to challenge the prosecution and would move to suppress the July 3 and 5 interviews with Murphy since he was not being held for murder during the interviews. The police and DA desperately needed those interviews, which had been conducted prior to the arrest warrant, as Murphy made incriminating statements that day without an attorney present.

With the March trial on the first-degree charges looming, Murphy seemed to hold leverage. He received different treatment than other prisoners from both his public defender and Judge Hansen, while Olt seemed unwilling to complete basic duties, such as adhering to the schedule and providing discovery. In January 2002, Murphy's public defender submitted motions for a stenographer, change of venue, suppression of statements, and sequestering of the jury. All were approved. Additionally, Judge Hansen ruled Murphy would not wear a stun belt (an electronic restraint device) at court, and a plainclothes officer would sit near him, not behind him. Judge Hansen also limited court coverage, insisting the press would have to get a pass from her office. When Murphy's attorney complained about jail conditions for Murphy, Judge Hansen suggested she draft an order for her client, listing all requests. Judge Hansen signed off on the request, giving Murphy four times the amount of visitation as other inmates and a private room with his attorney during visits, unlike other inmates. The reasons for these accommodations are not explained in the court filings or media reports.[29]

At the January hearings in preparation for the March trial on first-degree charges, Olt seemed determined to prevent disclosure of evidence. Even by the end of the month, Olt still had not prepared or submitted discovery, signaling yet another clue that he was not merely unprepared but possibly hiding something. Murphy's attorney pleaded for at least Olt's list of witnesses, which she did not receive. But perhaps most important of all, Olt contradicted himself on the matter of the blood and DNA test results.

The shoes, belts, and shirts deposited in the trash in Farmington and collected by Detective Wynes on July 3, 2001, still had not been tested by the CBI more than six months later, at least according to Olt. Officers took Murphy's DNA on July 12, 2001, yet Olt assured the court in January 2002 that the CBI had not tested the materials. On January 2, he told Murphy's attorney that CBI "will shortly begin testing." On January 9, he told her that the results would be ready February 1. By January 22, Olt suddenly announced a "problem" with the testing but would not clarify. Olt seemed to have blocked the defense's access to the CBI; the agency told her they could not speak to Murphy's attorney without Olt's permission.

Olt and the CBI continued to stall on the lab results to be delivered February 1. Suddenly, on February 7, Olt offered a plea deal on second-degree charges. Murphy accepted. His pleading guilty on second-degree charges wiped away the threat of the March trial and the disclosure of the February 1 lab results. Based on this series of events, the shoes, belts, and shirt may have contained DNA implicating someone other than Murphy. The absence of these DNA results from the court record leaves a critical, unanswered question: Why were items that could have contained another person's DNA not tested or their results not presented? This gap in the evidence supports an alternative narrative that the crime may have involved more than one perpetrator.[30]

The March trial, which would have exposed the interviews and evidence, got replaced with a May sentencing hearing, which got delayed to June, once again, because of Olt. With Murphy's sentencing six weeks away, he suddenly penned a letter to the court asking to withdraw his guilty plea. Once his attorney learned of the letter, she immediately filed a motion to withdraw the guilty plea on May 6. On May 22, just eleven days from sentencing, Murphy asked to withdraw his withdrawal and to proceed on the guilty plea. The media seemed to praise him for facing the consequences: "Murphy told the court he would stand by the plea after all."[31]

This convoluted dance—a letter written without counsel, a swift withdrawal by the public defender, and a final reversal—exposes the fissures in the official narrative. Murphy's reckless move suggests a moment of clarity, panic, or even outside manipulation. Perhaps he chafed at taking the sole blame for a murder he may not have committed alone. He may have realized the case against him rested largely on the testimony of Clint Sanchez. Brown's immediate damage control reveals the plea may have been fragile, an arranged outcome that Murphy may have questioned. The prosecution, seemingly desperate to avoid a trial that would have forced a public accounting of exactly what happened in the canyon, needed a single perpetrator, Murphy, and a tidy narrative: Murphy killed Martinez. Murphy pleading guilty to lesser charges served as the linchpin for their blurry narrative. The media's final framing of Murphy as someone who would "stand by the plea after all" laundered this narrative chaos into a story of resolve, effectively erasing the telltale signs of the deal that may have been struck to bury the evidence and alternative narratives.[32]

By pleading guilty to second-degree murder, Olt avoided a trial, and Murphy avoided a harsher sentence. The lack of a trial preserved the narrative of Murphy acting alone and left it a mystery as to how exactly Murphy came to be alone with Martinez in the canyon, what exactly Murphy did to Martinez, and whether any of it was premeditated. Both Olt and Murphy seemed eager not to dissect any details of June 16, 2001.[33]

At Murphy's June 3 sentencing hearing, his female relatives delivered yet another spectacle. The day began at 9:38 a.m. with Detective Harmon's testimony. He testified to seeing splattered blood, and DA Olt admitted exhibits 1 through 17 and played a videotape from the evidence. At 10:54 a.m., public defender Brown began her cross-examination of Detective Harmon, using Wynes's testimony to challenge him. Brown centered her examination on Clint Sanchez and his being taken into custody while her client was arrested. Judge Hansen again chastised Murphy's relatives for frequently exiting and reentering the courtroom as she had at previous hearings, ruling that they could leave only once. Brown continued her cross-examination of Detective Harmon. At 2:43 p.m., Shaun Murphy's mother, who was now out of jail, gave a statement defending her son. At 2:50 p.m., Brown presented her closing and cited letters written in support of Murphy. Suddenly, Murphy's grandmother screamed, collapsed to the ground, and was removed from the courtroom. At 3:23 p.m., Murphy's attorney began her closing once again and finished at 3:58 p.m. DA Olt rendered a fifteen-minute closing, declining to read the victim impact statements from Martinez's parents, which had been on the record since July and August of the previous year. At 4:15 p.m., Shaun Murphy made a statement on being "attacked" and acting out of "defense." After a short recess, Judge Hansen sentenced Murphy to forty years in an undisclosed prison. Olt could have requested no or limited possibility of parole, but he did not. Nor did he request that the name of the prison be disclosed.[34]

THE COUP OF 2018

Once sentenced, Murphy immediately made plans for his appeal, getting permission to use Brown again and filing notice July 17. He remained in Cortez at the Montezuma County Detention Center on appeal until August 13. According to John Peters-Campbell, the

Cortez LGBTQ+ leader and spokesperson for the case, Murphy vandalized the center more than once in his short time there. The state of Colorado moved Murphy repeatedly during his incarceration, a highly unusual pattern. On August 13, he was transferred to Buena Vista Correctional Complex under medium security until October 15, 2003, when he was taken to Colorado State Penitentiary under a status indicating the inmate needed management. The Colorado Court of Appeals affirmed his sentence on March 11, 2004. On April 17, 2004, Judge Sharon Hansen ordered the return of exhibits 15 and 16, rocks with blood evidence, to the Montezuma County Sheriff to be held until further order of the court.[35]

Murphy's attorney pursued every avenue of appeal. She filed a writ of certiorari with the Colorado Supreme Court, but it was denied on July 6, 2004. On February 7, 2005, Murphy's motion for reconsideration of sentence was denied. While his attorney fought, the state of Colorado continued to move Murphy to other facilities. On his third move, Murphy was taken to Centennial Correctional Facility on August 5, 2005, back to medium-security status. But just a few months later, on November 21, 2005, Murphy was switched to "close status," a high-security classification, again indicating some problem that could have been the fault of Murphy. He remained at close status for almost a year until August 29, 2006, when he went back to medium security—but only for a few days. On his fourth transfer, he was taken to Colorado Territorial Correctional Facility in Cañon City on September 5, 2006, with the general population under medium security. After two stints on heightened security and only six weeks at the Cañon City prison, Murphy got into his first documented fight. Sergeant Debra Minjarez, who stopped the fight, ended up with blood spatters on her clothes. A month later, on November 20, 2006, Murphy was moved for the fifth time to Arkansas Valley Correctional Facility in Ordway, Colorado, with the general population under medium security. Prison moves are unusual and normally done in response to behavioral problems.[36]

Murphy's sentence was affirmed for the last time on December 27, 2006, and he remained in the Ordway prison until 2018. Perhaps coincidentally, President Donald Trump's 2017 inauguration initiated a flurry of activity for Murphy's incarceration. In the first act of the coup of 2018, the Colorado Department of Corrections (CDOC)—exercising its authority under state law C.R.S. § 17-22.5-403—gave Murphy a parole eligibility date of April 30, 2017. But that state law seems to have allowed the Colorado DOC to assign parole eligibility after an inmate served either 50 or 75 percent of their term, depending on context. This would equal twenty or thirty years in Murphy's case. Yet Murphy had only served fifteen or sixteen years. The Colorado DOC holds no records that show when Murphy was assigned his parole eligibility date or by whom. At Murphy's 2017 parole hearing, the panel denied parole, citing the seriousness of his crime, and suggested a second parole hearing in 2018. But in the second move toward a coup, prior to the second parole hearing in 2018, the CDOC moved Murphy on January 20, 2018, back to Buena Vista—the facility where he began—this time under minimum security.

The third act in the coup took place over February and March 2018. On February 13, Montezuma County court clerk Felicia Canzona logged a receipt documenting the release and destruction of exhibit 17, a videotape provided by Mary Lobato. Because no attorney claimed the exhibit after thirty-five days, Judge Plewe approved the notice on March 23. On March 27, Murphy's parole was approved by Denise Balazic during a ten-minute video meeting, although the record shows approval by the full parole board. With the board's official approval, Murphy walked out of prison on May 15, 2018. Not a single media outlet noted his release until September 2019.[37]

To summarize these events: The CDOC gave Murphy a parole eligibility date that seemed to be short of the required time served. Their official logs show nonsequential entries—for example, actions from 2018 logged before decisions made in 2017. In December 2017, after Murphy's parole denial, the CDOC moved him to minimum security at Buena Vista, a facility for inmates nearing parole. Yet the 2017 parole board mandated that he be kept at level 3 medium-security custody. Being moved to minimum security before the 2018 parole hearing suggests the outcome of his 2018 parole may have been predetermined. Many state actors may have coordinated a series of actions on behalf of Murphy. State workers may have given

Murphy an early parole eligibility date and moved him in violation of the 2017 parole board mandate, but this has not been reported nor investigated.

The only names associated with the series of events leading to Murphy's release are Judge Plewe and Denise Balazic. The anonymous CDOC officials who seem to have moved mountains on behalf of Murphy remain unnamed. Balazic, while named, is a relatively unknown entity. Judge Plewe remains the only person on record who does have a significant history and profile. Judge Plewe has donated his leadership to the J. Reuben Clark Law Society, a powerful Mormon legal network. Plewe's religious identity as a member of the Church of Jesus Christ of Latter-day Saints (LDS) likely has little to do with his intervention in the case, but it is important to note the power of the LDS in Diné history. Martinez's mother attended the LDS Intermountain Indian High School in Brigham City, Utah. In the 1970s, the school operated as a federal boarding school designed to replace Navajo language, culture, and religion. She also narrated that she lived with an LDS family near the school, dislocating her from her own Diné roots and kin during her development into a woman. Those individuals from the LDS Church remain in her life even today.[38]

The bigger questions still stand: Was the parole eligibility date outside of legal restrictions? Was Murphy moved against the parole board's recommendation? Was Murphy's parole hearing outcome predetermined?

CLOSING ARGUMENT

The people of Cortez do not want to dwell on the 2001 murder of Martinez, nor do they want to be equated with the homophobic rage in places like Laramie, Wyoming, where Matthew Shepard was murdered in 1998. Cortez insists the town has changed: Judges and police no longer engage in corruption, use drugs, solicit favors, or tamper with court records. Its citizens, they claim, have progressed and hold no ill will toward queer Coloradans. Perhaps there has been some progress, but some things have stayed the same. This legacy of bigotry does not confine itself to the past. In 2022, Odis Sikes ran for the office of Montezuma County Sheriff on a platform opposing trans rights and critical race theory. He ran a campaign promising to deliver sheriff deputies to libraries and schools to stop children from being educated about queer rights or the history of racism in America. Sikes used a publicity photo styled in the rugged, law-and-order image typical of the television show *Yellowstone*. He lost to Steve Nowlin. But Montezuma County hardly stands alone in its homophobia or anti-Indigenous violence. The 2022 shooting at Club Q in Colorado Springs, where five people were murdered with an AR-style rifle, and the popularity of the city's Dragonmans gun store, bear testament to the continued inner rage of some Coloradans.

The full scope of the events of June 16, 2001, remains suppressed. This chapter shows the police immediately turned Martinez's mother, Pauline, into a scapegoat. The July 4 affidavit exposed her address but withheld the names and addresses of the suspects, placing her in danger—a pattern repeated in other documents. The police presented Pauline as a derelict mother who never phoned police about her missing child. This deliberate mischaracterization, a racialized trope, shifted blame onto Pauline and painted her as complicit rather than victimized. Combined with three separate publications of her home address, this rhetoric effectively sanctioned hostility toward her, significantly increasing her danger by signaling she was undeserving of protection or empathy. The police also undermined community concern for the victim by representing them negatively. The police used a system—and continue to use a system—that allows citizens to report missing individuals to police without generating records of the phone calls. This allowed them to portray the victim's mother as a liar.

The police also downplayed Murphy's utterances of slurs like "fag" and "*joto*," squelching queer voices who wanted attention paid to the gendered nature of the crime. The police contradicted themselves about not knowing who the victim was but admitted they took their identification card and a personalized mirror monogrammed with Martinez's name into evidence. The police never charged Clint Sanchez, the man with a car who drove Shaun Murphy to Cortez and reported Fred/FC/Fredrika/Beyoncé being in the car with him and Murphy. Nor did they ever charge Melissa Glover Scharnhorst, the woman who knew Murphy may have killed someone. Murphy was never charged for lying to police about his alibi or lying about being jumped, nor did the legal structures ever make clear that Martinez was attacked from behind, disrupting Murphy's claim of self-defense. No one ever questioned whether the police and Sanchez coordinated a narrative and evidence in exchange for dropping all charges against Sanchez. The police never charged Sanchez for illegally carrying a concealed weapon. When Murphy's mother committed a felony in the courtroom during a hearing, the charges were dropped.

The district attorney made a seemingly poor effort at prosecution, took numerous vacations over the crucial year, and refused to admit the homophobic nature of the crime. Forensic pathologist Kurtzman signed and released an autopsy report indicating no known cause of death, making it easier for Olt to avoid pursuing first-degree murder charges. DA Olt began the case with second-degree charges and seemed all too willing to return to second degree, accepting Murphy's plea bargain. Judge Hansen placated Murphy's every request for privileges.

Murphy's 2018 release may have been carefully planned. He served only sixteen of the forty years sentenced. The parole board said Murphy had no disciplinary problems as a prisoner, but he was put on special status twice and engaged in one recorded fight that resulted in bodily fluids on an officer. The parole board stated he had never violated parole, but Murphy violated parole when he left Farmington, New Mexico, for Cortez, Colorado, in 2001. Additionally, he damaged the Montezuma County Detention Center during 2001 and 2002 as he awaited sentencing, a fact left out of his parole and prison records.

The Cortez police, the Montezuma County Sheriff, the CBI, the Cortez media, and Cortez district attorney Joseph Olt seemed to deal with the June 16, 2001, crime as expeditiously as possible, potentially to control the narrative and suppress the narrative of a second assailant. Reexamining the July statements of Sanchez and Murphy allows us to reconstruct an emergent narrative: Sanchez and Murphy saw Martinez at the party. Sanchez—enraged upon realizing Martinez was assigned male at birth and presented as female—insisted on following Martinez. Sanchez may have coerced Martinez into the car under the false pretense of getting pizza. Murphy admitted he did not know where Martinez wanted to go, the first thing discussed when giving someone a ride. Murphy also admitted that Martinez became angry, which may have been in reaction to not being let out of the car when they passed Martinez's home. Sanchez admitted to mocking Martinez and asking about their "exotic name," clear signs Sanchez openly expressed homophobia in the car. Sanchez may have refused to let Martinez out of the car and instructed Murphy to drive to the isolated canyon, where they could have murdered Martinez together.

Martinez refused to occupy the category of cishet male as demanded by the town. The town residents—including teachers, administrators, middle school and high school staff, and the Adult Education Center—punished them for that choice. Martinez wore a backpack through the entire murder, and evidence suggests they tried to escape. Sanchez could have been involved, but the police let him go. Because of the plea deal, DA Olt never had to release test results or discovery. The plea deal allowed Olt to avoid a careful narration of the moments between the party and the killing in the canyon. With no lab results from the CBI, no one could ever know definitively if the shoes, belts, and shirt held DNA from Murphy.

Fred/FC/Fredrika/Beyoncé Martinez died at the hands of a rageful homophobic and white supremacist violence brought to Diné lands and its environs by settlers steeped in genocide and slavery. Someone acted on the historic impulse to destroy the Native and the Two-Spirit. Through the narrative warfare that followed the murder, the convicted perpetrator seems to have received support from attorneys, judges, and state agents.

THE MACRO CRIME SCENE

As a person who embraced gender fluidity, Fred/FC/Fredrika/Beyoncé Martinez lived within a very high statistical possibility of encountering deadly violence. Two-Spirit, queer, and nonbinary Natives experience even higher levels of violence than cishet Native women. This vulnerability represents not just a statistical reality but also a theoretical blind spot. Scholars like Kai Pyle critique the additive logic of the acronym MMIWGT2S as reinforcing marginalization, while professor Dean Spade warns that state-centered solutions fail gender-nonconforming Indigenous people. The term "femicide," though pivotal in Latin America, falters in Native contexts due to its binary framing, a tension that Chickasaw scholar Jodi Byrd and Driftpile Cree scholar Billy-Ray Belcourt tie to settler academia's erasures. Byrd notes Indigenous studies' "queer problem," and Belcourt rejects its "universal male subject," both speaking to the ways in which queer Native experiences are erased in Native Studies. Fred/FC/Fredrika/Beyoncé's story disrupts these silences.[39]

Fred/FC/Fredrika/Beyoncé's murder must be understood within the four-century continuum of settler violence against the Diné, beginning with Spanish incursions in the 1500s and intensifying under US occupation. This systematic violence sought to erase Indigenous lifeways, particularly targeting those who defied imposed gender binaries. Prior to colonization, Diné society recognized a spectrum of gender identities, including *Asdzáán* (female), *Hastiin* (male), *Nádleeh* (feminine man), *Dilbaa* (masculine woman), *Nádleeh Asdzaa* (lesbian), and *Nádleeh Hastii* (gay man). European colonizers expressed disdain at this complexity, with Catholic, Protestant, and Mormon missionaries actively suppressing traditional gender expressions. The nineteenth century brought successive waves of violence: The Mexican-American War resulted in the US acquisition of Diné homelands through the 1848 Treaty of Guadalupe Hidalgo, followed by Kit Carson's brutal campaigns, which culminated in the Long Walk of 1863–66, during which hundreds of Diné perished in the forced removal to Bosque Redondo. The 1868 treaty allowed their return, but at the cost of cultural genocide through boarding schools, Christian conversion, and resource extraction. By the twentieth century, uranium mining poisoned the land while cases like *Haaland v. Brackeen* continued the assault on Diné families. Through this history of dispossession, Fred/FC/Fredrika/Beyoncé's murder emerges not as an isolated hate crime, but as the logical endpoint of settler colonialism's gendered violence against Native bodies that refuse to disappear. But their story also underscores how Diné people continue to resist erasure, maintaining the largest tribal nation in the US with 170,000 fluent Navajo speakers and unbroken connections to their land, despite centuries of calculated destruction.[40]

Leaving the reservation posed a danger for Fred/FC/Fredrika/Beyoncé because of the history of colonization and the settlers living near the reservation. But leaving the reservation became a necessity in the twentieth century as raising livestock became unsustainable, and some Navajos were compelled to seek wage labor elsewhere. Diné began moving outside the reservation to work as day laborers on massive farms, for the Southern Pacific Railroad—like Fred Martinez Sr.—and in border towns. Navajos rely on border towns for supplies, and the border towns want Navajo dollars, yet some hate their presence. Many people living in border towns near the Navajo reservation—across Utah, Colorado, New Mexico, and Arizona—see Navajos as people who should not occupy space in US cities. Some non-Natives in these border towns resent that Navajos possess a reservation with a significant land base. That resentment can result in violence against Navajos—not only from US citizens but also from city and county police officers.[41]

Border towns see the reservation and Native people as the source of violence. White citizens of border towns learn a US history in which Kit Carson—a US military leader responsible for scorched-earth campaigns that led to the Long Walk—represents a hero who defeated the Navajo. The erasure of Carson's genocidal practices allows white settlers to imagine that they are hunted and haunted by Navajos. They imagine themselves surrounded by violence and justify their violence against Diné, blaming them for their own victimization. But in reality, border towns and their settler residents pose the greater danger. These towns create a dangerous environment of risk, hostility, and punishment for simply existing in the US as a Diné. Farmington, New Mexico, operates as an important node in settler violence against Navajos in a border town, a town where white and Latinx boys were rumored to dismember Navajos and place their body parts in their lockers at Farmington High School. In Farmington, the city government allows for more liquor stores than city codes allow, with permits given to wealthy Latinx families who profit from alcohol dependence. Then the liquor store owners, along with Farmington citizens, cry over the effects of alcohol dependency on unhoused Navajo in Farmington. In the late 1950s, white firemen in Farmington poured red paint on men who were Native and drunk, and this racist violence made its way into the newspaper, only to be treated glibly with a poll asking white citizens whether they approved of the violence.[42]

The violence continued. In 1974, three teenagers bludgeoned three Navajo men: Benjamin Benally, John Harvey, and David Ignacio. The teens fixated on their faces and reproductive organs, placing explosives inside the Navajo men's noses and atop their genitals. They then burned the Navajo men and hid their corpses in Chokecherry Canyon on the border between the town and desert. The Chokecherry Canyon of the 1974 massacre exists as a different place from the canyon where Martinez was murdered, yet the two operate on symbolic parallels. The word "canyon" itself became a recurring site of anti-Navajo violence over the twentieth century.[43]

When the Navajo relatives of Benjamin Benally, John Harvey, and David Ignacio were not allowed into the courtroom for the hearings, Navajos organized a Farmington demonstration against violence only to encounter whites dressed in the uniforms of cavalry officers—the same officers their ancestors would have seen in the nineteenth century—to remind Navajos of the past violence and the present threat of violence from surrounding whites. These men dressed as cavalry blocked the protest parade, and a riot broke out because of their threatening presence. The federal government followed up with a massive budget for a very expensive study with a simple conclusion: Institutional racism and discrimination function as realities in border towns. In Farmington, the study pointed especially to the hospital, those in charge of creating districts, and the city's hiring practices as key sites of discrimination. Three decades later in the 2000s, the federal government congratulated themselves for money well spent and a job well done, making official reports of progress since the first report, and considering their goals accomplished. Yet the racism and violence never stopped despite the expensive study.[44]

In 1978, a white hitchhiker shot Duane "Chili" Yazzie, who lost his arm because of the attack. In 2000, Betty Lee, a thirty-six-year-old Navajo woman, was bludgeoned to death like the Navajo men in the

Chokecherry Massacre. In 2004, George Arthur's son encountered white male high school students who beat him and attempted to set him on fire, violence identical to that of the Chokecherry Massacre. Also in 2004, on June 4, three white men from Farmington patrolled the streets looking for Navajos to attack. They found William Blackie and tricked him into getting in their car. As they drove out of town into the isolated desert, Blackie asked to get out to relieve himself. They clubbed him in the head, then left him there to die. He survived only because he was able to use his phone. Six days later, on June 10, 2004, a white officer, hired and trained by the city of Farmington, murdered Clint John, a Diné man, in a Walmart parking lot.[45]

In 2014, another attempted murder of three Navajo men—eerily like the Chokecherry Massacre—took place in Albuquerque. Three Latino teens brutally attacked three Navajo men: Allison Gorman, Kee Thompson, and Jerome Eskeets. Only Eskeets survived and reported that the homicidal teens used metal pipes, wooden sticks, and cinder blocks to destroy and bludgeon the Navajo men. As in the Chokecherry Massacre, the male teens mutilated the bodies and faces of the Navajo men to the point where the corpses could not be identified by visual observation. The killers glibly admitted that in 2014, they had beaten at least fifty others. The prosecution refused to consider race a contributing factor and steered clear of any assertion that the teens committed a hate crime.[46]

On March 27, 2016, white police officer Austin Shipley shot and killed Navajo mother Loreal Tsingine in the border town of Winslow during a thirty-second interaction that resulted in the six-foot-tall officer shooting Tsingine six times. Tsingine's family filed a claim against the city of Winslow, which trained, employed, and authorized Austin Shipley to carry a gun. Navajo Nation filed separate lawsuits on behalf of Tsingine, one against the city of Winslow and another against the federal government. All three suits were decided against Tsingine's family and Navajo Nation and ruled in favor of the respondents. Police killings continued. In 2018, Montezuma County Sheriff officer Edward Oxley murdered Fordell Hill, a twenty-six-year-old Navajo man, on the Navajo reservation outside of Montezuma County. On June 1, 2019, Cecilia Finona disappeared in Farmington.

A grandmother and an army veteran, Finona was hit in the head by her non Native boyfriend with a large object, thrown into her own car, and then driven through New Mexico, Arizona, California, and Nevada as she bled to death. Her boyfriend eventually hid her corpse in a culvert outside of Las Vegas, Nevada. The violence against Fred/FC/Fredrika/Beyoncé in 2001 fits into this pattern of border town hate and violence toward Navajo people.[47]

In the next chapter we stay in the 2000s but move south to Mexico where a group of male soldiers murdered an Indigenous elder. These men knew they had the full backing of their country to perform their gruesome violence, and they were right. As officers of the occupying military, they unleashed a violence upon her and enjoyed complete impunity, with even their president lying on their behalf to protect them from the consequences of their actions. Ernestina Ascencio Rosario's story centers on Indigenous communities in Mexico in 2007. What followed in the aftermath of her murder demonstrates the power of the state's narrative arbitrage to shield non-Native perpetrators and preserve their impunity.

GUIDE TO KEY FIGURES IN CHAPTER 4

ERNESTINA ASCENCIO ROSARIO: A seventy-three-year-old monolingual Nahua elder of Tetlatzinga, Veracruz. A beloved mother. Murdered in 2007.

MARTHA INÉS ASCENCIO: Ernestina's daughter. A monolingual Nahua speaker who witnessed her mother's dying words—*pinome xoxome* (men in green/soldiers)—and carried them as a sacred duty. Court filings with the Inter-American Court of Human Rights spell her name as "Martha." Mexican journalists spell her name as "Marta."

JULIO INÉS ASCENCIO: Ernestina's son. Served as a translator for his mother and family, conveying her words to Spanish-speaking authorities and media.

ALFREDO: Ernestina's twenty-one-year-old great-nephew. Helped carry her to a truck to seek medical help after the attack. Last name unknown.

FRANCISCO INÉS: Ernestina's son. Drove the truck that transported her to multiple medical facilities in a desperate attempt to save her life.

MAYOR PASCUALA: The Indigenous leader (mayor) of Soledad Atzompa. Filed early complaints against the soldiers' behavior and helped organize community resistance after the attack. Was offered a bribe and also set up to be assassinated.

RENÉ HUERTA: A leader from Centro de Readaptación Osocial Indígena Santiago Zacatepec (CROISZ). Alerted the community and helped the family initially. Later co-opted by the state to deny the military's involvement. Participated in the abduction and silencing of Ernestina's family.

JULIO ATENCO VIDAL: A former official of Soledad Atzompa and CROISZ representative. Helped file the initial complaint against the soldiers and witnessed the military's deceptive tactics.

LUISA HERNÁNDEZ: A nurse and neighbor who briefly examined Ernestina and urged the family to take her to a hospital.

DR. MARIO ALBERTO GANTE: A doctor at the private Clinica Los Ángeles in Ciudad Mendoza. Examined Ernestina and confirmed she needed emergency hospital care.

DR. MARÍA CATALINA RODRÍGUEZ ROSAS: A gynecologist from the Veracruz Attorney General's Office specializing in sexual crimes. Documented Ernestina's catastrophic injuries at the hospital and was later suspended for her report.

DR. JUAN PABLO MENDIZÁBAL: The forensic doctor for the Veracruz Attorney General's Office. Performed the first autopsy that documented the sexual assault and violence. Was coerced, suspended, and later won a Supreme Court case for his pension. He still has not received his pension.

JOSÉ SOBERANES: An officer of the Sixty-Third Infantry Brigade. Lied to Indigenous protesters, claiming soldiers had been arrested to gain access to the road being blockaded the night of the murder.

SERGIO ARTURO ARAGÓN: Commander of the Twenty-Sixth Military Zone. May have used a deceptive tactic of presenting civilian-clad soldiers as detainees to the family.

FELIPE CALDERÓN: President of Mexico (2006–12). Announced a finding by the Comisión Nacional de los Derechos Humanos (CNDH), or National Human Rights Commission, before they had begun investigating, that Ernestina died of gastritis, setting the official narrative and forcing other state institutions to conform to it. His administration's "war on drugs" rhetoric provided the pretext for the militarization of Indigenous zones that led to the crime.

FIDEL HERRERA BELTRÁN: Governor of the state of Veracruz. Oversaw and orchestrated the abduction of Ernestina's family.

ABRAHAM KUNIO GONZÁLEZ: A federal undersecretary. Attempted to bribe Mayor Pascuala and later met with René Huerta to pressure the family into changing their testimony.

DR. IGNACIO GUTIÉRREZ VÁZQUEZ: The Veracruz state examiner who performed the second autopsy on Ernestina's exhumed body in the cemetery. Was also suspended.

JOSÉ LUIS SOBERANES FERNANDEZ: The ombudsman of the CNDH. Led the CNDH's reversal, siding with the military's narrative and attacking the credibility of the doctors and family.

DR. FERNANDO CERVANTES DUARTE: A CNDH doctor who authored the final report, cynically ignoring the evidence of sexual assault and claiming Ernestina died of gastritis.

GUILLERMO GALVÁN: The secretary of national defense. Admitted to testing semen samples from the crime, a statement the military later retracted.

BARBARA YLLÁN RONDERO: Former senator, attorney, and writer. Provided a clear legal analysis that the cover-up was a desperate attempt by the military to manufacture jurisdiction over the case.

LUCIA MELGAR: Mexican scholar interviewed by the author. Provided analysis on state complicity and the myth of motherhood in the cover-up of Ernestina's murder.

VALENTINA VALIA BATRES GUADARRAMA: A federal deputy from the Party of the Democratic Revolution. Introduced a constitutional reform decree in response to the case and other military crimes against civilians.

MARCELA LAGARDE: A prominent non-Indigenous Mexican feminist scholar. Coined the term *feminicidio* (femicide) to describe state-enabled, gender-based murder.

RITA SEGATO: An Argentine feminist theorist.

CHAPTER 4

ERNESTINA

On Sunday, February 25, 2007, at nearly 5 p.m., Ernestina Ascencio Rosario's relatives found her, lying on her right side, her hands and legs bound together, her clothes pulled over her head, her huarache sandals scattered nearby. The elderly woman told her rescuers about the soldiers, how they tied her up and got on top of her. The bullets in their cartridge belts dug into her chest during the attack. Her family raced to save her.[1]

PINOME XOXOME

Before sharing the rest of the incident, it is necessary to understand the role of the Mexican government and military in Indigenous-majority territories of Mexico. The soldiers who tortured Ernestina were enlisted as members of the Mexican Army's Sixty-Third Infantry Battalion based at the San Antonio military barracks in Orizaba. Military leaders stationed their unit at the Base de Operactiones Mixtas "García" just five days before they attacked Ernestina. But soldiers belonging to the Twenty-Sixth Military Zone had been in the region since 2005. And before that, soldiers from other locations arrived in the 1980s as Mexico embraced a militarization process—especially in rural and poverty-stricken areas with large Indigenous populations—to surveil, patrol, and control Indigenous communities. These policies had nothing to do with drugs and cartels. According to Amnesty International, Mexican soldiers sexually attacked at least sixty

Indigenous women since the mid-1990s, though the numbers could be much higher.[2]

The Mexican government targeted Veracruz for its history of Indigenous activism, an activism that goes back to the 1970s. Several organizations in Nahua-dominant regions of Veracruz included the Nahuatl Indigenous Organization of the Sierra de Zongolica, the Regional Coordinator of Indigenous Organizations of the Sierra de Zongolica, the Indigenous Peasant Organization of the Sierra de Zongolica, and the Union of All Poor Peoples (TINAM, for its acronym in Nahuatl). Gloria Arenas served as one of the founders of TINAM in the '80s. Her arrest in 1999 in Guerrero for her involvement in a different group reinforced the Mexican state's equation of Veracruz with armed Indigenous resistance, much as the Txompaxtle brothers' case did. Gerardo and Jorge Txompaxtle Tecpile worked as Nahua campesino activists from the Sierra de Zongolica, Veracruz, devoting their lives to defending communal land, forests, and Indigenous self-determination in the region since the 1970s. In January 2006, Gerardo, Jorge, and another Nahua activist were arrested by federal police and incarcerated for nearly three years. Along with Arenas, the Txompaxtle brothers became symbols of Indigenous activism in Veracruz, an Indigenous resistance the state found threatening. In 2020, the Inter-American Court of Human Rights (IACtHR) found in their favor and ordered comprehensive reparations for the state's campaign against them.[3]

The Mexican militarization of Indigenous communities created a continuity of surveillance and invasion by the settler state. The Mexican military aimed its counterinsurgency and militarization efforts in the Sierra Mountain range of Veracruz and in other areas populated by Indigenous people, including the Zapatistas farther south, as part of a widespread campaign against leftist groups such as the People's Revolutionary Army and the Revolutionary Army of Indigenous Peoples. By the time the military murdered Ernestina Ascencio Rosario, these groups of soldiers overlapped as did their directives, which blurred the line between cartels and Indigenous activists.[4]

The soldiers who assaulted and tortured Ernestina arrived in Veracruz on February 1, 2007, setting up camp in Teotlalco. The military men walked about town with rifles, harassing locals for food, water, firewood, and livestock. Mayor Pascuala at Soledad Atzompa sent a message to the military camp on behalf of the Indigenous leader at Teotlalco, asking why soldiers were stationed in their autonomous zones. They sent him on a bureaucratic errand, telling him to visit the provisional barracks rather than the camp. The following day, February 2, Mayor Pascuala, René Huerta of the Centro de Readaptación Osocial Indígena Santiago Zacatepec (CROISZ), and Julio Atenco Vidal—a former official of Soledad Atzompa's city council and later representative of the CROISZ—presented their written complaint in person at the military barracks at Orizaba. They received no reply. Unbeknownst to them, just weeks before Ernestina's murder, journalists in Veracruz were already investigating nearly identical reports. Norma Trujillo, a journalist in Xalapa, had interviewed locals from the northern Huasteca region who denounced the military's rape of Indigenous women. When Trujillo confronted Governor Fidel Herrera Beltrán with these findings at a press conference, he not only confirmed that he had authorized the military's presence but personally threatened her for asking the question. The state threat against Trujilo confirmed the violence resulted from a systemic, state-sanctioned strategy, not an isolated incident.[5]

On February 20, the camp of about 150 soldiers moved from Teotlalco to Tetlatzinga, a small village of 736 individuals, about three hundred feet from Ernestina's home. Pascuala and others believed the military repositioned the soldiers in retaliation for their letter. In the days leading up to the murder, residents reported seeing soldiers spread throughout their mountains and hills, an action that has nothing to do with a war on drugs and everything to do with terrorizing Indigenous people.[6]

Pen and paper became weapons against the state, and Mayor Pascuala wielded them alongside others. Three weeks before the attack on Ernestina, the Indigenous leader at Mexcala, Modesto Antonio Cruz, penned a letter to Lieutenant Colonel Alejandro de Jesús Orozco. Like Pascuala, he documented the behavior of Mexican soldiers and their harassment and violence toward Indigenous locals. Infantry Corporal Edwin Martinez responded brazenly: "We come with superior instructions and, here, we do as we want." Martinez's statement captured the essence of the settler mandate: "Here, we do as we want." Though this phrase cannot be found in Mexican Army manuals, constitutions, bylaws, or procedures, it nonetheless resides there—as if written in invisible ink. Martinez knew this truth so well he felt confident announcing it to an Indigenous leader in response to documentation of military crimes.[7]

Under the direction and leadership of newly inaugurated President Calderón, the Mexican Army set up the Garcia base just five days before the murder of Ernestina at Tetlatzinga. Although Calderón employed the "war on drugs" and "Plan México Seguro," or "Safe Mexico Plan," phrasing to suggest his militarization policy targeted drug trafficking and promoted safety, his predecessors had already fused the fight against cartels with the repression of leftists—especially Indigenous leftists—and even Indigenous people in general. By the time Calderón ordered more soldiers to the Sierra de Zongolica, the mostly Nahua community had grown furious with the constant theft of their firewood and food, abuse of military authority, and disrespect for Indigenous locals. Some demonstrated against the infusion of still more soldiers by Calderón. Ernestina participated in those protests.[8]

After enduring torture and being thrown down a hill, Ernestina spoke two words, in addition to others, in Nahua to her daughter, Martha, which continue to haunt the powers that be in Mexico: *pinome xoxome*, meaning "men in green," or "soldiers." These words uttered in Nahua from mother to daughter, have been carried by Martha, a monolingual Nahua speaker, as her sacred duty and burden to share with the world, despite the costs to her own life and safety. Martha shared these words with her older brother, Julio, who spoke some Spanish. Julio stood in the position of translator, sharing his mother's words with reporters and government officials. Other relatives with them on the day of the attack on Ernestina also spoke some Spanish—including her great-nephew, twenty-one-year-old Alfredo—and they, too, translated Ernestina's utterance of *pinome xoxome* into Spanish.

After being discovered, Ernestina could not walk. At the scene, Alfredo sought the help of Ernestina's daughter, Martha. Martha convinced a cargo truck driver to stop for them. The driver and Ernestina's sons, Julio and Francisco, carried her to the truck in hopes of saving her life. The envoy with Ernestina passed three military trucks as they left Tetlatzinga. The soldiers witnessed the medical emergency and did nothing. Perhaps some of the soldiers who watched her being swept away were her attackers who notified superiors that she had been rescued.[9]

Seeking medical intervention for Ernestina as quickly as possible, her family made several stops in their search. They decided to head to the Clinica Instituto Mexicano del Seguro Social in Acultziapa, as it was the closest facility, but it turned out to be closed as it was Sunday in the predominantly Catholic country. They stopped at the local home of nurse Luisa Hernández, who briefly examined Ernestina and urged them to quickly get her to a hospital. They set their sights north to Ciudad Mendoza for help at the private Clinica Los Ángeles. When the blue truck carrying Ernestina passed through Soledad Atzompa on the way to Ciudad Mendoza, the group alerted Mayor Pascuala and other key figures in the community what the Mexican military had done to the beloved Nahua elder, and locals began organizing instantly. Completing the trek to the Clinica Los Ángeles, Ernestina was briefly examined by Dr. Mario Alberto Gante. He repeated what Hernández had said: Ernestina must be seen by physicians in a hospital. While she was at the clinic, Francisco raced to the CROISZ office to alert leader René Huerta of the news. Huerta informed his network of the emergency and later joined the family at the hospital.[10]

At their final stop, Ernestina and her relatives entered Río Blanco Regional Hospital in Río Blanco, Veracruz. Hospital staff failed to perform the emergency surgery and to provide a Nahua translator. The only intervention Ernestina received at the hospital came from her relatives, not the hospital staff: Her family and Huerta notified the Veracruz Attorney General's Office to at least ensure documentation of the assault. The office sent María Catalina Rodríguez Rosas, a gynecologist of the Specialized Agency in Sexual Crimes. She approached Ernestina around 11 p.m. Dr. Rosas, who did not speak Nahua, examined her injuries and documented: "Radio folds of the anus were observed with dermal-epidermal excoriations, anal sphincter with recent tear with layer bleeding and transabundant bleeding, probable rectal perforation, life-threatening injuries, taking more than fifteen days to heal, requiring urgent management of general surgery and/or coloproctology." Crucially, Dr. Rosas also recorded an abundance of seminal fluid. Dr. Rosas was suspended for her report on her examination of Ernestina. Her professional character was assassinated, and authorities later falsely accused her of failing to collect semen samples. She claims otherwise.[11]

As the Río Blanco Regional Hospital staff made no interventions, Ernestina fell into a coma. She died in the early morning hours of Monday, February 26. As with Levina Moody, her murder can only be understood as death by sexual assault. The violence enacted upon her body exemplifies the intersection of militarization, gendered colonial logics, and racialized state power. After Ernestina's death, a forensic doctor from the Veracruz Attorney General's Office, Dr. Juan Pablo Mendizábal, transported her body to a funeral home where he conducted the autopsy, documenting her injuries thoroughly and methodically. He documented the genital destruction: "concentric lacerations to the labia majora at 3, 5, 7, and 11 o'clock positions, with deep ecchymosis in the vaginal canal, indicating repeated blunt-force penetration with a rigid object." Dr. Mendizábal's report also notes "anal atrocity: full-thickness tearing of the anal sphincter with active hemorrhage and probable rectal perforation, requiring emergency surgery and fifteen days of healing time." Altogether, Mendizábal attributed her death to a traumatic brain injury, spinal fracture, vaginal and anal assault, and acute anemia. These injuries bear the hallmarks of weaponized rape.

The state of Veracruz released her body to her relatives on Tuesday, February 27, 2007. Her community at Tetlatzinga held her burial and funeral the next day. She received all the holy rites of the Catholic Church, including a public rosary, funeral Mass, and rites at her burial, with blessings of the grave, sprinkling of holy water, prayers, and a novena offered by her entire community. But within days, the very military that killed her would dig her up for another autopsy.[12]

NARRATIVE WARFARE

The events that followed the murder of Ernestina reveal the narrative warfare between the military, state government, human rights organizations, local Indigenous leadership, Nahua locals, and the family of Ernestina. Indigenous people protested; the president and the independent human rights commission sided with the military; the state of Veracruz changed its position; the Mexican government divided the Indigenous community using local Indigenous leaders to gain direct access to Ernestina's family; and those who spoke out in support of Ernestina's utterance of *pinome xoxome* faced manipulation, threats, suspensions, and slander. These actors could not erase the military killing of an elderly Nahua woman and, instead, sought to erase the words she spoke, the belief in her words, and the outrage over her words, which continues even now. Ernestina's dying words, witnessed by her community, her son Francisco's desperate alerts, and the evidence gathered by Rosas and Mendizábal converged within just forty-eight hours into a formidable threat to the Mexican military and the nation itself.

Indigenous protests in Tetlatzinga began immediately and continued for days. The very night that followed the discovery of Ernestina on Sunday, February 25, thousands of Indigenous people gathered in front of city hall in Soledad Atzompa in a spontaneous show of anger. By the next morning, their outrage had solidified into organized action. Protesters deliberately blocked the road entering the Orizaba Valley, as they knew the soldiers from Tetlatzinga would be trying to head north to Orizaba. This road provided the only way out for the military. During the blockade, a Mexican military Hummer approached the crowd. Inside the vehicle was Officer José Soberanes of the Sixty-Third Infantry Brigade—no relation to the similarly named National Human Rights Commission official later involved in the case—accompanied by four soldiers wearing civilian clothes. To make his way through the blockade, Soberanes likely lied to Mayor Pascuala, claiming the blockade was preventing him from traveling in order to arrest the guilty men. The community now believes the four men in the vehicle may have been the assailants. Indigenous protesters also blocked the secretary of public security, Juan Manuel Orozco, prosecutor Emeterio López, and other unnamed authorities. Julio Atenco

Vidal, an Indigenous activist from Soledad Atzompa, later remembered that moment. In Vidal's telling, just hours after the crime, Soberanes stood in front of three hundred people and claimed that four soldiers had been arrested and were the subject of an investigation. The trusting crowd let the military convoy through, believing that giving access would support the investigation of the four soldiers.[13]

This military stunt to deceive Indigenous peoples did not occur in isolation. The next day, the deceitful pattern repeated. As reported by *La Jornada* on March 10, Commander Sergio Arturo Aragón of the Twenty-Sixth Military Zone visited the homes of Ernestina's relatives with four soldiers dressed in civilian clothes, presenting them as detainees. Parading four unnamed, civilian-clad soldiers to different audiences on subsequent days exposes it not as a legitimate investigation but as a coordinated strategy to manufacture a narrative of accountability where none existed. This narrative gesture was meant to placate outrage, create confusion, and protect the assailants, the military, and the nation. Despite the early theatrics, the Mexican Army never detained or arrested even one soldier for the murder of Ernestina.[14]

In the aftermath of state-sponsored brutality, the lie meant to contain the fury instead became the spark that mobilized a nation's conscience and brought a region to the edge of war. Upon hearing they had been lied to about the arrest of the four soldiers, six thousand Indigenous protesters gathered in a trench in the tiny village of Tetlatzinga. Less than a third of a mile separated them from the military camp that hosted the barbarism against their Nahua relative. The soldiers of Garcia Operations Base, about 120 in all, minus the four who had been shepherded away by an officer, entrenched themselves, fully armed with weapons purchased by Mexico and manufactured in the United States. The mayor of Soledad Atzompa led the Indigenous vanguard, claiming a defiance that preceded the Zapatistas: "Since the mid-eighties, we began to defend our territories and our rights." The state's governor, Fidel Herrera Beltrán, suddenly appeared in a helicopter, an extraordinary privilege when compared to the poverty of most Nahua in Veracruz. Declaring his intent to support peace, Governor Herrera chose to land inside the military camp, a calculated decision that made his stance unmistakably clear: He stood with the

Mexican soldiers, not the Nahua. His dark tailored suit and polished leather shoes spoke volumes of his privilege; his choice to physically stand behind army lines told the rest.[15]

Attempting to divide the Indigenous community from their leadership, the military set out to co-opt the Indigenous mayor of Soledad Atzompa. Within days of the murder, Mayor Pascuala was subjected to an intense campaign of intimidation by the Mexican military and government to support a cover-up. They detained him for hours in a locked room where military officials and the state public prosecutor interrogated him. They intended to convince him to retract his statement that Ernestina had been raped and killed by Mexico's soldiers. Pascuala refused to bend. After the first detention, he received new instructions to attend another meeting with Federal Undersecretary Eng Abraham Kunio González. For this meeting, Pascuala was explicitly instructed to come to the meeting alone—an order he refused by bringing a witness. At the meeting, González launched the official cover story of Ernestina's death, attributing it to "gastritis," and offered him a suitcase full of cash as a bribe, which Pascuala refused. This coordinated effort involved containment, harassment, threats, and attempted bribery from authorities at multiple levels of government, but they all failed.[16]

Once two reports by highly skilled state representatives (Drs. Rosas and Mendizábal) documenting the assassination of the Nahua elder were submitted, accepted, and filed with the state of Veracruz, the narrative warfare centered on defanging those reports. Only later did it become clear that the military led the discrediting campaign. The president took the charge first. Then La Comisión de los Derechos Humanos (CNDH), or the National Human Rights Commission. Then the state of Veracruz. Veracruz administrators forced Dr. Mendizábal to sign a false report after his factual one had already been submitted. Signing it under severe duress, Dr. Mendizábal later recanted and publicly insisted he had been coerced. His refusal to stay silent and his public whistleblowing led to his 2010 inactivation, a measure that barred him from holding office or exercising his role as a forensic doctor. Veracruz blamed his inactivation on a lack of professionalism connected to the autopsy, including contamination of blood samples, erroneously certifying sexual assault, and performing her autopsy in an unauthorized location in the presence of unauthorized individuals. Dr. Mendizábal waged a long legal battle against the state of Veracruz to receive his pension. In 2019, Mexico's Supreme Court ruled in his favor, ordering the state of Veracruz to pay him his full pension and back pay. As of 2026, he still has not been paid and continues to speak out regularly in defense of his original report and findings on the murder of Ernestina Ascencio Rosario.

Much of the case rests on the two doctors' findings and the testimony of her relatives—especially the two words *pinome xoxome*. These two non-Indigenous state representatives, Drs. Rosas and Mendizábal, supported a Nahua elder by stating the evidence according to their training, skills, and expertise. The doctors went against the unwritten mandate of the settler state—denying settler and state violence—which supports the other state mandate: "Here, we do as we want." The two doctors provided documentation of Ernestina's vaginal and anal injuries as well as the injuries to her rib cage, spine, hips, and skull. Without their documentation, the legion of individuals pushing for justice in Ernestina's case would have only the testimony of her Nahua relations, words rejected by the state. The Nahua relatives of Ernestina who translated on her behalf, as she lay dying an excruciating death, stand defiant in the face of a settler legal apparatus that weaponizes those very translations against them.

The investigation into Ernestina's murder reflects historic and systemic issues faced by Indigenous peoples since the beginning of colonization. Ernestina never learned Spanish, and that inaccessibility put a target on her back, giving Spanish-speaking authorities a path toward silencing her. Martha and other family witnesses testified to Ernestina's Nahua words, including "Many, many. They tied my feet. They tied my hands. It hurts," along with other statements. State actors attempted to neutralize her Nahua words. They aimed especially to relegate her identification of Mexican soldiers to the realm of the unspoken. For the Mexican military and government, Ernestina's Nahua words—in particular, *pinome xoxome*—indicted state soldiers, and that accusation had to be denied and erased by the settler state. The government went so far as to hire a Nahuatl linguist from the prestigious National Autonomous University of Mexico who parsed the words of Ernestina, her daughter Martha, and other relatives, suggesting that either Ernestina had misspoken or one of Ernestina's relatives had mistranslated. But her daughter, Martha, and other relatives have repeated themselves since 2007, insisting that Ernestina indicated she had been sexually assaulted by soldiers.

No force of nature made the cover-up of Ernestina's murder inevitable. State employees did. Throughout early March, some governmental agencies initially held their ground that Ernestina had been sexually assaulted, making their subsequent about-faces sudden, remarkable, and all the more telling. Over the month of March, the Mexican Army, the state of Veracruz, the CNDH, and the president battled over the narrative of weaponized rape. At the hospital, military officers appeared out of nowhere and made their presence felt at every stage of the investigation. On February 26, the CNDH opened a case into the investigation of the murder, perhaps earnestly. On March 3, the commission supported the reports by Drs. Rosas and Mendizábal, admitting Ernestina "died due to the lesions she received." But the military changed the CNDH's methods and position within days of their March 3 utterance. In short order, the CNDH sought to clear the military of any wrongdoing—not by proving they had committed no wrongs, but by providing false evidence.

The military led the narrative warfare from the start, beginning their campaign of lies from the day of the murder. Unlike the CNDH and the state of Veracruz, the military never once supported the work of Drs. Rosas and Mendizábal or the statements of Ernestina's relatives. In early March, they created a facade of investigation. On March 3 and 6, they tried to quell angry protesters by claiming they had questioned four military officials and seventy-nine soldiers, examining their penises for lacerations or "signs of sexual activity." They confidently proclaimed that none of the men had had sex within the last seven days, a ludicrous conclusion. They also informed the press that the Garcia base sat ten miles from Tetlatzinga (not the actual one-third mile away), and that the criminals wore stolen military uniforms, if there was, in fact, a sexual assault. These statements amounted to fabrications.[17]

From the very start, the military stood against the Indigenous community and its claims. One by one, others fell under military control, adopting its viewpoint and cover story. The president of Mexico spoke first. Although the state of Veracruz held jurisdiction from the moment Ernestina entered the hospital, the CNDH claimed a shared jurisdiction beginning the day after her death due to the accusation of human rights violations by the military. The military held no jurisdiction yet claimed otherwise on March 8 and ordered an exhumation and second autopsy of Ernestina's corpse to be performed on March 9. Three days later, President Calderón either made a grave error or followed a predetermined script when he preemptively announced the CNDH's findings, which did not yet exist: "The CNDH intervened, and what resulted from the necropsy was that she died of untreated chronic gastritis. There is no trace of being raped." President Calderón either blundered by telling reporters what the military and the CNDH had already agreed to, or he made this announcement to force the CNDH's hand toward the gastritis cover story. The military seemed to be influencing President Calderón by telling him what the CNDH would conclude, and the president seemed to be influencing what the CNDH would conclude.

The state of Veracruz clung to the doctors' reports, while the CNDH surrendered to the military's narrative. Although the CNDH had supported the Veracruz doctors' reports on March 3, it did an about-face in response to President Calderón's leak. By March 18, José Luis Soberanes, CNDH ombudsman, supported Calderón's unfounded assessment, refusing to acknowledge the possibility of rape, military involvement, or any evidence suggesting murder by soldiers. By March 30, Soberanes had moved into an offensive posture, threatening to sue the Veracruz forensic officers for "badly done" reports. But the state of Veracruz continued to hold strong against the narrative warfare of the military and president. In response to Soberanes, Governor Herrera waved the death certificate before the press, stating emphatically: "It was a crime, not natural death." The Veracruz State Commission of Human Rights concurred: "I don't believe [the natural death story] at all."[18]

One might uncharitably observe that Soberanes's fidelity to the fabrications proved to be a far more lucrative career move than steadfastness to the evidence and testimony. Today, he holds the title of full-time senior researcher at Universidad Nacional Autónoma de México's Institute of Legal Research, holds Level III status in Mexico's National System of Researchers, serves as a distinguished professor at the National University of San Marcos in Peru, works as an academician of Spain's Royal Academy of Jurisprudence, and enjoys a visiting professorship at the University of Social Sciences in Toulouse, France—positions involving little, if any, teaching.[19]

While the CNDH's complicity, led by Soberanes, constitutes a massive contradiction of its stated mission, Mexican soldiers committed the crime, and the military covered it up and hid the felons. They failed to gather evidence from the crime scene where Ernestina was assaulted. They failed to log, document, and test the evidence, such as the orange peels Ernestina mentioned as having been left by her killers. The DNA could have been gathered from these items, and it may have been, but the location of those items and any test results that may exist have never been shared with any entities determined to ascertain the names of the killers. Perhaps most importantly, the Department of Defense held no jurisdiction over the murder of Ernestina. Yet they intervened as though the case was theirs. Had the soldiers attacked Ernestina on the base, the Department of Defense would have held jurisdiction; however, the attack took place off base—a fact not contested by the Department of Defense—which meant the state of Veracruz held legal authority over the case. Yet the Department of Defense controlled the second autopsy and made themselves a presence at the hospital when Ernestina died. What exactly they did to manipulate, hide, or destroy any evidence remains unknown but is speculated on frequently.

The Mexican military, the state of Veracruz, and the CNDH formed a grim, unholy alliance to carry out the gruesome and macabre task of unearthing Ernestina's buried body on March 9, 2007. They conducted the second autopsy in the cemetery, next to her open grave. This delegation arrived at the tiny hamlet of Tetlatzinga and its even tinier cemetery at 6 a.m. They had left Orizaba around 4:30 a.m., traveling before sunrise to avoid being seen. The standoff that Governor Herrera had tried to suppress—arriving by helicopter in his tailored suit—never stopped; Indigenous protesters still flooded Tetlatzinga and Soledad Atzompa, demanding justice. Fearful of the armed protesters, the officials on their way to the cemetery called them "rioters" and chose the early morning hour to avoid them.[20]

Beyond the violation of the act itself loomed its horrifying public spectacle. This state-sanctioned dissection did not occur in the sterile privacy of a morgue, but in the heart of Ernestina's community, in the tiny cemetery of Tetlatzinga, a place of intimate mourning and sacred transition into the afterworld, now transformed into a stage for grotesque, theatrical violence. Under the gaze of armed military observers and passive CNDH officials, Dr. Vázquez cut into her and photographed her genitals, all within potential sight and earshot of the community members and protesters who had gathered to defend her dignity. This exceeded the macabre; it functioned as a calculated act of terror, a visceral assertion of state power intended to show the Nahua people that even in death, their elders enjoyed no safety from violation and that even their sacred spaces belonged to the state.

The second autopsy became a master class in state obfuscation, a deliberate shell game of responsibility and interpretation. The events that followed prove they brought her body back to the surface to displace the reports by Drs. Rosas and Mendizábal. Dr. Ignacio Gutiérrez Vázquez, the state of Veracruz's examiner, performed the gruesome exhumation and autopsy without any of the tools or protocols customary for the task. He performed his work under the watchful eyes of military officers and CNDH representatives, feeding him suggestions and directives. Dr. Vázquez's findings did not fully erase the violence done to Ernestina, as he was likely instructed by the military. Yet he documented the injuries to her vagina and anus: "Recent tears at approximately 4, 5, 8, and 9 o'clock . . . at the anal region . . . [and] lacerations and erosion, with vulvar edema." Dr. Vázquez made a clinical admission of traumatic injury to her genitals, but he backed away slightly from the findings of Drs. Rosas and Mendizábal by rejecting the injuries to the rest of her body. Dr. Vázquez was suspended for his report on March 29 along with Drs. Rosas and Mendizábal.[21]

In the comfort of an air-conditioned office in Mexico City, Dr. Fernando Cervantes Duarte of the CNDH used Dr. Vázquez's autopsy findings to write a report on Ernestina's death that erased the findings of Drs. Vázquez, Rosas, and Mendizábal. Dr. Duarte blamed Ernestina for her own death: "Acute anemia secondary to hypovolemic shock due to upper gastrointestinal bleeding." The CNDH doctor looked at the evidence of a brutal sexual assault and declared it irrelevant. He did not contradict the truth; he bureaucratically ignored it on orders from above, making her death a mere administrative matter. Soberanes, Dr. Duarte's boss, concurred on April 6, plainly asserting that no crime had been committed: "There was no violation. There was no homicide. There was an autopsy done poorly and with negligence." By April 20, Soberanes went further, denouncing the translator for mistranslating Ernestina's testimony, insisting she had not claimed to have been attacked by soldiers. Soberanes and the university Nahuatl specialist were parsing *pinome xoxome* and other words uttered in Nahuatl—a language not conducive to describing weaponized rape—to undermine the family's statements. The CNDH included a condemnation of Dr. Rosas in this press announcement as well for her documentation of Ernestina's injuries. The CNDH systematically destroyed every piece of evidence pointing to sexual assault and the military.[22]

The second autopsy unfolded as a coordinated comedy of errors, a terrorizing performance designed to obscure the truth. The military and the CNDH collaborated to demand the exhumation, yet the CNDH only filed paperwork for an exhumation, not an autopsy. Military doctors observed his work, while the CNDH staff stood by passively, their occasional questions and suggestions seeming to be guided by their military counterparts. The commission's stated role required ensuring compliance with proper protocols, including those mandated by the United Nations. They raised no objections during the autopsy. Instead, they ambushed Dr. Vázquez only after he filed his report, issuing a condemnation so thorough that their own stated concerns would have logically required a third autopsy, which they never intended to perform.

But a greater horror awaited. Beyond the violation of digging up Ernestina's body to perform a second autopsy beside her open grave, Mexican Army representatives took photographs of Ernestina's genitals. Those photographs could be anywhere, as the military never opened their files to investigators. The CNDH also obtained and distributed photos in 2007, as did the state of Veracruz. The violation continued. In 2021, a CNDH doctor admitted he had taken photos of her corpse, which never became part of the official file. Someone failed to enter all photos into the file. If they were not placed in the file, where are they?

As a final, grotesque insult, the CNDH's own 2021 report republished the photographs of Ernestina's vagina and anus for general distribution. In its online version, the commission only partially redacted the images; the inadequate black bars and captions left enough visible that the photos' violent purpose could not be mistaken. Much like the display of Cindy Gladue's vaginal tear in a Canadian courtroom in 2015, and the potential theft of Levina Moody's "female parts" by an RCMP officer in 1969, the CNDH seems to have engaged in the trafficking of Indigenous women's body parts in 2007—specifically targeting their reproductive organs under the guise of investigation—revealing motives at once punitive and voyeuristic. The trafficking of images of her violated body acted as a form of postmortem sexual violence, showing the continuation of the original crime, now enacted and facilitated by the state and even the human rights commission designed to protect the vulnerable.[23]

The men running the narrative warfare campaign played games not just with invasive photos of Ernestina's genitals but also with the semen evidence that could have convicted her torturers. The semen narrative began with the secretary of national defense, Guillermo Galván, who admitted on March 6 that forensic experts were "comparing samples of seminal fluid taken from the body of the dead woman with blood samples taken from military personnel." The following day, he elaborated, proclaiming two sets of semen had been found and would be sent to a Mexico City lab to collect DNA and genetic markers.

The semen story collapsed when the CNDH took over. Where Dr. Rosas had documented an "abundance" of seminal fluid in the hospital, the commission's Dr. Duarte reported a total absence. He claimed utter ignorance, stating he did not know if the army or hospital had ever collected samples, or if any had been preserved. The CNDH's position was clear: There was no semen.

Yet weeks later, on April 5, the CNDH performed a stunning reversal. It now blamed the failure of the case on the "degradation and contamination of the semen samples," the very samples they had previously claimed never existed. This new lie trapped the military. Having already admitted the semen's existence, the army was now being implicated in losing it. The very next day, a military spokesman emphatically declared in *La Jornada*: "The Ministry of National Defense does not have any sample of seminal liquid . . . and has never had it."[24]

This official obfuscation falls apart against the testimony of Dr. Juan Pablo Mendizábal, the forensic doctor for the state of Veracruz. Mendizábal authored the first autopsy, a report so forensically sound and damning that it cost him his job and represented a liability of catastrophic proportions for the Mexican state. He insisted he found "the prostate antigen . . . in the rectum and vagina" and that samples were verified at a state lab in Xalapa. According to his analysis, the presence of "seminal fluid" was "clearly appreciated" and contained "chromosomes of at least three people," a finding confirmed by a second lab in Mexico City. But the lab results do not carry the danger alone. Mendizábal's living memory and testimony of the evidence—the semen tested and verified twice, in two different labs, with conclusive results—remains an active, un-erasable threat. His report became their kryptonite; its very existence, and his unwavering testimony, threatened to unravel the entire official narrative. Journalist Norma Trujillo later verified this, reporting that the first autopsy included semen collection.[25]

Who holds the results of the semen testing from the labs? The evidence confirms the tests were done successfully. The results were known but then made to vanish to support the state narrative that Ernestina died of gastritis. Dr. Rosas, the doctor who examined Ernestina while she was still alive, testified in 2021 that the samples were tested in Mexico City, confirming Dr. Mendizábal's memory.

Additionally, Dr. Rosas was present at the meeting where the Mexico City chemist who tested the semen presented her findings on the semen and conclusion of rape. The chemist and Soberanes of the CNDH "clashed" over her results. The next day, the CNDH announced Ernestina had died of gastritis. The semen existed. The test results existed. The state needed both to disappear.[26]

The inconvenient results of the semen tests became just one more piece of evidence smothered within the immense, deliberately constructed archive of the state's making. The CNDH's investigation did not perform some cursory review; it functioned as a massive bureaucratic operation. The original complaint file, 2007/901/2/0, swelled to twenty-four volumes, comprising 9,594 pages and thirty-seven CDs. To generate this mountain of paper, the commission deployed a small army of specialists: seven assistant investigators, a forensic doctor, specialists in sexual crimes and surgery, a pathologist, an internist, a chemist, a geneticist, a criminologist, and a translator. By May 2, the Veracruz attorney general used this mountain of paper to justify the commission's work: 1,200 sheets, 5 volumes, and 210 annexes. And this constitutes the output of a single, supposedly independent agency; it excludes the undoubtedly vast files generated by the state of Veracruz and the Ministry of National Defense.

This immense effort, however, served something other than the preservation of the facts for the record. Preservation operated as the machinery of obfuscation. The thousands of pages and CDs did not illuminate the crime but buried it, creating a labyrinth of contradictory reports and technical jargon so dense that the simple, brutal facts—*pinome xoxome*, the documented tears, the seminal fluid lab results—could be declared "lost" within it. The volume of the file matches the state's fear of Ernestina's words.[27]

What powered that narrative machine? According to attorney and former senator Barbara Yllán Rondero, the entire operation boiled down to a single, desperate objective: to manufacture jurisdiction. She laid bare the legal mechanics of the cover-up for me with clarity—even as a man with a speaker planted himself at our restaurant table in Mexico City, screeching into his microphone. Her testimony cut through the chaos, revealing that the military's own actions—its request for lists of soldiers and its own investigative materials—proved both its belief in the guilt of its personnel and its illegal attempt to seize a case that fell under civilian authority. This jurisdictional panic, Rondero argued, powered the engine behind the second autopsy. The CNDH's request for an exhumation, not an autopsy, served as a tactical move in this illegal power grab. By executing a full autopsy in the cemetery with military doctors present, the commission used the puppet agency to discredit the findings of the civilian autopsy and thus destroy the state of Veracruz's case. In essence, the Mexican military, lacking all jurisdiction, ran a parallel investigation using the CNDH and others as their puppets. The CNDH acted on its behalf, using the grotesque theater of the graveyard autopsy to speak and act according to the military's wishes.[28]

The military took actions instantly to protect the killers by lying to Indigenous protesters and manufacturing evidence to hide the murder. Their efforts to co-opt or assassinate Indigenous leader Pascuala failed entirely. They next targeted Indigenous leader René Huerta of CROISZ. Huerta had been present at the hospital, had alerted the Indigenous community to Ernestina's condition, and had notified the state of Veracruz to send an investigator to the hospital. But by April, the state of Veracruz joined the military's team in the narrative warfare. In the period between the second autopsy in March and the official reports and public announcements made in April, Veracruz officials worked behind the scenes to divide the united Indigenous community. In early April, the state sowed more discord by flooding Tetlatzinga with material inducements—small houses, bicycles, buses, and building materials such as cement and sheet metal, and money to build a gas station. They started a rumor that Ernestina's family had been offered six million pesos, suggesting the family was paid off. After a meeting in President Calderón's office about Ernestina's case, on April 9, Undersecretary González, the same González who met with Pascuala, met with Huerta. He met him again the next day. As a result, Huerta spoke on behalf of Ernestina's family, telling the press that the family no longer pointed to the military as the culprits, completely denying her words of *pinome xoxome*. Whether through coercion or consent, González held a meeting with Huerta and Ernestina's family on April 19. Five days later, CROISZ members formally requested Huerta's dismissal from the organization. The request cited his meetings with González, his claims of speaking for the family, and his attribution of an alleged change in testimony to them.[29]

Ernestina's family took back the narrative, refusing the control of González and Huerta. On April 26, 2007, Ernestina's family published their first and only statement to the press, titled, "We Didn't Sell Our Mother." In it, they assured the public they had not been bought or manipulated by Huerta, and they condemned him for making requests on their behalf "without their consent." They insisted that "all the offenses we are receiving is precisely because we have not allowed them to use us." The offenses included control: being told they were not allowed to speak to anyone without the approval of the authorities. They included threats: On April 21, someone shot a gun at 1 a.m. very close to their home; the next night, again at 1 a.m., a van full of ten armed men illuminated their house with an extremely bright light. The offenses also included destruction of property: The family's milpas (roughly translated from Nahuatl as cultivated land using polyculture) had been "destroyed by vehicles."[30]

Ernestina's children paid dearly for using their voices and speaking directly to the press on April 26. In response to the statement of independence by the family, the state of Mexico abducted Ernestina's entire family, including her grandchildren, on April 30. René Huerta coordinated the abduction with the state government. *Proceso* called it a "mysterious disappearance." A bus arrived in Tetlatzinga "without prior notice" staffed with numerous "state security" officers who barred the family from speaking to anyone before they boarded the bus. State security drove them four hours north to Xalapa to hear the state prosecutor's findings. But they did not release the family after the meeting.

Some knew of the family's captivity. Journalist Norma Trujillo, who had been doggedly tracking the case, managed to locate them during their stop in Xalapa. In an interview with me in Mexico City, Trujillo recounted how she discovered their hotel room, its hallway lined with police. Pretending to be a friend dropping something off, she found the entire family crowded into a single room. Ernestina's oldest son told her they had signed documents promising not to speak to the press and could tell her nothing. This firsthand account confirms the family found themselves in Mexico City not as guests of the state, but as prisoners under surveillance and coerced into silence.[31]

For days, they were held captive, driven from city to city. They were held overnight in Ixtapan, a bit north of Xalapa, before being driven five hours north to Tampico, making the abduction look like a voluntary tour of Mexico. From there, they endured a five-and-a-half-hour drive to Mexico City, where reporters witnessed the family visiting the Basilica of our Lady of Guadalupe. In total, Huerta and security agents held them in captivity for twelve days.

Governor Herrera controlled the abduction. His office announced the family would be at the Basilica around May 8, and encouraged the press to document their "visit." But *La Jornada* confirmed this was no visit. The paper reported seeing Veracruz government staff at the Basilica as well as the deposed René Huerta, claiming to protect the family at their request. The family repeatedly hid and turned from reporters. The private Fundación Cordobesa del Golfo paid for the abduction, and the foundation's director held close ties with Governor Herrera.[32]

The state abducted Ernestina's relatives as punishment for their crime of speaking out and on the record, but they also intended to contain them while they made a major press release. One day after forcing them into their custody, the Attorney General's Office closed the case, stating "she [Ernestina] was not raped or murdered." The Veracruz office dismissed Ernestina's family's words, calling them "witnesses of hearing and not eyewitnesses." Even *La Jornada* misled the public by posting a photo of Ernestina's son, Julio, in Tetlatzinga, implying that he was at home, while the state announced the case was closed. By the time Huerta and the state released them, the deadline for appeal had passed.[33]

The narrative warfare reached its bureaucratic conclusion within months of the murder. On June 27, 2007, with the public pacified, the family manipulated, and the medical evidence successfully muddied by the CNDH and the state of Veracruz, the military public prosecutor issued its final resolution: the definitive closure of the preliminary investigation into Ernestina's death. The official reason cited was a "lack of evidence of probable criminal conduct." This formal decree fulfilled President Calderón's premature declaration months earlier. The machinery of the settler state had done its work, not through a dramatic confrontation, but through the cold, administrative act of filing a case away. The message rang clear: The murder of a Nahua elder counted not as a crime but as a closed file.[34]

This bureaucratic closure represented not an anomaly, but a predictable outcome of a system designed to protect itself. As Mexican scholar Lucia Melgar explained during an interview in Mexico City, reflecting on the gendered patterns of state impunity, "In order for immunity to continue, you need accomplices." The Ernestina case proved this true: The military, the state government, the CNDH, and the presidency all acted as accomplices in a scheme to protect the assailants, the army, and the nation against consequences.

Melgar explained that the state was primarily motivated to "maintain the myth of the army's perfection, its role as the uncorrupted fatherland, which requires covering up any crime." To admit the army's barbarity in the sexual torture of an Indigenous female elder would shatter this foundational myth of institutional purity and national honor. Instead, the state chose to sacrifice the truth of Ernestina's death to maintain the fiction of the army's fatherly perfection.

This accomplice network relied on a profound national contradiction, which Melgar identified. "Symbolically, there is respect for motherhood in Mexico," she noted. "The problem is that there's a breaking point between the symbolic order or law for the mother and the hate for real women, even if they are mothers." Ernestina, a seventy-three-year-old Nahua elder and mother, should have been sacrosanct within both myths—the protective army, or father, protecting the sacred mother. Yet the state's machinery revered the symbol but brutalized the real woman. Her body became the site where this national hypocrisy was exposed, a hypocrisy that leads, as Melgar observed, to the horrific outcome in which violence against women becomes "naturalized."[35]

Over the next decade and a half, the case moved through national and international organizations propelled along by the family, their attorneys, and nongovernmental organizations. In 2017, the CNDH admitted that Ernestina had faced discrimination based on race, gender, class, age, language, and limited access to medical care and translation—but also discrimination within the investigation itself, which resulted in impunity due to the cover-up. But the commission did not admit fault. In 2021, it admitted to supporting the president's preemptive claim that Ernestina died of stomach problems: "Thus, the Commission sought to position itself improperly and hastily, and therefore issued Recommendation 34/2007, which is inadmissible and contrary to the nature of the responsibility of the CNDH." Although written to absolve the commission, the 2017 and 2021 National Human Rights Commission reports nonetheless assisted the family in their case against Mexico.[36]

Standing before the Inter-American Commission on Human Rights (IACHR) and the Inter-American Court of Human Rights (IACtHR), the family's attorneys summarized her case in 2023. They bore witness to her family members' testimonies about finding Ernestina sexually injured and spending hours driving to various medical facilities before landing at the Río Blanco Hospital. They validated the findings of Dr. Rosas's exam and Dr. Mendizábal's initial autopsy, findings that verified that sexual torture was listed among the causes of death. They noted the military's and the CNDH's manipulations of the case. They reminded readers of their 2021 report, which identified Ernestina as a victim of both the Mexican Army and the nation of Mexico, noting that both entities violated Articles 4, 5, 11, and 26 of the American Convention (under Article 1.1); Article 7 of the Belém Do Pará Convention; and Articles 1, 6, and 8 of the Convención Interamericana para Prevenir y Sancionar la Tortura (CIPST) by failing to carry out a thorough investigation, deal honestly with the family, or make a sincere effort to charge the assailants. The commission also condemned the Mexican government for its failure to provide requested documents to attorney Suárez, violating 13.1 of the American Convention. Although the IACHR filed notice in 2021, it filed again in 2023, as the Mexican government did nothing in response to the 2021 filing. The 2023 IACHR report requested that the Inter-American Court issue several reparations, including individual reparations to the family, a criminal investigation, the provision of case files to Attorney Cabrera, protection for the family and their attorneys, and measures to prevent gender-based violence by the state.[37]

On January 30, 2025, the IACtHR held a public hearing in the case of *Ernestina Ascencio Rosario v. Mexico*, marking a pivotal moment in the long pursuit of justice. The court examined allegations of sexual violence and torture committed by members of the Mexican Army, the state's failure to provide adequate medical care that contributed to her death, and the racial and gender-based discrimination she suffered as a monolingual Nahua woman. Other central issues under review included testimony mishandling due to language barriers, the obstruction of her family's search for justice, and the concealment of key public information to shield perpetrators. The hearing—held in San José, Costa Rica, and broadcast publicly—followed the IACHR's referral of the case in mid-2023 and represents a significant step toward international accountability.[38]

On September 30, 2025, the Inter-American Court of Human Rights confirmed what the family of Ernestina has claimed for nineteen years: that Mexico was responsible for the violations surrounding the rape, torture, and death of their mother, Ernestina Ascencio Rosario. The judgment was publicly notified in December 2025. The Court affirmed that Ernestina's children "were subject to pressure and intimidation to prevent them from continuing to seek justice." The Court further ruled that Mexico must "perform an exhaustive and serious criminal investigation on the rape, torture and death of Ernestina in order to identify, prosecute, and punish those responsible." On February 25, 2026, human rights organizations called on Mexico to comply with and implement the Court's ruling. Mexico has yet to announce a plan for fulfilling the order of the Court, although President Claudia Sheinbaum has insisted they will.[39]

Behind the IACHR and its court lies the history of fascism in Europe and the Americas. The Organization of American States (OAS), founded in 1948 in Bogotá with the signing of its charter, functions as a regional body dedicated to peace, democracy, human rights, security, and development. The thirty-five member states of the OAS created the IACHR in 1959. Ten years later, the IACtHR was established. Crucially, only countries that ratified the OAS treaty, which created the court, fall under the court's binding jurisdiction, and the United States and Canada never ratified. Ironically headquartered in Washington, DC, the OAS created both the IACHR and the IACtHR, but the court cannot enforce rulings against the United States.[40]

Born of antifascism, the OAS was established in Latin America where countries feared the potential rise of fascism. The United States feared the same for those countries, but not for itself. Many countries in Latin America, having fought alongside the Allies in World War II, wanted regional guarantees that fascism would never again go unchecked. At the same 1948 Bogotá conference that founded the OAS, the American Declaration of the Rights and Duties of Man was adopted, becoming the world's first international human rights instrument. The declaration was born out of the atrocities of World War II, Latin America's struggles with authoritarianism, and a desire to lead the global push for democracy and rights before the UN's Universal Declaration of Human Rights later that year. These initiatives were driven mainly by Latin American democracies like Costa Rica and Chile. The US backed the human rights language and housed the organization on its turf but refused to provide its own citizens with protections of human rights and safeguards against fascism.[41]

This international pursuit of justice stands in stark contrast to the impunity enjoyed in the US and Canada, where the architecture of inter-American law has been deliberately neutered. Lydia's family, Levina's family, Martinez's family, and Savanna's family cannot receive help from the IACHR. The United States set itself up to control and surveil the OAS but to never allow its own citizens to be protected in the way that citizens all over Mexico, Central, and Latin America are protected. The very mechanism designed to provide justice in the Americas was structured to be incapable of addressing the crimes happening in the United States and Canada, the two wealthiest, most powerful settler states on the continent. With the OAS headquartered in Washington, DC, in the very heart of empire, the US and Canada refuse to be subject to its rulings. Settler states create and control systems designed to shield them from accountability, yet Mexico, Central, and Latin America—a vast region depicted as substandard by US power brokers—voluntarily subjects itself to international oversight. The true commitment to justice and human rights, the courage to submit to a higher law, has been demonstrated by the very nations the US often depicts as chaotic or corrupt.

THE MACRO CRIME SCENE

The sheer scale of state violence in Mexico can make this single case seem like merely an entry in a long ledger of horror. The 1968 Tlatelolco massacre, the unresolved femicides in Ciudad Juárez, and the 2014 disappearance of forty-three students from Ayotzinapa stand as defining tragedies that rightly haunt the national conscience of Mexico. However, to collapse these events into a single narrative of state violence ignores the supporting, gendered logic of violence. The sexual assassination of Ernestina Ascencio Rosario reveals the intimate, gendered, and bureaucratic mechanics of a state performing a different function—not just repressing dissent or enforcing order, but actively working to eliminate the Indigenous presence that threatens the settler state's fantasy of legitimacy. This violence enacts itself not just on the body but on the very fact of Indigenous existence. To focus on Ernestina isolates and examines the core engine of that elimination—an engine that powers the state's other, more publicized crimes.[42]

As a monolingual Nahua woman born in 1934, Ernestina had lived her life under surveillance. The state perversely agreed with Indigenous communities on one thing: that speaking one's native language forms the core of Indigenous identity. It therefore assiduously tracked language use and trained scholars to speak Nahuatl, not to foster understanding but to perfect its surveillance and control over people like Ernestina. Unlike in the United States, where tribal nations use treaties to negotiate their relationships with the government, the Mexican state's constitutional framework defines Indigenous rights through individual land tenure, a system that ultimately fails to protect communities from state-sponsored extraction and violence. The Mexican state equates Native people with their land, especially land they inhabit, rather than seeing Indigenous peoples as a collective. The Mexican constitution strives to protect the rights of individual Indigenous land inhabitants from the state but does little for the whole of Indigenous peoples. Indigenous peoples in Mexico seek precisely what the state does not offer: protected collective autonomy, thus giving rise to the international human rights movement in Mexico and Latin America.[43]

As James Baldwin wrote of "captive populations," their poverty proves "extremely expensive," placing their feet "on the treadmill forever." This same relentless poverty—rooted in Indigenous subsistence practices of grazing animals and gathering wood—placed Ernestina in the soldiers' path. The state did not merely overlook this reality. The state weaponized her poverty. By positioning its army there, it turned Ernestina's daily struggle to survive into the delivery system for a colonial violence that ended her life.[44]

Ernestina's case embodies the collective outcry of Indigenous women across the Americas, with those women theorizing from their lived experience to redefine justice and security. They understand the state's true project: using the pretext of the drug war to attack communities that resist extraction on their ancestral lands. This violence is compounded by linguistic imperialism: the state's refusal to provide interpreters, a right enshrined in Mexican law but systematically denied. For Ernestina, this meant facing her torturers and her would-be healers in a language she could not understand, a final, fatal marginalization. Her death does not sit in the margins as an isolated incident; her death exposes the blueprint of state violence.[45]

Ernestina's murder tells a hemispheric story. To analyze it solely within the context of Mexico replicates the colonial myopia that, as Muskogee and Shawnee scholar Victoria Bomberry argues, marginalizes Indigenous peoples south of the US border. Instead, following Maya K'iche' scholar Emil Keme's call for a "transhemispheric Indigenous bridge," this chapter places Ernestina's case in direct conversation with parallel cases in the US and Canada. This does more than comparison; this generates a political alignment that reveals the shared logics of settler violence across the Americas. Ernestina's body becomes a site not only of trauma but of relentless transnational solidarity.[46]

This transhemispheric Indigenous bridge not only connects parallel cases of violence but also provides the critical framework for understanding them, a framework powerfully articulated in Spanish by feminist theorists in Mexico and Latin America. Non-Indigenous Mexican feminists like Marcela Lagarde have provided the essential vocabulary for understanding violence like that inflicted on Ernestina. Lagarde's concept of *feminicidio* reframes these murders not as isolated crimes but as "state crime[s]" enabled by a patriarchal system where authorities and assailants enjoy "ideological and political complicity." Her analysis, forged in the context of the murders in Ciudad Juárez, exposes a fundamental truth: Even when violence against women operates outside the bounds of the legal, it often fails to be treated as a crime by the state tasked with prosecution.

This framework functions less as an academic tool than a diagnostic one. For Ernestina, this complicity took literal form: Soldiers served as the assailants, and the state military and human rights apparatus became the co-conspirators in the cover-up. When Lagarde writes of the state's refusal to recognize or investigate "gender status," she could be describing many of Mexico's responses to Ernestina's murder. They inspected soldiers' penises for scratches. They declared she died of stomach problems. Both acts refused to see what actually happened: a woman killed by men, men dispatched by the nation, protected by a patriarchal state. The term *feminicidio*, which Lagarde coined to specify a genocide against women, rejects the gender neutrality of *femicidio* and precisely names the systemic, political annihilation inflicted on women like Ernestina Ascencio. Yet, as much as Lagarde diagnoses the state as the problem, she also offers a blueprint for the solution: a rebellious "feminist acculturation" born from transgression and sustained by affective bonds between women. This feminism operates not through state institutions, but through "deep, political confrontation" with a culture saturated in patriarchy. In the aftermath of Ernestina's murder, we see this very praxis in the thousands of Indigenous protesters who blocked roads, the doctors who refused to stay silent, and the family who endured abduction rather than recant their testimony. Their solidarity embodies the kind of feminist affection Lagarde theorizes: a powerful, confrontational love that becomes the necessary antidote to state-sponsored death.[47]

If Lagarde provided the term *feminicidio*, Argentine scholar Rita Segato provided its grisly semiotics. From her work interviewing convicted rapists in Brazil, Segato concluded that sexual assault functions less as a sexual act and more as a "language between men," a performance of power meant to build community among perpetrators. This insight exposes the sexual torture of Ernestina not as a crime of passion but as a brutal form of masculine communication, a ritual of solidarity that state soldiers enacted upon the body of an Indigenous elder. Segato further theorizes a "Second State": a shadow network of "Creole men" who operate with the state's implicit permission, blurring the line between official and criminal violence. This framework perfectly describes the impunity of the Mexican soldiers whose actions were followed by a coordinated cover-up involving military command and government officials. Ultimately, Segato and Lagarde converge on a terrifying truth: that patriarchy operates through a "communication system with a violent alphabet." Ernestina's violated body became a text on which that violent alphabet was written.[48]

The state's violence against Indigenous people operates like a single system, what Mexican theorist Rossana Reguillo Cruz, thinking alongside feminicide theorists, identifies as a necropolitical logic where neoliberalism functions as an "occupying power" and an "insatiable stomach." This system does not distinguish between the young and the old; it consumes whatever lies in its path. It swallowed the students of Ayotzinapa and vomited them into hidden graves. Just as surely, it consumed Ernestina Ascencio. Her elderly, Indigenous, female body held a different kind of "value" for the state, not as fuel for a *maquila* (a duty- and tariff-free factory) or a cartel but as a site to demonstrate absolute impunity, to enact a lesson of terror, and to be metabolized into nothingness by a bureaucratic cover-up. Whether targeting the young or the old, the state's consuming hunger remains the same.[49]

The struggle for justice for Ernestina Ascensio reflects a broader, transhemispheric pattern of Indigenous women confronting state sexual violence. Just as Ernestina's community fought for accountability in Mexico, Q'eqchi' Maya women in Guatemala waged a landmark legal battle in the 2016 Sepur Zarco trial, which delivered a delayed reckoning for sexual enslavement by the military during the US/CIA-fueled civil war (1960–1996). Their historic victory offers a powerful counterpoint: It proves that state violence can be exposed in court. In a stunning act of jurisdictional courage, Guatemala's national courts convicted former military officials for crimes against humanity in the Sepur Zarco case.

The Q'eqchi' Maya women's victory also exposes the global hierarchy of North and South. The Sepur Zarco trial addressed crimes from a conflict ignited by the US 1954 CIA coup. This layered irony seemed lost on a Canadian film crew that descended on postwar Guatemala to document its "macho culture" and femicide epidemic. As Canadians failed to show the hand of the US in the crisis, so too they denied Canada's ongoing epidemic of missing and murdered Indigenous women, reacting with shock to the situation in Guatemala. This performance of horror—critiquing a catastrophe manufactured by the US while ignoring the colonial violence perfected throughout Canada, as if male violence features as uniquely Guatemalan—exemplifies the hypocrisy enabled by the OAS architecture. The US and Canada critique human rights abuses, positioning themselves as adjudicators rather than participants, all while refusing the jurisdiction of the Inter-American Court that could hold them accountable.[50]

The theoretical framework that made the Sepur Zarco victory possible also reveals a feminism far different from mainstream Global North movements. At the trial, Argentine feminist theorist Rita Segato testified that rape functions to solidify military power and enact territorial control, a sophisticated analysis of violence that moves beyond individual pathology to expose its structural and communicative function. This insight provides the precise lexicon for understanding the murder of Ernestina: not a random crime but a calculated performance of settler power by soldiers on Indigenous land. This connective tissue of theory and praxis, of Indigenous women's testimony amplified by a radical feminist analysis of state power, stretches across borders, linking Veracruz to Guatemala and beyond.[51]

This divergence in confronting state power emerges most clearly in the reception of a transnational feminist performance that shook Latin America but barely registered in the United States. Inspired by Rita Segato's theories, Chilean women created "A Rapist in Your Path" in 2019, a protest song that directly accused the police by subverting the very anthem used by the police. Their revised song spread rapidly across Latin America, where critique of state forces remains central to feminist resistance, but the song stalled in the United States after just a handful of sanitized performances stripped all references to law enforcement. The performance's failure to translate northward underscores the same hemispheric divide that allowed Ernestina's killers to operate with impunity: a refusal to acknowledge that the state—its soldiers, police, attorneys, and judges—acts less as a protector of victims and more as a protector of assailants.[52]

While academic, journalistic, and activist accounts often focus on machismo, state violence, and drug wars in Mexico, Central, and Latin America, they can fail to center Indigenous lives and deaths. This chapter suggests that the erasure of Indigenous women in dialogues about gendered violence recreates a colonial practice. Ernestina was born in the mountains of a small Indigenous community in 1934. There, in the state of Veracruz, not far from where Hernán Cortés landed in 1519 on his way to conquer her nation's empire, Ernestina came of age in the years after the Mexican Revolution, a period that gave hope to the Indigenous people of Mexico. Yet, despite the revolution, Ernestina Ascensio Rosario's murder exposed what was already a well-known fact in Indigenous communities in Mexico: Mexican soldiers continued to act with brutality toward Indigenous people in spite of the revolution. Like the United States and Canada, the Mexican military physically manifests the ongoing settler project that is Mexico. Although Mexico, like the United States, achieved independence from its European colonizer, the Mexican Revolution hardly turned the country over to Indigenous people. Much like Native people in the US, Mexico's Indigenous communities remained nearly as marginalized by the Mexican government as they had been under the Spanish colonial regime.[53]

Mexico might disagree with this assessment. In 2019, President Andrés Manuel López Obrador sent a letter to the King of Spain asking him to take responsibility for human rights violations during colonization and to offer apologies. At the same time, President López

Obrador certainly did not recognize Mexico as a colonizer of Indigenous peoples, as he requested no apologies from the state of Mexico. This read as a radical move by many, but the Indigenous people of Mexico may say otherwise.[54]

The bureaucratic machinery of the Mexican state, having worked to erase Ernestina Ascencio Rosario's words and the evidence of her murder, demonstrates how settler colonialism operates through official channels, legal obfuscation, and the systemic devaluation of an Indigenous elder's life. Yet this logic of elimination does not confine itself to state institutions or national borders. It travels, mutating to fit different landscapes and legal systems, but always retaining its core function: the reduction of Indigenous life to something expendable.

As we turn north back to the US in the next chapter, this same logic manifests with brutal intimacy in a humble apartment building in North Dakota. There, the targeting of a Native woman's pregnant body shifted from state-sanctioned violence of soldiers to the private, predatory violence of neighbors. There, too, the state fought to control the narrative, battling the woman's family and community for the story from the moment she vanished.

GUIDE TO KEY FIGURES IN CHAPTER 5

SAVANNA LAFONTAINE-GREYWIND: Spirit Lake Dakota and Turtle Mountain Band of Chippewa woman, beloved daughter, and soon-to-be mother to Haisley Jo. Eldest of her siblings. Murdered in 2017.

ASHTON MATHENY: Savanna's boyfriend and the father of her unborn child.

JOE GREYWIND: Savanna's father.

NORBERTA LAFONTAINE-GREYWIND: Savanna's mother.

KAYLA GREYWIND: Savanna's sister.

BROOKE LYNN CREWS: The white upstairs neighbor who murdered Savanna and abducted her baby.

WILLIAM HOEHN: Brooke Crews's live-in boyfriend and accomplice.

SAMUEL BOLLMAN: A Fargo Police Department officer who entered Crews and Hoehn's apartment twice on Saturday.

PHIL SWAN: A Fargo Police Department officer and detective who entered Crews and Hoehn's apartment on Sunday evening.

JIM VANLITH: A Fargo Police Department detective who entered Crews and Hoehn's apartment on Sunday evening.

JOE ANDERSON: Deputy Police Chief of Fargo.

DAVID TODD: Police Chief of Fargo.

DETECTIVE LOOS: A Fargo Police Department detective involved in the interrogations and investigation.

DETECTIVE KJONAAS: A Fargo Police Department detective involved in the interrogations and investigation.

DETECTIVE NELSON: A Fargo Police Department officer and detective.

SANDRA SALISBURY: The woman who discovered Savanna's body in the Red River.

CHRISTOPHER HAGEN: A journalist from *The High Plains Reader* who retrieved Brooke Crews's personal items from a dumpster.

STEVEN MOTTINGER: Brooke Crews's public defender.

DANIEL J. BORGEN: William Hoehn's first privately paid attorney.

KIARA KRAUS-PARR: William Hoehn's second privately paid attorney who handled his appeal.

JEROD E. TUFTE: North Dakota Supreme Court justice who ruled that William Hoehn had not physically harmed Savanna's baby by murdering her mother.

SCOTT PATRICK BRAND: William Hoehn's third privately paid attorney.

BETTY JO KRENZ: A white woman on the Spirit Lake Reservation who was running an illegal adoption ring targeting Native moms and their children.

AUTYM BURKE: A buyer who paid Krenz for an illegally obtained Native baby.

SAMUEL DUTTON HINMAN: An Episcopal priest who molested a Dakota girl at Spirit Lake.

DR. WILLIAM WORRALL MAYO: Founder of the Mayo Clinic. Exhumed and dissected the bodies of Dakota men executed in 1862.

MARPIYA OKINAJIN (CUT NOSE): A Dakota man whose body was exhumed by Dr. Mayo and rendered into a skeleton.

CHAPTER 5

SAVANNA

Saturday, August 19, 2017. North Dakota felt heavy. In January, Trump's first presidency began. On February 22, the Oceti Sakowin camp at Standing Rock had been ordered to evacuate, a brutal end to a prayerful stand that had drawn global attention to the defense of Indigenous land and life. In theaters, the problematic *Wind River*, produced by Harvey Weinstein (later convicted of rape), depicted missing and murdered Indigenous women using graphic violence and centering white characters over Indigenous ones. But in Fargo, North Dakota, on this Saturday, Savanna Greywind's mind leaned toward a restorative weekend at home.

With no nursing shifts scheduled at Eventide, she had a rare day to herself. After eight months of pregnancy, her feet ached. Her parents and siblings were busy with errands, cleaning, and laundry. Savanna helped some, but she also needed to rest. She missed her boyfriend, Ashton Matheny, the father of her unborn baby, who was not yet living in Fargo. They had met at Spirit Lake Reservation and began dating in high school; raised with strict parents, he had been her first and only boyfriend.

As a young woman relentlessly pursuing her goals, she graduated high school in 2013 and immediately obtained her Certified Nursing Assistant license. Born on the Turtle Mountain Indian Reservation, she had moved to Fargo with her family in 2016, transferring her skills from Eventide at Spirit Lake to their facility in the city. She was building a life, a family, a future.[1]

And on that quiet Saturday, she was simply looking forward to relaxing.

Her boyfriend had been living and working in Minneapolis, Spirit Lake, and Grand Forks, as work was available, but he made the trek to Fargo to visit Savanna regularly. Savanna enjoyed living with her parents, Joe and Norberta, and her siblings. Although her doctor said her baby would arrive around September 13, 2017, her ambition led her to consider enrolling at Rasmussen College to pursue her registered nurse license, allowing her to earn more money. With $700 saved between herself and Matheny, she met with nearby landlord Margaret McIntosh of McIntosh Properties LLC on August 4, 2017, to pay the security deposit for the one-bedroom apartment she would share with Matheny and her baby. Margaret McIntosh gave Savanna a move-in date of September 1, 2017. Although nervous about living on her own for the first time as a new mother, she viewed August 2017 as a time of change and anticipation. On August 9, 2017, she celebrated her twenty-second birthday with Matheny and her family. The young Native couple excitedly waited for their baby's birth and their seven-year anniversary. On August 18, 2017, Savanna went shopping with her sister, Kayla, for baby clothes. Savanna and everyone who loved her built their lives around the birth of Savanna and Matheny's baby girl. The baby shower was planned for Sunday, August 20.[2]

Savanna's family, nurturing, tight-knit, and loving, stood in stark contrast to her upstairs neighbors. Her family worked hard, saved, and stayed in constant touch, giving each other meals, rides, and emotional support. The couple upstairs, however, fought regularly, used drugs, and worked sporadically or not at all.

In her father's nation, the Spirit Lake Dakota, a baby's maternal grandmother should be present for births and the first to hold newborns. Savanna's mother and her entire family were denied that moment. Savanna was murdered by her white neighbors on August 19, 2017, the day before her baby shower.

HOME

This horror occurred at the family's home. Savanna's father, Joe, last saw his daughter at 1:24 p.m. on Saturday, August 19, 2017.

Their white female neighbor, Brooke Lynn Crews, came to the family's home, apartment 2, at about 1:15 p.m., offering to pay Savanna twenty dollars in exchange for Savanna modeling a dress Brooke needed to tailor. Brooke had come to their apartment a few weeks earlier, asking Savanna to join her in smoking marijuana. August 19 constituted her second attempt at spending time alone with Savanna. Savanna's father discouraged his daughter from going to Brooke's apartment, but Savanna wanted the money. She ordered a pizza from Deek's, texted her mom, then Matheny, then said goodbye to her father.

Between 2:30 and 4 p.m., Savanna's father and mother texted Savanna repeatedly and knocked on Brooke's door more than once, asking about Savanna. Brooke lied each time, saying they had not finished, then claiming Savanna had left. On Joe's last visit, around 3:45, he asked to come in and look. Brooke acted frightened of Joe, although he remained calm, and refused him entry, creating the facade that he was behaving in a violent manner. This foreshadowed her use of white womanhood against Joe with Fargo police. Brooke Crews's portrayal of herself as frightened caused the Greywinds to fear that Joe would be perceived as a threat and arrested, a common and historically documented risk for Native men interacting with law enforcement.[3]

By 3:45 p.m. on Saturday, Joe stood defeated outside Brooke's door, trapped in a cage built by her narrative and by history itself. He intuited something terrible had happened to his daughter inside that apartment, yet he saw no path forward aside from forcing entry to search. Brooke expertly wielded her role as a besieged white woman, casting him as the threatening Native man. She knew that if he so much as raised his voice, she could cry to the Fargo police and have him arrested, a threat that loomed large because of his identity as a Dakota man. By lying that Savanna had simply left, Brooke turned apartment 5 into a private zone of terror protected by settler impunity. Returning to the family's home in apartment 2, Joe knew he would have to navigate the Fargo police without getting arrested for simply being Native and distraught. Brooke knew exactly what she was doing.[4]

While Joe was met with hostility and lies at apartment 5, Savanna's mother, Norberta, decided the only way to gain access to apartment 5 was through the Fargo police. Norberta called 911, explaining that her daughter had been gone for several hours, without her car or wallet, and was eight months pregnant. Instead of declaring an emergency and sending officers to the apartment, the dispatcher asked, "Is she vulnerable?" This marked the first invocation of a vulnerability narrative that state employees would repeatedly rely on to shift blame onto Savanna for her own disappearance. Norberta replied with intensity, notable given her quiet nature, and explained that Savanna was not vulnerable, but she was only a month away from her due date and her car and wallet remained at home.[5]

Settler cities hire, train, and pay police and thus bear responsibility and liability for their actions. From the moment Savanna's family realized she was missing, City of Fargo employees treated Savanna and her family as a problem. Fargo police deemed the visibly pregnant Savanna as a runaway, a criminal classification and justification for a lack of action. Additionally, the police treated Savanna's terrified parents almost as criminals. Dispatchers later admitted to raising their voices at Savanna's mom during one or more of the calls. Mrs. Greywind desperately called 911 several times that Saturday afternoon and evening to beg the police to search apartment 5. Savanna's mother had written proof of her daughter's last known whereabouts in text messages, yet Norberta's phone calls seemed to elicit the irritation of the 911 dispatchers.

When the police finally gave in and made a personal appearance at the apartment building at 2825 Ninth Street North that fateful Saturday afternoon, they did so only because Mrs. Greywind was indefatigable and called them repeatedly. It seemed that Fargo police came to the apartment building more to convince Norberta to stop calling 911 than to find Savanna. But just as the police clung to their narrative of Savanna's criminality, Savanna's mother clung to her desire to find her child and grandchild.

Fargo police created a narrative that ignored Mrs. Greywind's maternal love, ultimately delaying and harming the investigation. But her love made her willing to endure police harassment and criminalization for the sake of her missing child and unborn grandchild. Fargo police officer Samuel Bollman remembers hearing dispatch ask for an officer, and his report showed he arrived at the apartment building at 4:37 p.m. A thirty-year-old white male, he had joined the Fargo Police Department when he was just twenty-one years old, almost the same age as Savanna, who was twenty-two at the time of her disappearance. City of Fargo employees hold no records of Bollman's video or audio recordings, if he made any, during his visit with Savanna's parents or with Brooke Crews and her live-in boyfriend, William Hoehn, that Saturday afternoon.

Bollman did not proceed directly to the scene of Savanna's last known location, which Savanna's mother had begged police to do. Instead, he questioned Savanna's family at their apartment. Bollman spent valuable time reading Savanna's text messages. In them, he saw that Savanna had expressed frustrations. The runaway theory solidified in his mind after reading the texts. He reiterated the dispatcher's earlier claim to Norberta: Savanna had run away due to problems with her parents and boyfriend. But what stood before Bollman was a loving, close Native family whose daughter had disappeared under highly suspicious circumstances, without her wallet or car, after a simple trip upstairs. Yet he focused on a runaway theory. Only at Norberta's persistent intervention did Officer Bollman reluctantly walk upstairs to apartment 5, where Crews would later confess that Savanna's corpse was hidden in the bathroom closet.[6]

Listening to the police interact with Savanna's murderers provides a study in narrative warfare. The combination of white police officers and white suspects reveals how the police-criminal binary breaks down when both law enforcement and criminals are white, and the victims are Native. When Officer Bollman knocked on the door of apartment 5, he appeared without a search warrant and was convinced the Native family downstairs had driven their daughter away. Crews had already unlocked the door, essentially leaving it open, signaling innocence. When Bollman tapped on the door, it opened, and she was standing in the doorway. Crews lied to the officer, saying Savanna had left, a lie he found entirely plausible because of Crews's pleasant demeanor and Savanna's texts about her frustrations. Officer

Bollman asked Crews if he could come in and look. Crews consented, which he also took as a sign of her innocence.

State police often see the world in a binary that separates criminal from victim. Within this framework, agents of the state tend not to see Native people as victims or whites as criminals. Brooke Crews, a white woman who had just murdered a Native woman, embodied what police officer Bollman imagined to be the ideal Fargo citizen: friendly, clean, submissive, and white. Her unlocked door and consent to enter likely reminded Bollman of the belief that individuals who refuse to comply with officers are often guilty of crimes.

Once inside Crews's apartment, Officer Bollman turned to the right and went to the bedroom where he saw her boyfriend, William Hoehn. Officer Bollman did not inspect the bedroom but stood in the doorway and stated, "Well, you're not Savanna," both stating the obvious and underscoring the veracity of Brooke's claim. His failure to conduct a search or pose any questions made it evident that he did not suspect the couple of violence. When Bollman saw the sewing project on the couch, he asked Crews for confirmation that Savanna had modeled the dress for her. But Crews suddenly changed her story, noting that Savanna had helped her with the tailoring but had not modeled it, suggesting that Joe had lied. Bollman did not question this discrepancy, accepting Crews's story over Joe's.

Officer Bollman believed he had searched the crime scene, entangled in the historical narrative that whites exist as martyrs and Natives operate in the margins. He approached the apartment of Crews and Hoehn reluctantly due to his firm belief that Savanna fit the profile of a runaway: young, pregnant, Native, frustrated. For Bollman, Savanna's texts made her a suspect, not a victim. As a white couple, Crews and Hoehn embodied innocence in the officer's mind, despite their lack of money and Hoehn's criminal record. Bollman may have known that Hoehn had a warrant for his arrest and that he and Crews had an active protective order between them that they were breaking by being in the same residence.

Hoehn also had a criminal record of child abuse, and although his apartment had been the last location of a missing, pregnant woman, Officer Bollman did not see Hoehn as a criminal. He may not have been able to identify with the Native family downstairs. Instead, Bollman emphasized that the white couple's home was "tidy," and the white couple came across as "calm." Bollman's words set up a stark contrast in how he described the Native couple in apartment 2: upset, anxious, distraught, demanding, and insistent.

Steeped in the anti-Native narrative so common in North Dakota, it seems as though Bollman would have only been suspicious of Crews and Hoehn if he had found obvious signs of struggle—splattered blood or a corpse. His mind seemed to refuse to let him consider a narrative in which whites could kill Natives, that a murder scene could be cleaned, or that killers could act calmly after killing. We would learn later that both Savanna's body and her baby lay hidden in the apartment during Bollman's first Saturday visit to apartment 5. Officer Bollman received a promotion after his work on the Crews and Hoehn cases and now serves as sergeant. He still stands by the decisions he made on Saturday, August 19, 2017.

The Greywinds challenged police reticence from the beginning, and their challenges seemed to frustrate officers acting on behalf of the state. Bollman's Saturday late-afternoon visit only heightened the Greywinds' concerns, especially their concern about the bathroom closet, where they believed Savanna may have been hidden. Norberta felt certain that Crews knew exactly what happened to her daughter, so she called the police again after Bollman's visit. She demanded their help, but they rebuffed her, pointing her back toward other theories of Savanna's disappearance, theories involving Savanna's voluntary and silent withdrawal from everyone she loved. City of Fargo dispatch only reinforced the Native family's sense that the police refused to help, but their rebuff also shifted the family's strategy to find answers without Fargo police assistance.

Realizing that the police resented them and that they would have to find Savanna on their own, the Greywinds turned to friends and relatives. By 6:30 p.m., several made their way to the Greywinds' home to work as a community on Savanna's disappearance. This infuriated Crews and Hoehn who stood inside apartment 5 glaring at the gathering of mostly Native people below their window on the lawn.

Those who gathered that night felt the answers to Savanna's disappearance lay within apartment 5. Some of Savanna's relatives and friends climbed the stairs to knock on the door, but Crews and Hoehn refused entry. Seeking firsthand evidence, they asked to enter or at least to talk. Crews refused both. This left the gathering of friends and family no choice. Being Native, they understood that they would not receive any help from the Fargo police to find their pregnant, missing loved one. Being Native, they also knew they could not risk even a hint of violence toward the couple in apartment 5 or they would face arrest. While fearing for her daughter and granddaughter's lives, Norberta also had to worry that one of her Native relatives or friends would face incarceration for trying to find Savanna.

Crews and Hoehn aligned with the Fargo police that Saturday night: Control the Greywinds. Someone, likely Crews, called the Fargo police to complain about the Native people on the lawn shortly after 10 p.m. on Saturday, August 19. Officer Bollman and Sargeant Erbes returned at 10:30 p.m. in response to the call, labeling it a potential "disturbing the peace." Searching for Savanna had only brought one officer earlier in the day, but a call about "loud Natives" merited two. The officers tried to convince the Greywinds and their supporters to accept that Savanna had vanished and to leave the lawn below the window where Savanna vanished.[7]

Norberta refused to relent or comply, begging them to search again. With tremendous reluctance, Officer Bollman climbed the steps up to apartment 5 once more. When Crews spoke with Officer Bollman the second time, she reacted with indignation about the gathering of Natives. She asked incredulously, "What do I have to do to show you I don't know where that girl is?" Bollman returned to the lawn and told Savanna's parents he had searched and that Crews and Hoehn had nothing to do with Savanna's disappearance. His reassurances achieved Crews's goal of the concerned gathering of Natives leaving the lawn. But by staying so focused on controlling Savanna's family instead of finding Savanna's killer, the Fargo police had given Crews and Hoehn the time they needed to hide evidence of the murder and Savanna's stolen baby.[8]

After the two police visits to apartment 5 on Saturday, the Greywind family woke up on Sunday feeling even more distressed. They thought about how they had spent weeks planning a baby shower for that very afternoon. They were also determined to find Savanna and began planning a search. While Norberta made missing-person flyers, Savanna's sister, Kayla, called the district attorney's office, asking for help. Perhaps at their urging, Officer Phil Swan and Detective VanLith made an appearance for the third police visit to apartment 5. As Swan and Vanlith knocked on the door at around 6:30 p.m. that Sunday, Savanna's corpse very likely lay inside the apartment, as did her baby. Crews called out happily, "Who is it?" The police identified themselves, and Crews immediately opened the door.[9]

Crews expertly performed the role of the cooperative, cheerful white citizen, a strategic performance to gain credibility and cast immediate suspicion on the Greywinds. In opening the door quickly and happily each time, Crews built a narrative of herself as reasonable, calm, and self-assured. She cast the Greywinds as the opposite, and the police took her bait each time. Upon opening the door, Crews introduced herself as though she were interviewing for a job: "Hi. My name is Brooke Crews," then "Hello. Good evening," in her most polite and upbeat voice bordering on an Atlantic accent, according to the police recording.

Crews was also communicating whiteness, asserting sameness with the police officers, immediately connecting with them on a shared basis of whiteness: trust, friendliness, camaraderie, and even flirtation. Her demeanor softened the power dynamics between Crews and the officers who had the legal means to tear her house apart and arrest her. With each giggle, the police seemed to convince themselves that Crews was just a nice white lady. The officers could not see that she was playing on their own narrative biases, assuming the demeanor of a friendly, upbeat, flirtatious white woman who embodied innocence, while casting the upset Native mother downstairs as unhinged.[10]

Crews ably played this role during these three visits by Fargo police officers while Savanna lay dead in her apartment and her baby lay hidden in blankets. Crews had won over Officer Bollman the afternoon and night before, convincing him Savanna's Native family represented the only problem at the apartment building. At perhaps Crews's insistence, the police had cajoled or maybe threatened Savanna's family into leaving the lawn the night before. As soon as she opened her door to a new set of police officers that Sunday evening, the officers seemed to fall under her spell. They apologized more than once: "Sorry to bother you," which may have been a strategy to gain trust but may have been genuine. They obtained Crews's consent to search the bathroom, and Crews eagerly offered to let them search the entire home. They never opened the bathroom closet as Savanna's parents had requested, the closet the killers later testified they had used to hide Savanna. In audio recordings of the Sunday night interaction with Crews, the police officers laughed and joked with Crews. Officers Vanlith and Swan seemed more concerned about communicating to Crews that they were not in her apartment of their own will than they were about finding Savanna. Perhaps they rolled their eyes, silently indicating their exasperation with the Greywinds, a powerful cue to Crews, which would have escaped audio recording.[11]

Crews used every tool available to her as a white woman to come across as innocent. After letting the officers in, she immediately complimented Vanlith, gushing: "Oh my god. You're tall!" Vanlith, trained in psychological tactics, could have met her flirtation with silence or simply reminded her why he was there. Instead, he immediately quipped, "I try," making her giggle in response. This flirtatious interaction asserted Crews's equal footing with the officers. She took the initiative to speak unsolicited, flattering the officer's appearance. Crews acted as though she was playfully chatting with two white men in a bar. When asked if they could look around, she responded warmly, "Sure, come on in. Look around," switching the tone to one of a happy chat between neighbors. Crews boldly claimed her space as an innocent white woman, all of which was sustained and amplified by the police officers who refrained from treating her as a suspect. As the officers searched her home, she made small talk, shifting to the role of concerned white neighbor, and the officers seemed to comply with the farce. She asked about Savanna with seemingly earnest and sincere concern, "So what's going on?" Vanlith answered, "We're still looking." "I've been wanting to ask them," replied Crews, playing up the idea that they were all in this together, concerned about the Greywind family and Savanna's disappearance.

After flirting with Vanlith, Crews immediately referred to Saturday night, confirming her story that the 10:30 p.m. police visit was caused by the Greywinds. She referred to "the incident last night" to explain why she had not checked in with the Greywinds. Detective Swan spoke of the Greywinds with disdain: "They've probably got themselves whipped up into a grandiose idea." Officers spent six minutes and nineteen seconds speaking with Crews and looking at apartment 5, focusing on her kitchen cupboards, cupboards too small to hold a body, not the bathroom closet mentioned repeatedly and pointedly by the Greywinds.

As a profound counterpoint, the police spoke with Joe after the visit for two minutes and twelve seconds. Joe tried to give detailed instructions on the hidden compartment in the bathroom, but the police cut him off each time he spoke. They claimed their search to have been "thorough," but they would not directly address Joe's question about the hidden compartment. They also assured Joe that they were trained in spotting deception, and that Crews had told the truth. They indicated that their only lead, apartment 5, proved a dead end. The police gave him no kind words or reassurances of any kind, essentially demanding he accept their narrative. Calm and reserved, Joe Greywind thanked them and wished them a good night. They simply walked away without responding, failing to offer him a good night in return.

Crews's performance relied on the police's preexisting bias, which cast Joe Greywind not as a grieving father but as a menacing presence. This narrative made Norberta's maternal anguish invisible and allowed the police to interpret Joe's precise instructions as a threat to their authority rather than a path to his daughter and evidence of the crime.

The transcript of their interaction with Joe after the Sunday evening search lays bare the narrative in which they operated. Despite

Joe and Norberta insisting for days on a specific hiding spot in the bathroom, not a service panel, the police dismissed them:

> GREYWIND: You go in the bathroom. There's a closet on your right. That goes in behind, underneath the back.
>
> SWAN: [*Cuts him off*] Okay, so we just went up there and searched up there, and we didn't see anything . . .
>
> GREYWIND: [*Begins to speak but is interrupted*]
>
> VANLITH: Yeah, I mean, we found the area behind the tub, the service panel and all that.
>
> SWAN: We opened all that and looked back in there.
>
> GREYWIND: [*Begins to speak but is interrupted*]
>
> VANLITH: She's not showing any signs of deception. . . . She's now involved in something that has nothing to do with her. That's where we're at. We searched the whole apartment. We looked in her kitchen cabinets.
>
> GREYWIND: But you gotta understand—
>
> SWAN: [*Cuts him off*] I totally get it. I want to give you guys a little reprieve. We checked that box.
>
> GREYWIND: [*Begins to speak and is interrupted*]
>
> SWAN: If I can give you even the tiniest bit of reprieve for your feelings, then that's what I'm gonna do.
>
> GREYWIND: You guys have a good night.
>
> SWAN: Thank you.

The police refused to hear Joe out. Despite the family's pleas all weekend to check the bathroom closet, the officers interrupted him, talked over him, and willfully misdirected the conversation to a different feature entirely: a service panel. The officers did not fail to understand Joe; they deployed a strategy to silence the family's knowledge and maintain control over a narrative that excluded them. The officers did not want to understand the difference between the service panel they opened and the bathroom closet Joe wanted to describe that they had failed to open. They cut him off each time he began to speak. The police had full consent to search but chose instead to protect their own biases, likely standing just feet from where Savanna was hidden, inspecting a tiny service panel while ignoring the bathroom closet with Savanna inside.[12]

Her killers later confessed Savanna lay hidden inside apartment 5 on Sunday. She would have been in the bathroom closet or the dresser that Hoehn claimed to use. Had the officers tried to open a dresser with drawers nailed shut, this surely would have raised suspicion. Had the officers inspected the bathroom closet as the Greywinds had been demanding since Saturday, they might have found her. But the police barely searched. They never opened the bathroom closet. They opened kitchen drawers but not the sealed bedroom dresser where Savanna might have been hidden. The sentencing trial revealed that Hoehn bought duct tape at Ace Hardware on Sunday, the same tape used to seal the bags enveloping Savanna's body and later found to bear Hoehn's fingerprints once Savanna was found. Hoehn made the purchase at Burggraf's Ace Hardware on 2602 Broadway North at 1 p.m. on Sunday, well before the search of the apartment on Sunday night.

The exact location of Savanna's corpse on Saturday and Sunday and the removal of her corpse from apartment 5 remain unclear. Crews claims she and Hoehn placed Savanna's body inside the dresser on Sunday before the arrival of the officers, but she also insists they removed the dresser with her body in the middle of the night after the officers left. In some statements, Hoehn claimed he and Crews dragged the dresser hiding Savanna's corpse down the stairs in the dark of Monday morning. Hoehn's far-fetched story features him dragging the dresser down the stairs past Savanna's family's apartment, out to his car, which sits right outside the Greywinds' apartment, and down the driveway bordering Savanna's parents' home, then finally to the Red River, where they dumped her body. Yet neither the dresser nor remnants of a dresser were ever found. Taken together, their versions suggest Savanna likely remained hidden in apartment 5 during each of the three searches conducted by Fargo police on Saturday and Sunday.

NARRATIVE WARFARE

Over the third, fourth, and fifth days of Savanna's disappearance, police continued to interview Savanna's family, friends, and coworkers, still refusing to name Crews and Hoehn as persons of interest or bring them to the station for formal questioning. On Monday, Hoehn went to work and announced to coworkers that his girlfriend, Crews, "had a baby" over the weekend. While the police ignored Crews and Hoehn, the couple performed internet searches on flights, rental cars, and hotels, searches they were free to do because they lived under no obligation to remain in the state.

While the police exercised caution, the North Dakota media and community wasted no time. Norberta emailed a media outlet on Sunday morning, August 20, and searches organized by the family and community began immediately. As police approached Savanna's disappearance with a slower resolve, one detective called the volunteer community searches "rogue searches," revealing a disdain for those operating outside the control of the Fargo police. The family especially, but also the larger community responding to the family, faced a sort of criminalization for searching for Savanna, while the actual criminals were afforded the benefit of the doubt.[13]

The investigation operated on the deep-seated belief among Fargo police that Crews and Hoehn embodied a nice white couple on the third floor, and Savanna existed as a pregnant, Native runaway. Although police may have sought to hide their core beliefs about Natives and whites, those beliefs surfaced, nonetheless. The police made their opinions obvious when they spoke to reporters, even as they tried to claim they were investigating. On Tuesday, August 22, Deputy Police Chief Joe Anderson told reporters nothing suggested criminal activity on the part of Crews and Hoehn. Because Chief David Todd was vacationing out of state, the deputy made the announcement.[14]

With the Fargo community upset that the police chief remained on vacation during Savanna's disappearance, Chief David Todd made a public statement to the press on August 23. Dressed in his police uniform with a framed Blue Lives Matter poster behind him, Chief Todd sounded defensive. With the flag behind him sending a message about supporting police without question, Todd delivered a long list of facts to to make the case that the Fargo police were deeply committed to finding Savanna. Posted on the Fargo Police Facebook page, dozens of locals argued in the comments about whether the police were doing enough and whether private citizens should be searching for Savanna. Some in the comments spoke to the quiet threat that echoed the fear that had shadowed Native searchers from the start: Fail to agree with the police and the jail cell waits.[15]

The police campaign of narrative control extended from media announcements to the interrogation room, where officers subjected Savanna's boyfriend to a grueling and intimidating interrogation. On Tuesday, August 22, police interrogated Matheny for an hour and twenty-four minutes. He asked for breaks. He did not receive any. He asked for water. They never provided any. They asked for permission to physically take his phone out of his possession to another building where his data could be downloaded. Matheny asked for a time frame, worried that others could contact him about Savanna while his phone lay in their possession. They would not answer his question. He complied. They downloaded the data while his interrogation continued. They asked about his and Savanna's sexual history. They asked about his activities the night before her disappearance, demanding information such as exactly what types of alcohol he consumed and at what time. They asked him to share personal information about Savanna's parents related to alcohol. Matheny showed signs of intense and clear distress, but the police refused to relent. He begged to leave to continue the search, and eventually they let him go.[16]

Very late Tuesday and early Wednesday provided a breakthrough in the case. Although the police had interacted with William Hoehn three times on Saturday and Sunday—with means to arrest him each time—they arrested him around 1 a.m. on Wednesday for a warrant they knew about since Saturday. At the apartment building just after midnight as Tuesday became Wednesday, Fargo police found Hoehn and Crews pulling into their apartment parking lot, having just returned from a hit-and-run at Walmart, not in their Jeep Cherokee but in a red truck. Police took Hoehn into custody for the warrant that night but questioned him about the disappearance of Savanna.

During the detainment of Hoehn in the parking lot, Crews returned to her apartment. She held Savanna's baby hidden in a bag in front of the police officers and Savanna's family. Norberta and Joe begged the police to check her bag. Fargo police refused to ask Crews for consent to search her bag. Crews went up the stairs past the police and Savanna's family with Savanna's baby.[17]

Once at the station and mirandized for the hit-and-run, Detectives Loos and Kjonaas questioned Hoehn about Savanna. They allowed Hoehn to chew tobacco. He fidgeted, cursed, and waved his arms around. Like Crews, Hoehn acted within a narrative of an innocent white man surrounded by angry Natives. When asked about Savanna, Hoehn changed the subject. He lied about the Greywinds, telling police they were addicted to drugs. He labeled them as terrorists, a concept the police may have agreed with, as they saw the Greywinds as conducting "rogue searches" without police consent or assistance.[18]

Hoehn recalled Saturday night, describing to police a scene straight out of a Western, calling the gathering on the lawn a "fucking gang of fucking big-ass fucking Indians." Hoehn's strategy seemed to work. He drew on the Western metaphor of the circling of the wagons, telling a story of dangerous Natives on the front lawn, allegedly drinking. In Hoehn's telling, he became the victim of Natives. He and Crews were "trapped inside" because of what he saw as angry Natives on the lawn. His fear of what he saw as angry Native men seemed to make sense to the officers, although one openly identified with Joe being distraught. But Hoehn's constant assertions that he knew nothing of Savanna's disappearance or whereabouts seemed to satisfy police during the Wednesday interrogation. The detainment ended with his arrest for the warrant. He saw a judge that same morning when court was in session, paid $400, and returned home.[19]

But Fargo police later told a different story about the Wednesday 1 a.m. interrogation. Detectives related that they received notification from another officer that Hoehn had hit a car earlier that evening. Hoehn had borrowed the red truck from his boss, convicted sex offender Jesus Rios, and had driven the truck to Walmart, hit a car, and left the scene without exchanging information with the other driver. Detective Loos casually asked about the hit-and-run, and Hoehn confirmed it. Detectives Loos and Kjonaas interviewed Hoehn for two hours, listening to his lies about Savanna, appearing to sympathize with his racial slurs about the Greywinds, and failing to get clarity on why he borrowed a car. Later that Wednesday during the day shift, Detective Kjonaas interviewed Hoehn's boss, the man who had loaned the truck to Hoehn. Rios mentioned that Hoehn and Crews had had a baby that past weekend. Rios's mention of a baby changed everything. A newborn baby got the full attention of the Fargo officers, while an adult Native woman had received less.[20]

Despite these major revelations, police called Savanna's boyfriend, Matheny, back into the station at 11:30 a.m. on Wednesday for a second questioning. Matheny's older brother, who had been with him the night before the disappearance, came with him. Police reviewed the same details Matheny had provided the day before (Tuesday): exactly what kind of drinks they consumed, how many drinks, the exact intervals between drinks, and details about where they slept. But the police's real agenda seemed to be to further intimidate Matheny by taking his phone yet again.[21]

Although Fargo police downloaded his entire phone record the day before (Tuesday), causing him significant distress to be away from his phone during the search, they wanted access to his phone again on Wednesday. During the fifty-eight-minute questioning of Matheny and his brother, an officer spent forty of the fifty-eight minutes looking at Matheny's texts with Savanna on Matheny's phone. The officer seemed to be looking for particular texts. Although they had already downloaded the entirety of Matheny's phone contents, the officer brought out a professional-grade camera with a massive detachable lens just to snap pictures of six years' worth of texts on Matheny's tiny phone screen. Every shot came with a dramatic, echoing shutter click. The huge camera seemed like using a sledgehammer to crack a nut. Each time a picture was taken, the shutter produced an unnecessarily loud click, over and over for forty minutes, while Matheny often tried to self-regulate by laying his forehead on the desk. But police allowed no breaks for Matheny or his brother. No small talk. Just click, click, click.[22]

IGNORE THE WOMAN, SAVE THE BABY

When Fargo officers realized a baby lived in danger—rather than a Native woman—they sprang into far more intense action. At the Walmart where the hit-and-run took place, cash register footage showed Hoehn bought diapers, as confirmed by a video of him using self-checkout. Fargo officers obtained search warrants for apartment 5. Despite this advancement in the case, the public felt furious that the police obtained a search warrant on Thursday rather than Saturday when Savanna vanished into apartment 5.[23]

With a baby now at stake instead of a woman, Fargo police prepared to storm 2825 Ninth Avenue North, apartment 5, on Thursday, August 24, 2017. Around 1:30 p.m., Fargo police officers requested that the Greywinds vacate their home prior to the execution of the search warrant. While the Greywinds obediently stood across the street, police allowed all other building residents to remain in their homes. At 1:41 p.m., Fargo police broke down the door of apartment 5 when Crews would not answer. Buried in blankets on a queen-size bed lay Savanna's baby.[24]

Savanna's parents, siblings, and boyfriend learned of the birth of their daughter and granddaughter not in the joyful scene of a birth center or delivery room, and not even from the Fargo police, but as a huddled, segregated group across the street from their home. The Greywinds' neighbor, who lived below Crews and Hoehn, bellowed out their window, "They found a baby!" Joe and Norberta cautiously crossed the street, not directly in front of their home but using a neighbor's yard, to quietly ask the police for any information about the baby. Fargo police held to their vision of the Greywinds as a problem. Detective Nelson castigated the Greywinds for not following orders and remaining across the street where Detective Loos had placed them. To avoid arrest, Joe promptly placed his hands in the air, indicating compliance and submission.[25]

The Fargo police whisked the baby out of the building, past her grandparents, not stopping to allow the family to look at her even for a moment. The police swept the abducted baby into a government vehicle and drove her to an undisclosed Fargo hospital, where she was denied access to her entire family. She was then placed in an undisclosed location under the control of Cass County Social Services, likely with foster parents. Her relatives were forced to hire attorney Krista Andrews to gain access to their new family member. Her father "took her into his care" on September 6. On Tuesday, September 12, 2017, only as a result of their legal intervention, Ashton Matheny was granted custody at a custody hearing held by Cass County. The Greywinds were separated from the baby for two weeks after she was found. The family's separation from their granddaughter, which required them to hire an attorney, was experienced by them not as a rescue but as a profound reenactment of the historic trauma of child removal that the state has long perpetrated against Native families.[26]

From the start, Fargo police officers seemed to resent the case, a resentment possibly rooted in the Greywinds' refusal to passively accept and submit to the police narrative. In the reign of the first Trump presidency and the ascendancy of the Blue Lives Matter movement in Fargo, many Fargo officers held deeply conservative opinions with the full knowledge and approval of Chief Todd, himself seemingly a supporter of the Blue Lives Matter movement. Even after a Native baby was confiscated by the state, Fargo police still hesitated to admit that Crews and Hoehn had committed a crime. They instead believed Crews's claim that Savanna left the baby with her and vanished.[27]

The Fargo Police Department responded to the discovery of Savanna's baby with a campaign of narrative warfare designed to protect their image. Finding the baby on August 24—the baby who had been in the presence of police four separate times—exposed the City of Fargo's employees' colossal errors. During Crews's interrogation on August 24, video footage shows, one detective carefully placed his phone on the table, directly between Crews and himself, facing Crews so she could easily see his phone case, which depicted the Blue Lives Matter flag. Did his phone case send Crews a message?[28]

Perhaps gambling that the detective with the police phone case would support her, Crews lied. She had already convinced Officers Bollman, Vanlith, and Swan of her innocence. She told the detectives that Savanna asked her how to instigate labor, that Savanna gave birth at an unknown location, returned to Crews's home, left the baby with her, and then disappeared. Crews became the martyr in the story: She complained about the hard work of caring for Savanna's baby and how much she wanted to give it to the Greywinds. Detective Loos remained in the same physical position, completely still and silent, taking in Crews's testimony. Detective Kjonaas seemed unsure of the story, asking Crews about the instructions she gave on inducing labor. Crews explained that she told Savanna to insert a wooden kebab skewer inside her vaginal canal and past her cervix to start contractions. Detective Loos finally spoke in response to the skewer story, asking whether the skewer would have been the kind for barbecuing. Brooke eagerly agreed, as though this story did not beg reality, and he nodded vigorously, either trying to encourage her or actually believing it.[29]

Inside the interrogation room, Fargo police navigated the narrative of innocent whites and guilty Natives. Even after they found Savanna's body, they continued to engage in the narrative warfare that identified Savanna as a troubled Native woman from a troubled Native family. Onto this narrative structure, they merely layered on Crews's ridiculous story that Savanna had inserted a barbecue skewer into her cervix and uterus, delivered her baby, left her with complete strangers, and run away.

Hoehn received seemingly favorable treatment as well. After being brought to the police station in handcuffs, his guard worried about the tightness of the cuffs, offering to loosen them. The guard asked Hoehn if he wanted something to drink, a question never posed to Matheny. Hoehn requested a Sprite or water. The guard told Hoehn he could go to the "pop machine," but the guard wanted to know what to get Hoehn if there was no Sprite or 7 Up. Hoehn clarified: "Something on the clear side. Not any of the caramel-colored stuff." Then another officer got involved in the conversation, with a second discussion about his beverage preferences, with the second officer going to fetch Hoehn's drink. After ten minutes of friendly chat with the guard, the second officer delivered Hoehn his exact request: a cold Sprite. Police use strategies to gain trust, but the treatment of Hoehn stands in stark contrast to that of Matheny. The same system that showed such solicitous care for Hoehn, with not one but two officers fetching his preferred drink, had applied nothing but intimidation and dismissal to Matheny's profound distress.[30]

The disparity in police focus reached beyond the interrogation room. It extended to the very definition of who constituted a threat. Authorities struggled to locate William Hoehn's vehicle, asking the public for help, despite claiming to have the couple under surveillance. They even dedicated resources to monitoring the grieving Greywind family. According to Mr. Greywind, federal agents followed his family, watching them for over a week, from the Saturday Savanna vanished even up until the family stood at the edge of Red River wondering if she had been found. The police's operational priorities were laid bare: The inhabitants of apartment 5 were merely subjected to a passive, inefficient watch, while the Native family in apartment 2 were treated as active suspects requiring surveillance.[31]

Denied access by the City of Fargo's employees to their new relative, the Greywinds clung to the hope of finding Savanna alive, given the massive pressure from the police to believe Crews's story that Savanna was alive when Crews watched her leave her apartment. Tribal firefighters from Norberta's tribal nation, the Turtle Mountain Band of Chippewa Indians, came to Fargo to help organize the volunteer searches of creeks, rivers, and farms in coordination with Savanna's family members. Volunteers canvassed every neighborhood in Fargo, distributing thousands of flyers with Savanna's picture, details about the disappearance, and contact information. Crews and Hoehn sat in jail, insisting they had nothing to do with the disappearance of Savanna or the birth of her baby. In fact, they continued to play the role of white martyrs who had helped a troubled Native woman.[32]

In the late afternoon as the sun began to lower on the horizon on Sunday, August 27, Sandra Salisbury saw a body in the Red River near the Ninetieth Street Bridge on the Minnesota side of the river. Once police arrived and verified Savanna's tattoo, they informed her family of the terrible discovery of their deceased daughter. Because her body lay in Minnesota, Ramsey County prepared the death certificate and autopsy. This case fell under federal jurisdiction because Savanna's body had been transported across state lines, but the federal government declined to prosecute and Cass County took the case. The public pressured Cass County's prosecutor to seek murder charges. She never did.[33]

Fargo law enforcement left behind much of the treasure trove of evidence inside Crews and Hoehn's apartment. Fargo journalist Christopher Hagen of *The High Plains Reader* came to possess many items from Crews's apartment, including her journals, having been told by a neighbor that police dumped all of her belongings in the trash down the street away from the apartment building. Hagen jumped in the dumpster and took Crews's writings, which indicated in multiple entries that she had premeditated the murder of Savanna Greywind. Once Hagen publicized these materials, the police demanded them. He refused to hand them over, but he did allow police to photograph them for evidence.[34]

After months of a standoff in which Hagen held her journals and Crews held to her story of martyrdom, she broke. On December 7, 2017, Crews launched a new narrative: She was love-crazed and faked a pregnancy to keep Hoehn's love. Her attorney and police gave her an out: presenting herself as mentally ill. Such a tactic would blunt her responsibility and knowledge of her own actions. Prosecutors could have used the writings thrown away by the police to prove premeditation. Her writings showed a woman who planned to perform a C-section and who fabricated a detailed story of pregnancy, delivery, and even vaccines. Crews seemed to have planned the killing of Savanna and the abduction of her baby down to the last detail. She saw Savanna as disposable and her baby as highly desirable. Instead, she played lovesick, claiming she wanted a baby to keep Hoehn, and crazy, claiming her love caused her to lose her mind, taking Savanna's baby.[35]

The state privileged Crews's December narrative over the evidence. Crews and her attorney found a plausible narrative for her as a white woman: She lacked mental stability. As a male, Hoehn had other options. Both Crews and Hoehn qualified for a public defender, which Crews utilized, but Hoehn received private and paid counsel, paid for by an unknown source. On the advice of his attorney, Hoehn turned on Crews, asserting she killed Savanna, not him. Crews changed her plea to guilty in late November and rolled out the December confession. Flanked by public defender Steven Mottinger, Crews centered a lie she had told Hoehn: that she was pregnant. In this story, she claimed to believe she was, in fact, pregnant, succumbing to pressure from Hoehn who demanded she produce a baby. Then she murdered Savanna to take her baby and keep Hoehn. Prosecutors embraced this December 2017 story.

But Crews's journals, notes, shopping lists, and books provided irrefutable evidence of premeditation, detailing Crews's plan for the murder, the abduction, and even the future life she intended to fabricate for the child, including narratives she could use as a cover when interacting with pediatricians and schools and a list of items to purchase for a C-section and home birth. This evidence seems to prove Crews fully intended to kill Savanna. Yet the prosecution accepted her story of a love-crazed woman who performed this crime for Hoehn.

Prosecutors called Crews's actions a fetal abduction and chose not to consider other possibilities, including that Crews and Hoehn may have been intending to participate in the illegal trafficking of Native children. Such an operation existed just a few hours' drive from Fargo. Crews functioned on the edge of poverty, paying for her apartment in ways unknown to officials, perhaps with help from Hoehn, perhaps with remaining financial aid from the time when she had attended school. When Hoehn went to Walmart for diapers, he used his food-stamp card for a food purchase, but his debit card was declined for use on nonfood items. Clearly, neither of them had enough money.[36] With a profit motive in mind, they could have found buyers of Native babies and sold Savanna's baby to an illegal baby broker. This remains a possibility because a white woman, Betty Jo Krenz, was running such an operation on Spirit Lake Reservation in 2017. Autym Burke, a buyer from Facebook, paid for and made plans with Betty Jo Krenz to pick up a Native baby on August 8, 2017, just nine days before the abduction and murder of Savanna. Krenz made excuses for weeks when she did not produce the baby she had promised Autym. When Autym Burke never received the Native baby, one she felt she had paid for, she went to the police to complain. Betty Jo Krenz got caught. The dates Krenz was illegally trafficking Native babies overlap with the dates Crews attempted to get Savanna to consume marijuana with her and then to use Savanna as a model for a dress, a meeting that ended in her death. Betty Jo Krenz, a social worker, and Brooke Crews may have even been working together to abduct and sell Native children. While no direct connection between Crews and Krenz has been established on the record, the overlap in timing highlights a broader, documented context of illegal Native child trafficking in the region, a charged atmosphere in which the murder and abduction occurred.[37]

SHIELDING WILLIAM

If, as Kahnawà:ke Mohawk professor Audra Simpson argues, the state relentlessly finds and punishes Native women, then the case of William Hoehn proves it pursues settler assailants with equal zeal in order to shield them from the legal consequences of their actions.[38] The legal outcomes for the two defendants diverged starkly. The extensive appeals and eventual reduction of Hoehn's sentence demonstrate a legal process that functioned to greatly mitigate the consequences for him, consistent with a systemic tendency to devalue the lives of Native women. While Crews had to rely on a public defender, Hoehn somehow obtained a private attorney, Daniel J. Borgen, a well-connected former police officer and now a judge. The media never investigated who paid for Hoehn's attorney, and the prosecution avoided the subject as well. While the public defender pressured Crews to confess and change her plea to guilty, Hoehn's attorney instructed him to plead not guilty to the conspiracy to commit murder charge, the most serious of his three charges. A jury agreed and found him not guilty of conspiracy to commit murder. But the county prosecutor added a classification of "special offender status" to the remaining guilty charges (of conspiracy to commit kidnapping and giving false information to law enforcement) due to his 2011 child abuse conviction. At his sentencing, Hoehn received life in prison with the chance of parole in October 2018 because of his special status.[39]

But the machinery to shield him from a life sentence kicked in. Hoehn's special treatment culminated in a defense that echoed anti-abortion dogma: The mother does not matter, only the child. Hoehn received a second paid attorney, again from an unknown source. Kiara Kraus-Parr filed an appeal to overturn the special offender status and appeared before the North Dakota Supreme Court on his behalf. In defending Hoehn, Kraus-Parr made a fundamentally anti-abortion argument. She suggested to the North Dakota Supreme Court that William Hoehn had not harmed Savanna's baby. With a myopic lens like that used by anti-abortionists, Kraus-Parr made Hoehn out to be a white martyr: "The child was healthy. The child was given food, clothing, diaper changes. It was cared for." Kraus-Parr severed the murder of the baby's mother from the abduction of Savanna's baby much like Hoehn and Crews severed mother from child. Her argument—that you can kill a child's mother without harming her child—won the case. The anti-abortion movement, fueled by the Christian Right, centers adoption in the push to force women to give birth. Kraus-Parr borrowed from that thinking by downplaying the harm of killing a child's mother. Justice Jerod E. Tufte agreed with Kraus-Parr's logic, defining child abuse narrowly, writing: "Hoehn's conduct did not cause physical injury to the baby."[40]

The court's ruling in Hoehn's case operationalized the most extreme anti-abortion logic: that a pregnant woman serves as no more than a "host body" whose value ends when her child's life begins. This ideology contains a profound disregard for all women but also a racialized version that aligns perfectly with the settler-colonial need to control the reproduction of Native women such that they cannot keep their children. In the case of Savanna Greywind, the North Dakota Supreme Court created a powerful legal precedent for killing mothers and taking their babies. The court hearing marked the most important moment in the case: The justices made clear they believed Hoehn had not harmed Savanna's baby when he murdered her mother. In their view, the child's health neutralized the crime; the mother's death became irrelevant. For them, Crews's act of cutting Savanna's womb performed a reverse abortion: killing the mother and birthing the child. The unique horror of severing mother from child rendered the Native mother disposable, and the birth of the baby caused the horror to recede.

This disposability of the Native mother unlocks the case, revealing the intersection of anti-abortion misogyny and hatred of Native people. Native women are positioned as uniquely irrelevant in the settler schema, which has historically seized Native children while destroying Native families. For Christian nationalists and the alt-right, Brooke Crews's desire to abduct a baby made twisted sense; the murder required to do it presented merely a logistical hurdle. This mirrors the anti-abortion view that sees fetuses as possessing more rights than living women and the belief, especially, that Brown and Black babies should be raised by white families. What pregnancy means in Native communities, a celebration of community and relationality, stands opposed to this patriarchal, extractive, violent logic that values a woman's life only insofar as it reproduces children.

The reduction in sentencing for Hoehn, from a life sentence to twenty years due to the removal of the special offender status, served as the final payoff. Hoehn's attorney's defense strategy, bankrolled by anonymous sources, highlighted how the legal system consistently shields settler men from incarceration instead of seeking justice for Native families. After the Supreme Court of North Dakota removed the special offender status from his conspiracy to commit kidnapping conviction, Hoehn went back to county court with a third private attorney, Scott Patrick Brand—again, paid for by an anonymous donor. Scott Brand asked for a seven-year sentence. Instead, Cass County District Court sentenced Hoehn to twenty years in prison, which became seventeen because of time already served. Hoehn would have served life in prison were it not for the intervention of the North Dakota Supreme Court. To soften the blow, the court treated Hoehn differently from others, moving him out of state in March 2019 to an undisclosed prison where he remains today, free from scrutiny.[41]

Savanna and Matheny's daughter will be as young as nineteen years old when her mother's killer walks free, if he serves the full twenty-year sentence. If he is released early on parole, she may still be a minor at seventeen years old.

Despite having a clear path to seek maximum accountability, the prosecutor, Tanya Martinez, opted for the lesser charge of conspiracy that all but guaranteed William Hoehn's escape from a life sentence. North Dakota banned the death penalty in 1976, but the prosecutor could have argued that Savanna's kidnapping led to her death. This would have made the murder a federal offense, punishable by execution. The state, instead, chose to pursue a charge difficult to prove: conspiracy to commit murder. Crews took the fall by pleading guilty. Hoehn escaped the charge by pointing to Crews and obtaining privately paid counsel.

The tools for this narrative control reside within the state. Police and attorneys, often from the same insular communities, create a web of mutual protection. State attorneys must rely on police reports and cannot afford to alienate officers. They accept police reports, burying evidence that could help a defense or a victim's family sue for damages. This system operates above the law, vulnerable only to public exposure through community condemnation and a media willing to break from the official narrative.

In Crews and Hoehn's case, a rare breakdown in this narrative control occurred. Local media initially interviewed officers who made confusing statements; some, like Lieutenant Nelson, went on live TV and said it was not until August 23, the day police learned that Hoehn had spoken of his child's birth at work, that the police received information that made the apartment of Crews and Hoehn a potential crime scene. This erasure of Savanna's family's testimony that their daughter had been harmed in apartment 5 exposed the narrative warfare between the police and the community. Someone responded swiftly to this police interview by scrubbing it from the news station website, YouTube, the news site that posted the original, and the Internet Archive. State attorneys simply never questioned these tensions in the investigation in court as it would have only exposed the police, not the killers. City of Fargo employees seemed to have worked diligently to make it difficult to acquire the evidence that could challenge its preferred timeline—a timeline that made them into heroes who saved Savanna's baby.[42]

A profound sense of community relief that Savanna's baby was alive allowed a state narrative, based exclusively on the killers' testimonies, to become the accepted truth. This narrative remains unchallenged despite its gaping hole: No one other than the killers saw Savanna enter or exit apartment 5. The three police visits on Saturday and Sunday confirmed nothing because they searched superficially.

Only Crews and Hoehn know the fullness of what transpired in apartment 5, and their confessions probably lack veracity.

According to Crews and Hoehn, they murdered Savanna in the bathroom on Saturday. She was either dying, dead in the closet, or stuffed in a dresser during those police visits. The Greywind family specifically begged officers to look in the bathroom, namely the bathroom closet, knowing it was a potential hiding place. Due to a possible bias that framed Savanna as a criminal and not a victim, the police invalidated her family's pain and refused their requests.

This bias generated lethal consequences. Fargo police could have possibly saved Savanna; she may have been alive during the first search. Over the course of three separate searches, they walked within feet of her as she lay dying or deceased in a one-bedroom apartment because officers and detectives could not fathom the white couple as criminals. This failure of perception extended to the highest court in the state, which pardoned William Hoehn of special offender status. This case cannot be understood outside the framework of tribal dispossession. In the following section, chapter 5 examines how this structuring principle of settler colonialism shaped the investigation into the murder of Savanna Greywind, an Anishinaabe and Dakota woman.

THE MACRO CRIME SCENE

The severing of mother from child mirrors the dispossession of Native people from their land, a process rooted in the colonial view of Native women as expendable. The pervasive myth of Pocahontas, a sexualized figure whose story implies consent, acts as a synecdoche, erasing settler violence against Native women. This narrative works in tandem with the doctrine of discovery, framing both land and Native women's bodies as resources available for the taking. The violence of colonialism has always been met with Native resistance to these twin claims over their territory and their bodily autonomy.[43]

The larger history of Native America offers key insights into settler colonialism's elimination of Native female autonomy and motherhood, but the tribal histories in Savanna's lineage can tell us even more. The Spirit Lake Nation embodies the shock of settler colonialism. Prior to colonization, its citizens lived as bands of the Dakota Nation whose territory spread across the US and Canada, including the Red River Valley. Dakota peoples have always claimed portions of Canada as their original homeland, but Canada removed them and denied their presence, leaving them with no recognized lands there, despite their long history.[44]

The United States removed and incarcerated Dakota peoples, applying new group identities to those they confined to reservations. The enforcement of these new identities relied on violence. For Dakotas, the peak of that violence took place in the Dakota War and the forced relocations of 1862. As settlers invaded Dakota lands, traders and government agents targeted Dakota people, deceiving them and stealing treaty-guaranteed supplies already paid for by the federal government, then selling those stolen goods to settlers. The US government pushed them into treaties without their true consent, and settlers targeted Dakota women for sexual violence. This culminated in the public execution of thirty-eight Dakota men by the United States government on December 26, 1862, and the removal and death march of all Dakota people out of Minnesota.[45]

Settler violence and tribal dispossession ultimately confined Savanna Greywind's paternal ancestors to the Spirit Lake Reservation in North Dakota. Though some Wahpeton and Sisseton Yanktonai bands had avoided the 1862 Dakota War by fleeing Minnesota, they were still forced onto the reservation by treaty in 1867. The agreement created the Fort Totten Indian Reservation—a name reflecting its carceral purpose—and imposed the maliciously translated "Devil's Lake" on both the tribal nation and the lake, projecting paganism onto the Dakota people.

In 1993, the tribe reclaimed its identity, renaming itself the Spirit Lake Nation in resistance to this violent history. Yet the colonial name persists on maps and in the nearby, settler-dominated town, a continued erasure caused by displacement. Although geographically removed from the worst violence in Minnesota, Savanna's ancestors endured these waves of colonial destruction, and their community still bears the scars.

The confinement to reservations made Native communities targets for further violence, this time under the guise of salvation. Christian missionaries formed a core part of the governmental strategy to root out Native culture. At Spirit Lake, this intrusion took a horrific form with Episcopal priest Samuel Dutton Hinman, who molested a Dakota girl in 1876. The church convicted him of adultery to cover up the crime, devastating the Dakota community. The victim's family struggled to articulate the trauma, as there were no words in Dakota for what the priest had done.[46]

Savanna's maternal ancestors, the Turtle Mountain Band of Chippewa Indians, also endured removal and dispossession, leading to their confinement on the Turtle Mountain Indian Reservation. Like the Spirit Lake Dakota, they exist as part of a larger precolonial nation, the Anishinaabe (also called Ojibwe or Chippewa), whose vast territory once spanned the US-Canada border. Though the federal government created the reservation structure, the Turtle Mountain Band maintains its distinct identity as part of the enduring Anishinaabe people.

Like the Spirit Lake Dakota, the Turtle Mountain community claims complex identities as Anishinaabe and Métis. Their histories intertwine deeply; their lands overlapped, and they signed the 1858 Sweet Corn Treaty to solidify their boundaries against escalating settler pressure. This treaty recognized Turtle Mountain's claim to eleven million acres, lands the US later obtained. Settlers especially coveted the Red River Valley, the very river where Savanna's murderers would later discard her body.[47]

Settler colonialism's driving engine, territorial theft, systematically stripped Savanna's maternal ancestors of their land. The US government shrank its recognized territory from eleven million acres to a mere forty-six-thousand-acre reservation, a loss of over 99.9 percent of their homeland. This dispossession took place not as a single event but as a relentless campaign. It began with the coercive Treaty of Old Crossing and continued with executive orders that steadily reduced the reservation.

The theft culminated in the corrupt 1892 McCumber Agreement, where a handpicked council was manipulated into selling ten million acres against the will of the tribal nation. This calculated, decades-long seizure of land and resources created the generational poverty that still defines life for some at Turtle Mountain today, pressuring many young people to leave their community to survive.

This history of land theft binds itself to the assault on Native family and motherhood, which transforms Native women's uteruses into contested territory. Savanna's pregnant and autonomous body represented a profound threat: the reproduction of Native life within Native community. The US has rejected Native motherhood, while revering a submissive white motherhood. In analyzing the removal of a Lakota child in 1884 at Chief Hump's Camp, Nimi:pu: scholar Beth Piatote concludes: "An Indian mother could barely make her love legible even when she wrote it in her own blood."[48]

The same chilling dismissal unfolded in 2017. Crews and Hoehn targeted Savanna precisely because of her Native motherhood. Her murderers saw her not as a person but as a source of a desired baby, separating grandmother from mother, and mother from daughter. Their actions revealed the historic belief that Savanna's body and child belonged to someone other than herself, her family, and her community. While Norberta testified to the unutterable pain of losing her daughter, she reminded the court that William Hoehn nostalgically called the days he spent with the abducted child of Savanna "the best days of his life," openly reveling in the historic privilege that allowed him to steal her grandchild from her daughter's body.[49]

The crisis of missing and murdered Indigenous women emerges directly from centuries of policy designed to dismantle Native families. This systemic separation began with boarding schools and evolved into the widespread twentieth-century practices of forced adoption and foster care. This machinery of family separation, documented by scholars like Margaret Jacobs, operated on core colonial beliefs: that Native children fare better with white families and that Native mothers, by definition, fail. Savanna Greywind's story extends this logic to its violent extreme—not merely the removal of a child through government paperwork, but the eradication of the mother's ability to live or ever even touch her child. Savanna's child does not escape this cycle. Her child becomes its newest victim, growing up without her mother, her life shaped by a loss the state engineered. Yet her relations cling to an alternative, a futurity in which she is embraced, celebrated, and surrounded by love, family, and community, in spite of what happened to her mother.[50]

In a horrific echo of state-sponsored family separation, the first hands to touch Savanna's baby belonged to her murderer. This profound cultural and personal violation was articulated by Joe Greywind, who stated that in their Dakota tradition, the first hands to touch a newborn should be those of the maternal grandmother, a sacred role stolen from Savanna's mother. Instead, Savanna's baby's first days were spent in the arms of her mother's killers, hidden mere feet from her grieving family.

Tragically, this initial abduction was compounded by the state. When police finally recovered Savanna's baby, they completed the severing of family bonds. They carried the baby past her own grandparents without a word and placed her into undisclosed locations. For two weeks, the state held legal custody of the baby, forcing the father to hire a lawyer and sue North Dakota to get his own child back. The state did not perform a rescue. Taking the baby into county custody functioned as a bureaucratic extension of the killing—a second abduction that proved how easily the system replicates the very violence it claims to condemn. Without resources for a legal battle, the Greywind family could have permanently lost Savanna's baby to the state, fulfilling the enduring settler-colonial logic of taking Native children.

Native communities have consistently fought back against the state's assault on their families, with Joe Greywind's own Spirit Lake Nation at the forefront of this resistance. This fight was led by Native mothers. In 1968, five mothers from Spirit Lake traveled to New York City to testify about being systematically denied the right to raise their children. Their testimony, supported by the Association on American Indian Affairs, exposed a devastating fact: Over one-quarter of the children on their reservation were not living with their parents or relatives.

A distributed fact sheet laid bare the mechanics of this theft: 107 children lived in non-Indian foster homes, 93 lived in Bureau of Indian Affairs boarding schools, and 64 had been adopted, severing all tribal ties. This evidence of widespread family destruction, driven by state incentives, became the foundational catalyst for the movement that would eventually lead to the Indian Child Welfare Act (ICWA).

The courageous public testimony of Native women, beginning with the Spirit Lake mothers, provided the direct catalyst for the ICWA of 1978. This crucial legislation, which directly responded to their advocacy, was created to halt the widespread removal of Native children by establishing legal protections to keep them within their communities.

These women fought to reclaim their rights as mothers, countering the racist state narrative that labeled them unfit parents. They traveled to testify before Congress, bringing their children perhaps to protect them from being taken while they traveled. Their powerful stories exposed a system where social workers permanently placed Native children into non-Native homes, sometimes abusive ones, layering new trauma onto the trauma of family separation. This created a devastating legacy where multiple generations of Native people were raised by strangers, sometimes abusers.[51]

The settler-colonial logic of Native family separation persisted into the twenty-first century, facing continuous legal challenges despite the passage of ICWA. ICWA infuriates conservatives, and well-funded challenges from alt-right and Christian foundations have pushed to dismantle it. These attacks nearly succeeded. In the 2013 case *Adoptive Couple v. Baby Girl*, the US Supreme Court ruled in favor of non-Native adoptive parents, severing a Cherokee child from her father. This set a dangerous precedent for overturning ICWA and tribal sovereignty. A subsequent challenge, *Haaland v. Brackeen*, argued that the law discriminates against white parents. Though the court ultimately upheld ICWA in 2023, the ongoing assaults reveal a relentless commitment to the settler project of taking Native children.[52]

The deep-seated belief that Native parents provide unfit environments persists in the US psyche, enabling an illegal market for Native children. Even with ICWA, tribes must vigilantly protect their youth.

Joe Greywind's own Spirit Lake Nation hired a social worker for this purpose, only to be betrayed: The white woman they employed, Betty Jo Krenz, sold adoptions of Spirit Lake children online. Krenz targeted an unhoused Native mother, using Facebook photos of her child to broker an illegal adoption. She was caught only because her white client in Oregon felt swindled. This case exposes how the colonial impulse to take Native children has continued.[53]

Savanna's killers treated her as disposable, as mere collateral damage in their quest to take her child. This view continues a settler-colonial tradition that sees Native mothers as irrelevant vessels for valuable children, denying the mothers' sovereignty and humanity. The killers acted with confidence that they could murder a Native woman, keep her baby, and evade consequences by leveraging their whiteness. Even the police, by celebrating "saving" Savanna's baby while failing Savanna, repeated this historic violence. The separation of Native child from mother operates in the history of settler logics.

Crews and Hoehn's confidence stemmed not from historical knowledge but from an innate understanding of their white privilege within the settler-colonial system of North Dakota. When he went to work, Hoehn proudly announced to his coworkers that he and Crews had a new baby. Although no one recalled her showing signs of pregnancy, Hoehn felt comfortable speaking of their new baby because he knew he was not under investigation for murder. Hoehn knew he stood on the firm ground of settler privilege and its solid foundation of unquestioned innocence.

The severing of Savanna from her baby goes beyond the metaphorical. As gruesome and disturbing as this is, it must be addressed. Brooke Crews wanted the City of Fargo employees and Cass County to believe she existed in a delusional psychotic state, but Brooke Crews held a steady hand and premeditated and executed a cesarean section, a murder, and the delivery of an unborn child. Determined to kill the Native and save the baby, much like Richard Pratt's quote "Kill the Indian in him, and save the man," Crews used skill, dexterity, and calm to execute a C-section, despite having virtually no medical training or experience. To use her hands and arms in such a deadly manner, Crews drew on the long history of dismemberment and grave robbing of Native America to mentally withstand the actions she took upon the body of Savanna LaFontaine-Greywind. Like Crews, US medical doctors used Brown and Black bodies for their own purposes, disregarding the value and sacredness those bodies hold for individuals and their communities. While doctors did not murder to obtain corpses, medical schools relied on the poverty that made Black and Brown bodies more accessible than white bodies upon death.[54]

Grave robbing and body snatching of Native people undergird the US settler state. This tradition of desecration began with figures like Thomas Jefferson, who excavated Native bodies from a burial mound, framing this violation as scientific inquiry. This established a brutal economy where Native remains were treated as commodities. The US Army provided heads of Modoc people to colleges after executing them in 1872. Anthropologist Franz Boas robbed the graves of Indigenous communities in British Columbia in 1886, selling body parts for profit. Museums created a lucrative market for grave robbers, with the Harvard Museum of Natural History even writing to the secretary of war to request "the bodies of some Indians." The Inuit man Minik Wallace, whose father's bones were held by the American Museum of Natural History, named this practice correctly when he called its perpetrators "scientific criminals" in 1909. What they called science relentlessly desecrated Native bodies to feed the settler imagination.[55]

This trade in Native bodies played out with particular horror for the Dakota, Savanna's father's people. Settlers profited from Dakota pain at every turn: by starving them by diverting their treaty-guaranteed supplies to settlers for profit, and then by selling their corpses after the 1862 execution of thirty-eight Dakota men. The war and starvation that killed Savanna's ancestors created new business opportunities for the body trade. In the nineteenth century, medical schools wanted cadavers, and the bodies of Dakotas circulated within that market. In 1864, white soldiers shot and killed an unnamed Dakota man, then dragged his body to a fort where settlers beat and mutilated his corpse. After a shallow burial, a body snatcher delivered the remains to Dr. Alfred Muller, who mailed the man's body to the Army Medical Museum in Washington, DC. In a separate package, he mailed the man's severed hand. From there, the dismembered body was sent to the Smithsonian.[56]

The stealing, buying, and selling of Dakota bodies operated not as a fringe practice but as the work of renowned institutions, some of which remain powerful today. The Mayo Clinic, ranked as the best hospital system in the United States, is built on this foundation. Its roots lie in the theft of Dakota corpses following the largest mass execution in US history. On December 26, 1862, the US Army hanged thirty-eight Dakota men at Mankato and buried them in a mass grave. Late that night, Dr. William Worrall Mayo, who cofounded the clinic with his sons, paid a guard ten dollars to raid it. He and his companions exhumed four Dakota bodies, including that of Marpiya Okinajin (He Who Stands in the Clouds, but settlers called him Cut Nose). They loaded the wagons and covered the bodies with blankets. Dr. Mayo, the group's leader, then charged his accomplices a fee for access. He took the corpses to St. Peter, Minnesota, to sell three of them, completing the financial transaction of turning the bodies of Dakota defenders into gruesome commodities.

Dr. Mayo kept the body of Marpiya Okinajin. He transported it to LeSueur, Minnesota, where he stored the frozen corpse in a shed until he could host a dissection and viewing for local doctors. After the dissection, he saved pieces of his skin and then used a kettle to render Okinajin's body into a skeleton, which he then used as a primary teaching tool. His son, Will, learned anatomy by assembling the Dakota warrior's bones, a skill he later taught his brother, Charlie. Both sons would credit their foundational medical knowledge to this macabre practice. Dr. Mayo kept Okinajin's skeleton in his office for patient demonstrations as well, and after his retirement, the Mayo Clinic displayed the warrior's remains in its lobby and later in its Heritage Hall, a monument to its violent beginnings.[57]

A living Native person troubles settler colonialism; a dead Native body fuels it. This brutal economy built institutions like the Mayo Clinic and motivated the killing of Savanna and the theft of her child. The abduction of her child draws on settler colonialism and its history of grave robbing. Although Native bodies bore little to no value in the market when alive, their dead bodies fetched considerable cash in the nineteenth century especially. The medical field, archaeology, anthropology, and even the military all owe much of their knowledge and expertise to the deaths of Native people and the disarticulation of their bodies. Tribes have spent decades fighting settler institutions to return the bodies of their ancestors to the earth, only to be told, in essence, that those bodies constitute property—property owned by settler institutions, not by tribal communities from which they were taken.

CLOSING ARGUMENT

By reducing the murder of Savanna Greywind to simple conspiracy charges to commit murder and kidnapping, the Cass County court enacted the same logic that enabled her killers: that Native women's lives are disposable. Crews and Hoehn did far more than the court acknowledged. They stalked Savanna and premeditated her murder and the abduction of her unborn child. Their actions were rooted in the core tenet of narrative warfare born of history: that Native women lack value, while white perpetrators possess an inherent innocence that grants them permission to commit such crimes. They murdered and abducted Savanna because they knew they could, and they were right. During both the August 23 and 24 interviews with Fargo police, the man who admitted to dumping Savanna's corpse in the Red River repeatedly painted the Greywinds and other Native people in ways that invoke settler fears of Natives. Recalling the community gathering at the apartment building, he called them a "gang" along with expletives. His statement laid bare his strategy: a calculated reliance on the privilege that vilifies Native people and protects settler violence. Savanna died because of this privilege.[58]

The murderers dumped Savanna's corpse into the Red River, a place rooted in Native history but also settler violence, the very violence that killed her. Historically, the Red River Valley was held by the ancestors of both her parents: Spirit Lake Dakota and Turtle Mountain Chippewa. Settlers took this land by violence, just as her life was taken. A suburban kayaker ultimately found Savanna in the river that once belonged to her ancestors, a waterway that now marks the border between the two states that claim possession of it. Her body, disposed of in these waters, became the embodiment of the ongoing dispossession of Native people from their land and the ongoing disregard for their lives.[59]

The settler state in the Americas operates not as a neutral actor but as a structure that polices Native people, removes their children, and maintains access to their corpses. In Savanna's case, this meant that bias directly contributed to her murder, created a flawed investigation, and resulted in lenient sentencing for her male killer. The City of Fargo employees and Cass County used narrative warfare to, perhaps unwittingly, protect white criminals while silencing the advocacy of Savanna's Native family. By focusing on individual motive and psychopathologizing killers, the state obscured its own foundation: a history of land dispossession, war, and treaties that necessitates Native dispossession and disadvantage.

The state's narrative warfare enlisted law enforcement but also the law to control the story of who counted as victim and criminal. This narrative warfare operated not as a passive bias but as an active process of narrative arbitrage, where the value of a white life was inflated, and the value of Native life diminished. "Missing white woman syndrome" emerges from this very system of arbitrage in which white victims receive heightened urgency and concern from law enforcement, the media, and the public. In contrast, the state's narrative machinery treats Native and other non-white women and their families with dismissal and disgust, framing them as criminals from the outset. This one-sided hostility forces Native families to pursue justice alone, knowing they will anger the very institution meant to protect them and possibly face incarceration in the pursuit of justice.

The narrative arbitrage surfaces in the evident double standard: For many white victims, police act promptly and pursue suspects vigorously. For some Native victims and their families, they become suspects themselves. Authorities seem unable to perceive evidence, even when it sits in the room with them, within these narrative guardrails. Since many crimes against Native women are committed by settlers, this biased framework means that, in practice, killing Native women is only technically illegal. As Diné scholar Jennifer Nez Denetdale writes, "The fact of the matter is, in this country, it has never been a crime to kill an Indian. I find this fact also extends to law enforcement." The state's narrative warfare thus culminates in a brutal reality: The murder of Native women is not treated as a crime.[60]

Savanna Greywind's story ends where it began: in the logic of narrative warfare. This cold narrative logic does not merely devalue Native women's lives. It actively severs them from their children through policy and violence, commodifying their bodies even after death. From the grave robbing that built medical schools to the adoption industry that traffics Native children, the calculus remains consistent: Native life becomes disposable until possessed and used. Savanna's body, dumped in the river of her ancestors, became waste in her killers' eyes; her child became a commodity in the state's, rescued only once united with her relations. This final, brutal separation signified the core value of settler colonialism: the severing of Native people from their land, their children, and their own bodies.

EPILOGUE

Chapter 1 traced the Cherokee oral history of the attack on Lydia Kingfisher, suggesting that descendants preserved the memory of the violence by replacing a settler perpetrator with a Cherokee man in their retellings. Chapter 1 further suggested that that Cherokee man may have been falsely charged and convicted of murder prior to the attack, a victim of land fraud by the federal government. Chapter 2 laid bare the ongoing cover-up of the 1969 murder of Gloria Levina Moody, exposing suspicious deaths among the suspects, violent fates for officers who challenged the closed-case narrative, and a settler family with deep RCMP ties working to present themselves as heroes. Chapter 3 interrogated the archive to bring to light other possibilities in the closed case of the murder of Fred/FC/Fredrika/Beyoncé Martinez, presenting the potential suppression of evidence in the courtroom and the possibility that the convicted man was released from prison outside the bounds of state statutes. Chapter 4 presented the many layers of the ongoing cover-up of the murder of Ernestina Ascension, showing the potential destruction of evidence and tampering with state records to protect the assailants. Lastly, Chapter 5 called forth the closed case of the murder of Savanna LaFontaine-Greywind and the abduction of her baby, showing state actions that protected the assailants, with even the state supreme court saving one assailant from life in prison.

In these five chapters, the crime itself operates as the first wave of violence. The second wave arrives in cover-ups, tampered records, delayed requests, redactions, and the heroic narratives settlers craft for themselves. Committed afterward by the state, these secondary acts are framed as closure but often constitute separate crimes and bury the evidence. Bureaucratic systems routinely weaponize inefficiency to obstruct access to public records, as occurred in this case. Archivists and clerks delayed responses, refused to disclose inventory, and cited arcane procedures to block information requests. This exemplifies institutional gatekeeping that protects state narratives.

The system's power lies in its relentless, faceless operation against all who encounter it. These tactics manifest as delays that seemed calculated and can last weeks, months, and even years. Responses to records request might never arrive, even when the requested files are digital and could be transmitted in minutes. This pattern extends to systemic data extraction: Mandatory request forms collect IP addresses, physical addresses, and phone numbers. Such delays represent not inefficiency but intentional obstruction, denying families crucial information through bureaucratic warfare. Most family members endure significant harm when navigating the barrage of rules and procedures to access records about their loved ones.

The obstruction can transcend delay and escalate. Government agencies can provide records that are electronically inert, unusable, or contain corrupted headers. The weaponization of official records, potentially transforming documents meant for public accountability into digital threats, marks a profound corruption of the archival process. Turning records into viruses moves beyond gatekeeping into counterintelligence, where the very act of seeking evidence meets narrative warfare of a different kind.

Bureaucrats wield gatekeeping as a tool of control, enforcing a clear doctrine in which access to public records requires endorsement of state narratives. This expectation was made plain when a documentarian advised me that befriending police was a necessary step for obtaining materials. The state possesses no legal right to vet recipients, curate documents for release, or mandate engagement with its agents as a condition of access.

What bureaucrats can do with records, officers can do with bodies. Both can operate with impunity under the same logic. During the 2024 raid of Hind's Hall at Columbia University in New York City, a police officer simulated sexual assault against a detained woman, and in San Diego in 2023, police officer Anthony Hair intentionally locked himself in his car with a handcuffed woman after climbing into the backseat with her and turning off his body camera. They were only able to exit the car when another officer arrived to unlock the doors. These two examples from thousands function as expressions of the same ethos that treats bodies and information as territories to be dominated.[1]

Structural misogyny and racism ensure that Native women and Two-Spirit people remain the primary targets of genocidal logic. While public attention has waned since the peak of the movement to expose and end the crisis of missing and murdered Indigenous women and Two-Spirit people reached its peak around 2017, the emotional and communal toll of both historical and ongoing cases remains acute. Families are left navigating unresolved grief without answers, not due to a lack of evidence but because of systemic indifference. Social media posts garner little traction; interest rarely extends beyond affected Native communities and kin.

This work, however, confronts a powerful and pervasive form of ideological resistance. Dismissal recites itself like catechism. After a talk I gave at a women's college, a male professor shrugged, "It's sad. So what?" At an elite high school, a white woman teacher interrupted me during the lecture to interject, "But were they sex workers?" A prestigious university press editorial board reviewed my manuscript and asked if the book was a manual based on their interpretation of its title. These questions represent tactics: grief dismissed, the cruelty of settler violence mocked. In this climate of erasure, linking the crisis explicitly to legal structures becomes not just academic, but essential.

This system cannot solve the crisis it engineered. Even the archive showed itself to be a crime scene. The receipts of this violence exist, not as lost evidence but as actively suppressed testimony. This book unearthed them. They are now a matter of record.

Evidence alone cannot shift the narrative logic. But assembled, parsed, and read against the grain, it can light the way toward new narratives, narratives that stop settlers from getting away with murder.

ACKNOWLEDGMENTS

I want to first thank the families. Their testimony, witness, and research are the basis of all work on missing and murdered Indigenous people. All work starts with them. This book is because of them and for them.

Everything in chapter 2 stems from the knowledge, research, and expertise of Vanessa Moody Hans, daughter of Gloria Levina Moody. She shared records and notes from her meetings with RCMP officers, E-Pana, and her extensive research on the suspects and the Brecknocks. As a genealogist, researcher, and teacher, Hans devoted years to assembling information on the intricate relationships between the individuals in this chapter. Although this chapter contains dozens of endnotes and records, everything started with Vanessa Hans. I knew where to look and what to look for in the government archives because of her diligence and shared knowledge. I thank her and am honored she shared her knowledge with me.

I want to thank those who funded this project: Harvard Kennedy School and the Carr-Ryan Center for Human Rights graciously provided a fellowship at a key moment in the book project. The support I received there refined the project and propelled it into its final iteration. The Institute of American Cultures and the American Indian Studies Center at University of California, Los Angeles provided a fellowship at the crucial beginning stages of the research and provided the early framing of the project and initial interviews. The Institute for Advanced Study at Indiana University provided funding for research travel that was essential to the project and sustained the research.

I want to thank Beacon Press for believing in the book, especially my editor, Gayatri Patnaik.

I would also like to thank the Cherokee Scholars Group for their engagement, mentorship, and support. Thank you to my colleagues at Indiana University in the History Department, the Program in Native American and Indigenous Studies, and the First Nations Educational and Cultural Center for their collegial support and for fostering a stimulating intellectual environment: Judith Allen, Nicky Belle, Andy Bruno, Maria Bucur, Cara Caddoo, Thomas Chan, Andrea Sullivan Clarke, Nick Cullather, Deborah Delyannis, Arlene Diaz, Konstantine Dierks, Michael Dodson, Colin Elliott, Jennifer Foray, Janine Giordano-Drake, Sara Gregg, Clare Griffin, Peter Guardino, John Hanson, Ke Chin Hsia, Michael Ing, Sherene Ing, Karen Inouye, Carl Ipsen, Ben Irvin, Sarah Knott, Lara Kriegel, Alex Lichenstein, Pedro Machado, Michael McGerr, Jason McGraw, Juan Mora, Michelle Moyd, Amrita Myers, David Nichols, John Nieto-Phillips, Scott O'Bryan, Carolina Ortega, Roberta Pergher, Amy Ransford, Eric Robinson, Julia Roos, Mark Roseman, Tatiana Saburova, Eric Sandweiss, Jonathan Schlesinger, Leah Shopkow, Micol Siegel, Rebecca Spang, Fei Hsien Wang, Jakobi Williams, and Ellen Wu.

And a big thanks to the faculty, attorneys, and survivor family members who engaged with the project by reading, reflecting, discussing, replying, and bringing me out for talks, including Randall Akee, Gloria Allred, Karen Anderson, Desmond Ang, Steve Aron, Angelita Baeyens, Davarian Baldwin, Zada Ballew, Simon Balto, Cesar Barreras, Susan Bernardin, Ashlee Bird, Ned Blackhawk, Christine Bold, Amanda Takes War Bonnett, Kirby Brown, Kevin Bruyneel, Jodi Byrd, Cathleen Cahill, Colin Calloway, Luis Carcamo-Huechante, Marc Carpenter, Brenda Child, David Cornsilk, Amber Dean, Sarah Deer, Lucia Rafael de La Madrid, Adrian De Leon, David Shorter Delgado, Phil Deloria, Natalia De Marinis, Ashley Dequilla, Bill Deverell, Vicente Diaz, Alan Shane Dillingham, Rachel Dolan, Michael Thomas Ducey, Nick Estes, Freda Fair, Max Felker-Kantor, Johanna Fernandez, Darrell Redleaf Fielder, Estelle Freedman, Balraj Gill, Dina Gilio-Whitaker, Mishuana Goeman, Tao Leigh Goffe, Jennifer Graber, Robin Gray, Norberta Greywind, Wolf Gruner, Lauren Gutterman, Vanessa Moody Hans, Jeannette Haynes, Kelly Lytle Hernandez, Rosalva Aida Hernandez-Castillo, Elizabeth Hinton, Hi'ilei

Julia Kawehipuaakahaopulani Hobart, Anne Hyde, Usha Iyer, Michelle Jacob, Margaret Jacobs, Cat Jacquet, Joanne Jahnke-Wegner, Susan Johnson, Daniel Heath Justice, Amy Aisen Kallender, Regina Kunzel, Therese La Framboise, Mike Lambert, Jonathan Leal, Courtney Lewis, Patricia Nelson Limerick, David Palumbo Liu, Annita Lucchessi, Emanuele Lugli, Will Mack, Benjamin Madley, Nancy Marie-Mithlo, Lena Martinez, Michael McEachrane, Lucia Melgar, Inî Mendoza, Max Mishler, Pauline Mitchell, Maria Montoya, Dave Moody, Dean Moody, Marissa Moorman, Donna Murch, Mary Kathryn Nagel, Andrew Needham, Gene Norris, Jean O'Brien, John Peters-Campbell, Chris Pexa, Joseph Pierce, Eve M. Troutt Powell, Michael Ralph, Renya Ramirez, Sherene Razack, Karyn Recollet, Julie Reed, Mathias Risse, Jonathan Rodacay, Barbara Yllán Rondero, Jason Ruiz, Douglas Sackman, Claudio Saunt, Ellen Scott, Audra Simpson, Greg Smithers, Shannon Speed, Angela Spencer, Alexandra Stern, Corey Still, Rachel St. John, Rose Stremlau, Martha Stroud, Christopher Teuton, Brianna Theobald, Heather Ann Thompson, Coll Thrush, Mark Trahant, Libby Tronnes, Lauren Van Shilfgarde, Kiara Vigil, Yona Wade, Katie Walciexwz, Robert Warrior, Sharmaine Weed, Richard White, Hajar Yazdiha, and Melanie Yazzie.

To my friends and family, your love and devotion carried me through.

NOTES

INTRODUCTION

1. Eve Tuck, "Suspending Damage: A Letter to Communities," *Harvard Educational Review* 79, no. 3 (2009): 409–27.

2. Michel-Rolph Trouillot, *Silencing the Past: Power and the Production of History* (Beacon Press, 1995); Nuar Alsadir, *Fourth Person Singular* (Liverpool University Press, 2017).

3. Audra Simpson, "The State Is a Man: Theresa Spence, Loretta Saunders, and the Gender of Settler Sovereignty," *Theory and Event* 19, no. 4 (2016), https://muse.jhu.edu/article/633280.

4. Stephanie Rose Monesanti and Wilfreda E. Thurston, "Mapping the Role of Structural and Interpersonal Violence in the Lives of Women: Implications for Public Health Interventions and Policy," *BMC Women's Health* 15, no. 100 (2015), https://doi.org/10.1186/s12905-015-0256-4; Slavoj Žižek, *Violence: Six Sideways Reflections* (Picador Press, 2008), 14.

5. Billy-Ray Belcourt, "Can the Other of Native Studies Speak?" *Decolonization* (blog), Feb. 1, 2016, https://decolonization.wordpress.com/2016/02/01/can-the-other-of-native-studies-speak/; Simpson, "The State Is a Man"; Sierra Crane Murdoch, *Yellow Bird: Oil, Murder, and a Woman's Search for Justice in Indian Country* (Random House, 2020).

6. André B. Rosay, *Violence Against American Indian and Alaska Native Women and Men: 2010 Findings from the National Intimate Partner and Sexual Violence Survey* (US Department of Justice, National Institute of Justice, 2016), https://nij.ojp.gov/library/publications/violence-against-american-indian-and-alaska-native-women-and-men-2010-findings.

7. Sherene Razack, *Dying of Improvement: Inquests and Inquiries into Indigenous Deaths in Custody* (University of Toronto Press, 2015), 6.

8. Maggie Blackhawk, "Federal Indian Law as Paradigm Within Public Law," *Harvard Law Review* 132, no. 7 (May 2019): 1791–877.

9. Sarah Deer, *The Beginning and End of Rape: Confronting Sexual Violence in Native America* (University of Minnesota Press, 2015); Sylvia Van Kirk, *Many Tender Ties: Women in Fur Trade Society, 1670–1870* (Oxford University Press, 1983); Jean Barman, *French Canadians, Furs, and Indigenous Women in the Making of the Pacific Northwest* (University of British Columbia Press, 2015).

10. Ned Blackhawk, "'I Can Carry On from Here': The Relocation of American Indians to Los Angeles," *Wíčazo Ša* Review 11, no. 2 (Fall 1995): 16–30; Nicolas Rosenthal, *Reimagining Indian Country: Native American Migration and Identity in Twentieth-Century Los Angeles* (University of North Carolina Press, 2012).

11. Shannon Speed, *Incarcerated Stories: Indigenous Women Migrants and Violence in the Settler-Capitalist State* (University of North Carolina Press, 2019); Shannon Speed, "Public Comments," Theorizing Violence Against Indigenous Women, UCLA Law Library, Los Angeles, Mar. 8, 2023; Linda Tuhiwai Smith, *Decolonizing Methodologies: Research and Indigenous Peoples* (Zed, 1999), 24; Haley Duschinski et al., eds., *Resisting Occupation in Kashmir* (University of Pennsylvania Press, 2018); Mona Bhan and Haley Duschinski, "Occupations in Context—The Cultural Logics of Occupation, Settler Violence, and Resistance," *Critique of Anthropology* 40, no. 3 (2020): 285–97; Kelly Lytle Hernández, *City of Inmates: Conquest, Rebellion, and the Rise of Human Caging in Los Angeles, 1771–1965* (University of North Carolina Press, 2017).

12. Gwen Ifill is credited with coining the term "missing white woman syndrome" at the 2004 Unity: Journalists of Color conference, held Aug. 4–7 at the Washington, DC, Convention Center. See Gwen Ifill, "User Clip: Gwen Ifill Coins the Term 'Missing White Woman Syndrome,'" C-SPAN, Aug. 5, 2004, https://www.c-span.org/video/?c4666788/user-clip-gwen-ifill-coins-term-missing-white-woman-syndrome.

13. Jo-Marie Burt, "Military Officers Convicted in Landmark Sepur Zarco Sexual Violence Case," *International Justice Monitor*, Mar. 4, 2016, https://www.ijmonitor.org/2016/03/military-officers-convicted-in-landmark-sepur-zarco-sexual-violence-case/; "Guatemala Paramilitaries Sentenced for Raping Indigenous Women," *Al Jazeera*, Jan. 25, 2022, https://www.aljazeera.com/news/2022/1/25/guatemala-five-ex-paramilitary-members-sentenced-for-rape.

14. *Who Killed Alberta Williams* (CBC, 2018), audio podcast; *Missing and Murdered: Finding Cleo* (CBC, 2018), audio podcast; *Stolen: The Search for Jermain* (Gimlet Media, 2020), audio podcast; *Stolen: Surviving St. Michael's* (Spotify, 2022), audio podcast; *Stolen: Trouble in Sweetwater* (Gimlet Media, 2023), audio podcast.

15. I am thinking especially here of *Highway of Tears*, directed by Matt Smiley (2015). Although he had many interviews with First Nations peoples, the film is edited such that the narrative reads like victim blaming. This is less true of *Finding Dawn* (2006), directed by Christine Welsh, a film with many Native participants and tribal history but also very little sense of who the assailants are in terms of their ethnic, gender, and sexual identities.

16. Audra Simpson, "Consent's Revenge," *Cultural Anthropology* 31, no. 3 (2016): 326–33, https://journal.culanth.org/index.php/ca/article/view/ca31.3.02; Eve Tuck, "Suspending Damage: A Letter to Communities," *Harvard Educational Review* 79, no. 3 (Fall 2009): 409–28; Aileen Moreton-Robinson, *The White Possessive: Property, Power and Indigenous Sovereignty* (University of Minnesota Press, 2015); Max Liboiron, *Pollution Is Colonialism* (Duke University Press, 2021).

17. Shawn Wilson, *Research Is Ceremony: Indigenous Research Methods* (Fernwood, 2008); Lauren Tynan, "What Is Relationality? Indigenous Knowledges, Practices, and Responsibilities with Kin," *Cultural Geographies* 28, no. 4 (2021): 597–610.

18. Sherene Razack, "Keynote Address," Theorizing Violence Against Indigenous Women, UCLA Law Library, Los Angeles, Mar. 8, 2023.

CHAPTER 1: LYDIA

1. Personal conversation with David Cornsilk, Oct. 13, 2023.

2. Personal conversation with Cornsilk.

3. Personal conversation with Cornsilk.

4. Personal conversation with Cornsilk.

5. Cherokee County Clerk Land Records, Book 21, 87; Book 4, 561–62; Book 6, 575; Book 66, 449; Book 21, 87; Book 66, 449; Book 85, 8; Book 94, 71; Book 106, 504; Oklahoma and Indian Territory, US, Land Allotment Jackets for Five Civilized Tribes, 1884–1934; "Application for Allotment," Julia A. Thorne, May 18, 190[illegible], Ancestry.com, https://www.ancestry.com/discoveryui-content/view/13444:3999?tid=&pid=&queryId=fb2a7520-5e12-48a6-935b-c218dc53891b&_phsrc=Blf19&_phstart=successSource; personal conversation with Cornsilk; "Florence Blackbird Lyman Obituary," Dignity Memorial, https://www.dignitymemorial.com/obituaries/tahlequah-ok/florence-blackbird-lyman-10793725. For many other examples of Native women and girls in Oklahoma being swindled and coerced out of their land, see Zitkála-Šа (writing as Gertrude Bonnin) et al., *Oklahoma's Poor Rich Indians: An Orgy of Graft and Exploitation of the Five Civilized Tribes—Legalized Robbery* (Office of the Indian Rights Association, 1924), https://digitalprairie.ok.gov/digital/collection/culture/id/6553/.

6. "Frank Griffin Injured in Auto Accident," *Cherokee County Democrat-Star*, Mar. 4, 1932, 5; "Commissioners Proceedings," *Tahlequah Citizen*, Sept. 19, 1935, 7.

7. "Application for Allotment and Homestead, Department of the Interior, Commission to the Five Civilized Tribes, Cherokee Land Office," Aug. 20, 1903; "Bill of Sale, John Kingfisher to J. M. Warwick," 1903; "Order for Removal of Restrictions, Department of the Interior," Nov. 11, 1909; "Enrollment and Allotment Record for John W. Kingfisher, Memorandum for Official Use," n.d., Oklahoma Historical Society Records.

8. Oklahoma and Indian Territory, US, Land Allotment Jackets for Five Civilized Tribes, 1884–1934, Ancestry.com, https://www.ancestry.com/discoveryui-content/view/14985:3999?tid=&pid=&queryId=e9cf96e3-64ac-4f7f-8c6a-8960b374a936&_phsrc=xEm23&_phstart=successSource.

9. "13th Census of the United States: 1910—Indian Population," sheet 6, Supervisor's District 3, Enumeration District 55, Apr. 29, 1910, Saline Township, Delaware County, OK, Ancestry.com, https://www.ancestry.com/discoveryui-content/view/17591 5287:7884?ssrc=pt&tid=170525194&pid=402210192598; "Fourteenth Census of the United States: 1920—Population," sheet 8, Supervisor's District 2, Enumeration District 16, Jan. 26, 1920, Moodys Township,

Cherokee County, OK, Ancestry.com, https://www.ancestry.com/imageviewe /collections/6061/images/4384914_00907?pId=98774422.

10. Cherokee County Clerk Land Records, Book 42, 311.

11. Felix Ross, "Twelfth Census of the United States: 1900 Schedule—Population, Indian Population, Schedule 1, Enumeration District 29," Ancestry.com; John Blackbird, "Arbitrary Allotment," Feb. 3, 1906, in Oklahoma and Indian Territory, US, Land Allotment Jackets for Five Civilized Tribes, 1884–1934, Ancestry.com; *Tahlequah Arrow*, Jan. 1, 1909, 8; *Tahlequah Arrow*, Nov. 24, 1900, 2; *Tahlequah Arrow*, Feb. 9, 1907, 2; Grant Foreman, *Students of Cherokee Male Seminary, 1876–1909* (Star Printery, 1914), accessed via Oklahoma Historical Society Digital Collections, https://www .okhistory.org/research/digital/foremantrans/foreman.sup15.pdf.

12. "Arch Christie Attacked by Knife Toter," *Cherokee County Democrat-Star*, Aug. 23, 1935, 1.

13. John Blackbird, Allotment Packet, Record of Land Sales; "Fifteenth Census of the United States: 1930—Population," Ancestry.com; Department of the Interior, letter regarding allotment records, July 30, 1942; *Tahlequah Citizen*, Feb. 22, 1934, 1; Fairfax Chief, Apr. 22, 1937, 5; *Indian Journal*, Nov. 11, 1937, 2.

14. Personal conversation with Lydia's descendants: confidential (Feb. 1, 2024) and confidential (Mar. 20, 2023).

15. Crosslin Fields Smith, *Stand as One: Spiritual Teachings of Keetoowah* (Dog Soldier Press, 2021); Georgia Rae Leeds, *The United Keetoowah Band of Cherokee Indians in Oklahoma* (Peter Lang, 1996).

16. Sowande' M. Mustakeem, *Slavery at Sea: Terror, Sex, and Sickness in the Middle Passage* (University of Illinois Press, 2016), 153; Lauren Benton, "This Melancholy Labyrinth: The Trial of Arthur Hodge and the Boundaries of Imperial Law," *Alabama Law Review* 64, no. 1 (2012): 91–122. Theodore Dwight Weld, Angelina Grimké Weld, and Sarah Grimké describe a slave owner who would tie down an enslaved person and strike them with a paddle dipped in hot water to raise "whelks" on their skin as a common punishment for running away. See Theodore Dwight Weld et al., *American Slavery as It Is: Testimony of a Thousand Witnesses* (American Anti-Slavery Society, 1839), 120. On US soldiers using water to simulate drowning on Filipino soldiers, see Stuart Creighton Miller, *Benevolent Assimilation: The American Conquest of the Philippines, 1899–1903* (Yale University Press, 1982); Brian Linn, *The Philippine War: 1899–1902* (University Press of Kansas, 2000); and US Senate, *Affairs in the Philippine Islands: Hearings Before the Committee on the Philippines of the United States Senate* (Government Printing Office, 1902), 1556.

17. Diane Glancy, *Fort Marion Prisoners and the Trauma of Native Education* (University of Nebraska Press, 2014); Stephen C. Richards, "USP Marion: The First Federal Supermax," *Prison Journal* 88, no. 1 (Mar. 2008): 6–22.

18. Emmet Starr, *History of the Cherokee Indians and Their Legends and Folk Lore* (Warden, 1921); Donna J. Myers, *The Nighthawk Keetoowah Society: Symbols of Identity* (University of Oklahoma Press, 2017).

19. "A Murderer Captured," *Muskogee Evening Times*, July 30, 1903, 4; "Rattlingourd Arrested," *Tahlequah Arrow*, Aug. 1, 1903, 4; "Got Mr. Rattlingourd," *Fort Smith Times*, Aug. 4, 1903, 5; "At the Jail," *Vinita Daily Chieftain*, Aug. 5, 1903, 4; "Territorial Topics," *McAlester (OK) Capital*, Aug. 13, 1903, 6. Personal conversation with descendant of Looney Rattling Gourd's sister, Elizabeth Bird, Aug. 14, 2020.

20. Personal correspondence with Barbara Rust, lead archivist, National Archives, Washington, DC, Aug. 10, 2020; personal correspondence with Ketina Taylor, archivist, National Archives, Fort Worth, TX, Aug. 6, 2020; personal correspondence with Melissa Johnson, archivist, National Archives, Fort Worth, TX, Aug. 10, 2020; personal conversation with Kristin McCall Ryals and Linda Christie McCall, descendants of Sunday Christie, Apr. 5, 2023.

21. Tulsa County Clerk Land Records, "Oil and Gas Lease Record," book 1, p. 79 (Nov. 20, 1903), https://acclaim.tulsacounty.org/AcclaimWeb.

22. Cherokee County Clerk Land Records, book 6, p. 575; "Allotment Packet for Sunday Christie," Oklahoma and Indian Territory, US, Land Allotment Jackets for Five Civilized Tribes, 1884–1934, Ancestry.com; "Allotment Packet for Jennie Christie," Oklahoma and Indian Territory, US, Land Allotment Jackets for Five Civilized Tribes, 1884–1934, Ancestry.com; "Legal Notices," *Tahlequah Arrow*, Jan. 1, 1909, 8.

23. "Fourteenth Census of the United States: 1920—Population," record for Jennie Christie, Enumeration District 11, Grandview Township, Ancestry.com. Jennie Christie is listed as unable to read or write English; "Form No. 584, Letters of Administration," appointing Curtis E. Holderman as guardian for the deceased Sunday Christie by Judge William R. Lawrence, June 25, 1904, Tahlequah, Indian Territory, US Northern District, in Oklahoma and Indian Territory, US, Land Allotment Jackets for Five Civilized Tribes, 1884–1934, Ancestry.com, https://www.ancestry.com/discoveryui-content/view/25650:3999?tid=&pid=&queryId=f63a0439-a877-459f-96ce-aab3cec6167d&_phsrc=gUO1&_phstart=successSource; Department of the Interior, Commissioner to the Five Civilized Tribes, Cherokee Land Office, Tahlequah, Indian Territory, Cherokee Allotment Contest no. 3533, Jack R. Gourd by Samuel C. Pitts v. Daniel Christie, a minor, confessional of judgment signed by Jennie Christie (by mark), witnessed by Lorraine DeGroot and Veronica Harnage, filed Nov. 21, 1905, approved Dec. 13, 1906, by Tams Bixby, Commissioner in Oklahoma and Indian Territory, US, Land Allotment Jackets for Five Civilized Tribes, 1884–1934, Ancestry.com, https://www.ancestry.com/discoveryui-content/view/25650:3999?tid=&pid=&queryId=f63a0439-a877-459f-96ce-aab3cec6167d&_phsrc=gUO1&_phstart=successSource; "Sales Record for Jennie Christie, denied Feb. 5, 1918, Department of the Interior, US Northern District, in Oklahoma, US, Indian Land Allotment Sales, 1908–1927, Ancestry.com; "Notice of Guardian's Sale of Real Estate for Pearl Watie," *Welch Watchman*, June 24, 1909, 4; "Notice of Guardian to Lease," *Nowata Times*, Oct. 6, 1905, 5; "Notice of Guardian's Sale of Real Estate for Albert Watie," *Welch Watchman*, June 24, 1909, 4; "Guardianship of Elnora Keys," *Muskogee Times-Democrat*, July 13, 1910, 3; "Mrs. S. C. Pitts Dead," *Muskogee Daily Phoenix and Times-Democrat*, Dec. 4, 1918, 7; "Vote for a Winner,

S. C. Pitts, a Democrat for County Clerk," *Muskogee Times-Democrat*, July 25, 1914, 16; "Vote for a Winner: S. C. Pitts," *Boynton Index*, July 24, 1914; "Pitts for Register of Deeds," *Braggs Bugle*, May 30, 1912, 1; "S. C. Pitts Makes Statement," *Jay Record*, July 16, 1924, 1; "William Glory, Real Estate Sale," *Weekly Examiner*, Feb. 19, 1909, 3.

24. "Application for Allotment and Homestead," Looney R. Gourd, no. 21382, signed by George Benge, "Attorney in Fact," Aug. 6, 1903, Department of the Interior, Commission to the Five Civilized Tribes, Cherokee Land Office, in Oklahoma and Indian Territory, US, Land Allotment Jackets for Five Civilized Tribes, 1884–1934, Ancestry.com, https://www.ancestry.com/discoveryui-content/view/14985:3999?tid=&pid=&queryId=e9cf96e3-64ac-4f7f-8c6a-8960b374a936&_phsrc=xEm23&_phstart=successSource. For map, see Cherokee Nation Indian Territory Map (Indian Territory Map Co., 1909), Library of Congress, https://www.loc.gov/resource/g4021gm.gla00497/?st=gallery. On Rattling Gourd's delinquent taxes, see *Cherokee County Democrat-Star*, Oct. 17, 1940, 10.

25. Rebecca Nagle, host, featuring Matthew Fletcher (guest), *This Land*, episode 3, "The Opposition," Crooked Media, June 17, 2019, https://crooked.com/podcast/this-land-episode-3-the-opposition/. On Judge Gill's purchases of land from recent allottees, the guardians of others, and the children he held guardianships over, see Craig County Clerk Land Records: book 39, p. 247; book 20, p. 451; book 35, p. 480; book 149, pp. 420–21; book 15, p. 68; book 24, p. 283; book 80, pp. 215–17; book 90, p. 609; book 50, p. 108; book 50, p. 367; book 3, pp. 577–78; book 15, p. 426; book F, p. 237; book 149, pp. 416–17; book 156, pp. 735–36; book 24, p. 214.

26. "The fact early developed that fullblood or over half breed Indians sent to the U.S. prison at Leavenworth for a term of four or more years, either died or returned home, stricken with tuberculosis and for this reason Judge Gill and other U.S. Judges in Indian Territory always gave the Indians the benefit of the doubt and made the sentence as light as possible feeling that a five or ten year term usually meant in reality a death sentence." See Clarence Brown Douglas, *Some Men of Tulsa* (Dexter Publishing, 1922), 27.

27. Tulsa County Clerk Land Records, "Oil and Gas Lease Record," book 1, p. 79 (Nov. 20, 1903), https://acclaim.tulsacounty.org/AcclaimWeb; Sam Mitrani, *The Rise of the Chicago Police Department: Class and Conflict, 1850–1894* (University of Illinois Press, 2013).

28. "Prison Record for Looney Rattling Gourd (No. 4044)," National Archives at Kansas City, MO, received in digital form by author Aug. 6, 2020.

29. "Prison Record for Jack Downing (No. 4303)," National Archives at Kansas City, MO, received in digital form by author July 25, 2025; *Tahlequah Arrow*, Aug. 6, 1904, 1.

30. "Ask Pardon for Jack Downing," *Muskogee Times-Democrat*, Feb. 16, 1916, 2.

31. Timothy Wilcox, archivist, National Archives at Kansas City, email to author, Sept. 5, 2025, regarding search for Jack Downing (Teekahlanneesky). The search was conducted in Record Group 21, Records of the US District Court for the Indian Territory, Northern District (Vinita), specifically in the

series "Name Index–Criminal Case Files, 1894–1907" (OKTN33A), "Criminal Bench Dockets, 1889–1908," and "Judgments and Sentences Relating to Criminal Cases, 1890–1907." No record for Jack Downing or Looney Rattling Gourd was found in any of these series. This confirms earlier correspondence with the National Archives in Washington, DC, which also found no trial records for Looney Rattling Gourd or Jack Teekahlanneesky (Downing) in its holdings. See also Barbara Rust, lead archivist, National Archives at Washington, DC, email to author, Aug. 10, 2020; Ketina Taylor, archivist, National Archives at Fort Worth, TX, email to author, Aug. 6, 2020; Melissa Johnson, archivist, National Archives at Fort Worth, TX, email to author, Aug. 10, 2020; all in possession of the author.

32. "Special Letters," "Letters Sent," and "Letters Received," in Prison Record for Looney Ratting Gourd (no. 4044), National Archives at Kansas City, MO, received by author Aug. 6, 2020.

33. "Letter from George W. Benge to Major McClaughry," Feb. 28, 1906; "Letter from Major McClaughry to George W. Benge," Mar. 3, 1906; "Letter from George W. Benge to Major McClaughry," Aug. 31, 1906; "Letter from Major McClaughry to George W. Benge," Sept. 7, 1906, in Prison Record for Looney Ratting Gourd (no. 4044), National Archives at Kansas City, MO, received Aug. 6, 2020; Tulsa County Clerk. Land Records, "Oil and Gas Lease Record," Nov. 20, 1903, book 1, p. 79.

34. "Letter from George W. Benge to Major McClaughry," Sept. 10, 1906, in Prison Record for Looney Ratting Gourd (no. 4044), National Archives at Kansas City, MO, received Aug. 6, 2020.

35. "Letter from Major McClaughry to George W. Benge," Sept. 14, 1906, in Prison Record for Looney Ratting Gourd (no. 4044), National Archives at Kansas City, MO, received Aug. 6, 2020.

36. "Letter from Major McClaughry to Dana H. Kelsey, U.S. Indian Agent," Dec. 20, 1906, Prison Record for Looney Ratting Gourd (no. 4044), in National Archives at Kansas City, MO, received Aug. 6, 2020.

37. Tulsa County Clerk, Land Records, "Release," Feb. 18, 1908, book 41, p. 50; "Release," Mar. 10, 1908, book 41, p. 261; "Cherokee Allotment Deed," Mar. 31, 1908, book GG, p. 310; "Letter from Major McClaughry to Dana Kelsey, Indian Agent," Mar. 19, 1909, in Prison Record for Looney Ratting Gourd (no. 4044), in National Archives at Kansas City, MO, received Aug. 6, 2020.

38. "Letter from Dana Kelsey to Major McClaughry," Apr. 1, 1909, in Prison Record for Looney Ratting Gourd (no. 4044) in National Archives at Kansas City, Missouri, received by author Aug. 6, 2020; Tulsa County Clerk, Land Records, "Oil and Gas Mining Lease Upon Land Selected," May 19, 1909, book 53, p. 26.

39. "Letter from Major McClaughry to Dana Kelsey, U.S. Indian Agent," Aug. 4, 1910; "Letter from Major McClaughry to First National Bank in Leavenworth, Kansas," Sept. 21, 1910, in Prison Record for Looney Ratting Gourd (no. 4044), National Archives at Kansas City, MO, received by author Aug. 6, 2020.

40. "Letter from Major McClaughry to Mr. Looney R. Gourd, Gideon, Oklahoma," Nov. 25, 1910, in Prison Record for Looney Ratting Gourd (no. 4044) in National Archives at Kansas City, Missouri, received by author Aug. 6, 2020.

41. Oklahoma, US, County Marriage Records, 1890–1995, Cherokee County, "Marriage License, Lucinda Ketcher and Looney R. Gourd," June 29, 1912, County Court; "Fourteenth Census of the United States: 1920—Population," enumeration district 22, sheet 9A, Crittenden Township, Cherokee County, OK; "Fifteenth Census of the United States: 1930—Population," enumeration districts 11–14, sheet 7B, Peggs Township, Cherokee County, Ancestry.com; Lucinda Ketcher Rattling Gourd Grave, Swimmer Cemetery, Lost City, OK.

42. "List of Land Holdings," May 11, 1929, Department of the Interior in Oklahoma and Indian Territory, US Land Allotment Jackets for Five Civilized Tribes, 1884–1934, Ancestry.com; Tulsa County Clerk Land Records, "Oil and Gas Mining Lease Upon Land Selected," May 19, 1909, book 53, p. 26; book 441, p. 104 (1923); "Form A. Series 1908—Approved April 20, 1908, Amended February 6, and June 29, 1911," book 451, p. 323; "Release of Oil and Gas Lease," Apr. 10, 1923, book 977, p. 450; "Right of Way Deed," Feb. 8, 1932, book 1024, p. 565.

43. Personal conversation with confidential descendant of Looney Rattling Gourd, Nov. 11, 2020; Tulsa County Clerk Land Records, "Certificate Designating Lands Exempt from Taxation," June 21, 1949, book 2004, p. 183; "Certificate 2 Designating Lands Exempt from Taxation, Five Civilized Tribes, May 11, 1929," book 913, p. 476; *Tahlequah Citizen*, Mar. 11, 1937, 7; *Tulsa Daily Legal News*, Aug. 6, 1941; *Tahlequah Star-Citizen*, Dec. 23, 1948, 2; *Tahlequah Star-Citizen*, Dec. 8, 1949, 6; "Heirship of Adair County Land Will Be Determined," *Muskogee Times-Democrat*, Feb. 26, 1943, 3. On lawsuits after his death, see *Bartlesville Record*, Nov. 22, 1956, 7; *Bartlesville Examiner-Enterprise*, Apr. 17, 1963, 12; *Bartlesville Examiner-Enterprise*, Apr. 10, 1963, 12. For Washington County land records 1919–51, see Washington County Clerk Land Records, book 8, p. 256 (June 28, 1919); book misc. 41, p. 489 (Nov. 17, 1921); book 102, p. 25 (July 14, 1930); book 104, p. 606 (Mar. 11, 1931); book 225, p. 95 (July 15, 1949); book 256, p. 162 (Aug. 31, 1951). On the 1967 lawsuit, see book 513, pp. 422, 424, and 427.

44. Personal conversation with descendant of Looney Rattling Gourd's sister, Elizabeth Bird, Aug. 21, 2020.

45. On Val Lopez, see Renya Ramirez and Val Lopez, "Toppling Mission Monuments and Mythologies Conference," Critical Mission Studies, posted Aug. 13, 2020, YouTube, 21 min., 53 sec., https://www.youtube.com/watch?v=B5_GRq4moVo; Heidi Kiiwetinepinesiik Stark, "Criminal Empire: The Making of the Savage in a Lawless Land," *Theory and Event* 19, no. 4 (2016), Project Muse, https://muse-jhu-edu.proxyiub.uits.iu.edu/pub/1/article/633282.

46. Vine Deloria, *Custer Died for Your Sins: An Indian Manifesto* (Macmillan, 1969), 35; Robert Nichols, *Theft Is Property! Dispossession and Critical Theory* (Duke University Press, 2020), 9; Luana Ross, *Inventing the Savage: The Social Construction of Native American Criminality* (University of Texas Press, 1998).

47. Shiri Pasternak, *Grounded Authority: The Algonquins of Barriere Lake Against the State* (University of Minnesota Press, 2017), 3; Jasbir K. Puar, *The Right to Maim: Debility, Capacity, Disability* (Duke University Press, 2017), xviii.

48. Rose Stremlau, *Sustaining the Cherokee Family: Kinship and the Allotment of an Indigenous Nation* (University of North Carolina Press, 2011), 34.

49. Bonnin et al., *Oklahoma's Poor Rich Indians*, 5; Aileen Moreton-Robinson, *The White Possessive: Property, Power, and Indigenous Sovereignty* (University of Minnesota Press, 2015), xxiii.

50. Personal conversation with confidential descendant of Looney Rattling Gourd, Aug. 27, 2020.

CHAPTER 2: LEVINA

1. In-person conversation with Dean Moody, Apr. 25 and 26, 2026, Bella Coola, British Columbia. On Levina's father's hair turning white, see Eve Lazarus, *Cold Case BC: The Stories Behind the Province's Most Intriguing Murder and Missing Person Cases* (Arsenal Pulp Press, 2022), 99. On how Dan introduced himself, see Lazarus, *Cold Case BC*, 102.

2. Personal conversation with Vanessa Moody Hans, Apr. 19, 2022, and Feb. 17, 2024; in-person conversation with Dean Moody, Apr. 25 and 26, 2026, Bella Coola, British Columbia; in-person conversation with Vanessa Moody Hans, Apr. 25 and 26, 2026, Bella Coola, British Columbia; "Healing Process Impresses Judge," *The Tribune*, Jan. 24, 1995, 1; Angela Hall, "The Final Chapter in a Brutal Murder," *Coast Mountain News*, Jan. 9, 1999, 1.

3. Judith Butler, *Precarious Life: The Powers and Mourning of Violence* (Verso, 2004). I emphasize "biological" for a reason. In Vanessa's family, and among many Nuxalk and other Indigenous people, relations extend beyond the biological. For example, the people Vanessa calls her brothers were, in terms of biological relation to Levina, her uncles. In my conversations with Vanessa, we navigated the relationship identities Vanessa grew up with and uses today alongside helping me understand how these people relate to Levina biologically, or as non-Native people do. I use "biological" here to acknowledge that Daisy was, in fact, the mother of Vanessa and Dan while Levina was, in fact, their mother too. It is important to respect the role that Daisy played as mother to Vanessa and Dan while also documenting what happened to Levina, the woman who birthed Vanessa and Dan and should have been able to raise them.

4. Angie Mindus, "Case Closed on Brutal Murder," *The Tribune*, Dec. 22, 1998, A2.

5. In-person conversation with Dean Moody, Apr. 25 and 26, 2026, Bella Coola, British Columbia; in-person conversation with Vanessa Moody Hans, Apr. 25 and 26, 2026, Bella Coola, British Columbia; in-person conversation with Karen Anderson, Apr. 25, 2026, Bella Coola, British Columbia.

6. In-person conversation with Dave Moody, Bella Coola, British Columbia, In-person conversation with Dean Moody, Apr. 25 and 26, 2026, Bella Coola, British Columbia.

7. In-person conversation with Dean Moody, Apr. 25 and 26, 2026, Bella Coola, British Columbia.

8. Audra Simpson, "The State Is a Man: Theresa Spence, Loretta Saunders and the Gender of Settler Sovereignty," *Theory and Event* 16, no. 4 (2016): 10, https://muse.jhu.edu/article/633280.

9. Personal conversation with Vanessa Moody Hans, Apr. 19, 2022, and Feb. 17, 2024.

10. Province of British Columbia, County of Cariboo, Inquest into the Death of Gloria Levina Moody, Dec. 9, 1969 (Williams Lake, BC), GR-0419 (box 1, file 5), British Columbia Coroner Archives, Victoria, BC.

11. Angela Sterritt, *Unbroken: My Fight for Survival, Hope, and Justice for Indigenous Women and Girls* (Greystone Books, 2023), 88. In conversation with the author, Vanessa added that Levina's parents called the local radio station; personal conversation with Vanessa Moody Hans, Apr. 19, 2022, and Feb. 17, 2024.

12. Inquest into the Death of Gloria Levina Moody, Dec. 9, 1969.

13. Province of British Columbia, Coroner Archives, "Autopsy Report of Gloria Levina Moody," Oct. 27, 1969, and Inquest into the Death of Gloria Levina Moody, Dec. 9, 1969.

14. On Canada's history, see Susan Roy, *These Mysterious People: Shaping History and Archaeology in a Northwest Coast Community* (McGill-Queen's University Press, 2016); Elaine Dewar, *Bones: Discovering the First Americans* (Carroll & Graf, 2002); Jisgang Nika Collison et al., *Indigenous Repatriation Handbook* (Royal BC Museum, 2019); Vanessa Tünsmeyer, *Repatriation of Sacred Indigenous Cultural Heritage and the Law* (Springer Cham, 2022); and George P. Nicholas and Thomas D. Andrews, eds., *At a Crossroads: Archaeology and First Peoples in Canada* (Simon Fraser University Archaeology Press, 2017). On the United States, see Samuel J. Redman, *Bone Rooms: From Scientific Racism to Human Prehistory in Museums* (Harvard University Press, 2016). On Cindy Gladue, see Danielle Paradis, "Family of Cindy Gladue Says Province Has 'Misplaced' Her Remains," APTN News, Apr. 14, 2023, https://www.aptnnews.ca/featured/family-of-cindy-gladue-says-province-has-misplaced-her-remains/.

15. Megan Walter et al., "Trophy, Souvenir, or Simple Theft? Taking Items from the Victim in Sexual Homicide," *Behavioral Sciences and the Law*, 42, no. 4 (2024): 338–53; Janet I. Warren et al., "Collectors: Serial Sexual Offenders Who Preserve Evidence of Their Crimes," *Aggression and Violent Behavior*, 18, no. 6 (2013): 666–72.

16. In-person conversation with Dean Moody, Apr. 25 and 26, 2026, Bella Coola, British Columbia; British Columbia, Coroner Archives, "Registration of Death for Gloria Levina Moody," Oct. 26, 1969; Inquest into the Death of Gloria Levina Moody, Dec. 9, 1969; "Autopsy Report of Gloria Levina Moody," Oct. 27, 1969.

17. Harry Rankin, "The Fred Quilt Controversey [*sic*]," *Indian News* 14, no. 10 (1972): 10, https://winnspace.uwinnipeg.ca/bitstream/handle/10680/641/Volume%2014%20Issue%2010%20%201972.pdf?sequence=1&isAllowed=y.

18. Personal conversation with Vanessa Moody Hans, Apr. 19, 2022, and Feb. 17, 2024.

19. "Inquest Adjourned in Beating Death," *Vancouver Sun*, Oct. 29, 1969, 20; Lazarus, *Cold Case Vancouver: The City's Most Baffling Unsolved Murders* (Arsenal Pulp Press, 2016), 148. Lester Evans Blake applied to the city of Williams Lake for a lease of lands near Soda Lake to build a summer cottage

in 1961. See *Government Gazette British Columbia* 101, no. 28 (July 13, 1961): 1214, BC Archives. Eugene Elmer Johnson died Oct. 3, 2014. See "Eugene Johnson," *Williams Lake Tribune*, https://www.wltribune.com/obituaries/eugene-johnson-5467682.

20. Jeremy Deutsch, "'Case Closed' on Moody a Rumour: RCMP," *The Tribune*, Oct. 23, 2007, A2; Jason Proctor, "'A Rage in His Head': RCMP Spokesman's Widow Says, 'Attacks from Within' Got to Him," *CBC News*, Nov. 27, 2018, https://www.cbc.ca/news/canada/british-columbia/pierre-lemaitre-dziekanski-1.4921919.

21. Personal conversation with Vanessa Moody Hans, Apr. 19, 2022, and Feb. 17, 2024; Sterritt, *Unbroken*, 91.

22. Based on evidence from 1989, Eve Lazarus mentions one prime suspect who she says died in 1974 (Blohm died in 1972 and Weir in 1973). Lazarus details that the RCMP visited in the late 1990s, when they said there were three suspects in Levina's RCMP file. According to the officer, all of them were dead, one in 1972, one in 1974, and one in the 1980s. See Lazarus, *Cold Case BC*, 149–57. Lazarus also discusses the police questioning of David Moody. See Lazarus, *Cold Case BC*, 146.

23. "3 Convicted of Attack," *The Vancouver Sun*, June 2, 1955, 9; "$5000 Bail Set," *The Province*, Mar. 25, 1955, 12; "Guilty Plea in Robbery," *Vancouver Sun*, Oct. 17, 1958, 2.

24. "Divorces," *The Province*, May 11, 1959, 33; "Divorces," *Vancouver Sun*, May 15, 1959, 6; personal conversation with Vanessa Moody Hans, Apr. 19, 2022, and Feb. 17, 2024.

25. British Columbia, Coroner Archives, "Registration of Death for Albert William Blohm," Sept. 8, 1972.

26. British Columbia, Coroner Archives, "Registration of Death for Albert William Blohm," Sept. 8, 1972.

27. Archival searches on Al Blohm resulted in finding Albert Blohm's brother, Andrew Blohm, a.k.a. Allan Day. Andrew was beset with newspaper ads by a Vancouver social worker seeking contact, hinting at unresolved debts or crimes after Albert's death. Andrew's car was seized shortly after his brother's death, then Andrew was sued by a mortgage company. By 1995, Andrew resurfaced in Alberta, defending a convicted pedophile he housed in a mobile home, a detail that made local headlines. See "Information Wanted," *Vancouver Sun*, Oct. 16, 1973, 49; Oct. 17, 1973, 57; Oct. 18, 1973, 58; Nov. 17, 1972, 50; Nov. 18, 1972, 48; Nov. 16, 1972, 57. On the auction, see *The Province*, Jan. 23, 1959, 31. On the judgment, see *The Vancouver Sun*, Nov. 24, 1960, 66. His daughter seeks to unravel the mystery of her father on Ancestry.com, where she puts together scraps of data, including notice of her birth. See *The Langley Advance*, Jan. 4, 1962, 1, and "Marriage Certificate," state file no. 6300783, marriage license no. 3986, Mar. 3, 1963, Montana, US, Marriage Records, 1963, Ancestry.com, https://www.ancestry.com/imageviewer/collections/61478/images/47792_554328-00917?pId=151554. I was unsuccessful in locating a photo of Al, but I found one of Andrew through his daughter, who seeks information on her father via Ancestry.com. For Andrew's development permit, see "Development Permits," *Daily Herald-Tribune*, Oct. 5, 1995, 19.

On the pedophile tenant, see "Why Punish Me for Something I'm Not Doing?" *Daily Herald-Tribune*, Dec. 11, 1998, 1.

28. British Columbia, Coroner Archives, "Registration of Death for Darold Edward Weir," Feb. 12, 1973.

29. "Kelowna May Vote on 'Wide-Open' Hours for Stores," *The Province*, Oct. 27, 1960, 1; "Penticton," *The Province*, Oct. 28, 1960, 1; "Nine Months for Auto Theft," *Quesnel Cariboo Observer*, Dec. 15, 1960, A1; "Trial for Heathman Set for Assizes," *The Province*, Oct. 28, 1960, 1.

30. Angie Mindus, "Case Closed on Brutal Murder," *The Tribune*, Dec. 22, 1998, A2.

31. British Columbia, Coroner Archives, "Registration of Death for Darold Edward Weir," Feb. 12, 1973.

32. British Columbia, Coroner Archives, "Registration of Death for Darold Edward Weir," Feb. 12, 1973.

33. British Columbia, Coroner Archives, "Registration of Death for Darold Edward Weir," Feb. 12, 1973.

34. Wally T. Oppal, *Forsaken: The Report of the Missing Women Commission of Inquiry, Executive Summary* (Missing Women Commission of Inquiry, 2012) https://www2.gov.bc.ca/assets/gov/law-crime-and-justice/about-bc-justice-system/inquiries/forsaken-es.pdf.

35. British Columbia, Coroner Archives, "Registration of Death for Ronald Alexander McMillan," July 22, 1980.

36. Later in life, Buller, whose last name later changed to Zacharias, sat on the Williams Lake City Council for ten years and served as Cariboo regional director for three years. See Monica Lamb-Yorski, "Williams Lake City Council Pays Tribute to the Late Susan Zacharias," *The Tribune*, Sept. 14, 2023, 1.

37. "Wolf Gang," *The Tribune*, Apr. 6, 1976, 2; "From the Files," *The Tribune*, Apr. 9, 1996, 13; "Statton Pleads Guilty," *The Tribune*, Nov. 9, 1993, 2.

38. John Brecknock, "Birthday post," Facebook, July 12, 2019, screenshot in author's possession.

39. There is at least one documented instance of a publisher unwilling to publish work on police officers who have harmed Indigenous women. Indigenous author Maria Campbell wrote of the rape she endured at the hands of an RCMP officer in the 1940s in her 1973 book. But publisher McClelland & Stewart removed those pages during copyediting without her knowledge or consent—a fact only exposed in 2019 by a researcher. See Maria Campbell, *Halfbreed* (McClelland & Stewart, 1973); Deanna Reder and Alix Shield, "'I Write This for All of You': Recovering the Unpublished RCMP 'Incident' in Maria Campbell's Halfbreed (1973)," *Canadian Literature* 237 (2019): 1–6.

40. "Troop 6 Graduates at Penhold Training Division: Postings Listed," *Red Deer Advocate*, Dec. 18, 1967, 3; "Chilliwack Driver on Drink Charge," *Vancouver Sun*, Mar. 23, 1961, 16; "George Stanley Brecknock Buried at Alexis Creek," *The Tribune*, Apr. 14, 1983, 12; "Dog-Owner Evicted, SPCA Shelters Pets," *Edmonton Journal*, June 11, 1969, 83.

41. "Howard Lamb Obituary," Oct. 7, 2018, https://www.springfieldfuneralhome.com/obituaries/lamb-howard/; Angie Mindus, "Case Closed on

Brutal Murder," *The Tribune*, Dec. 22, 1998, 1, A2; Angie Mindus, "Unlikely Source Solves Crime," *The Tribune*, Dec. 24, 1998, 3.

42. Mindus, "Case Closed on Brutal Murder," 1, A2.

43. Mindus, "Unlikely Source Solves Crime," 3.

44. Mindus, "Case Closed on Brutal Murder," 1, A2; Mindus, "Unlikely Source Solves Crime," 3; "Sisters Set Brother A 'Blubbering,'" *The Tribune*, Apr. 27, 1999, 16.

45. "RCMP Plane Crashes," *The Tribune*, Nov. 9, 1989, 1; Angela Hall, "The Final Chapter in a Brutal Murder," *Coast Mountain News*, Jan. 9, 1999, 1; personal conversation with Vanessa Moody Hans, Apr. 19, 2022, and Feb. 17, 2024; Sterritt, *Unbroken*, 89.

46. On McIntosh, see Sterritt, *Unbroken*, 92–93.

47. Sterritt, *Unbroken*, 93.

48. Anne H. "Nana" Harvey Brecknock, 1914–1997, grave marker, Williams Lake, British Columbia, https://www.findagrave.com/memorial/158433211/anne-h-brecknock.

49. Personal conversation with Vanessa Moody Hans, Apr. 19, 2022, and Feb. 17, 2024, and receipt of Facebook messages, May 13, 2025; Sterritt, *Unbroken*, 93–96; Mindus, "Case Closed on Brutal Murder," 1, A2.

50. Personal conversation with Vanessa Moody Hans, Apr. 19, 2022, and Feb. 17, 2024, and receipt of Facebook messages, May 13, 2025; Sterritt, *Unbroken*, passim.

51. Susan Brecknock Bamford, "Obituary," Jan. 2, 2020, https://www.springfieldfuneralhome.com/obituaries/bamford-susan-alice-brecknock/; "Charged Out Record," RCMP file, Gloria Levina Moody, BC Archives. McIntosh claimed Toni's daughter worked at the detachment. Sterritt, *Unbroken*, 92.

52. John Brecknock, public Facebook page, Mar. 11, 2017.

53. Rachel Elsiufi (@RachelleElsiufi), "Chris Smiley Interview," Twitter, Sept. 23, 2020, https://twitter.com/Rachelleelsiufi/status/1308839028716904448; Emily Jaycox, "Staff Sgt. Chris Smiley on Murder of Chantelle Firingstoney," *Ponoka News,* Feb. 15, 2021, https://www.ponokanews.com/news/staff-sgt-chris-smiley-on-murder-of-chantelle-firingstoney-nobody-carried-a-sign-for-her-in-our-town-6711201; Emily Jaycox, "Discussions About Justice Continue as Ponoka Murder Victim's Case Proceeds," *Sylvan Lake News*, May 2, 2021 https://www.sylvanlakenews.com/news/discussions-about-justice-continue-as-ponoka-murder-victims-case-proceeds-6587432.

54. Personal conversation with Vanessa Moody Hans, Apr. 19, 2022, and Feb. 17, 2024.

55. Personal conversation with Vanessa Moody Hans, Apr. 19, 2022, and Feb. 17, 2024; in-person conversation with Dean Moody, Apr. 25 and 26, 2026, Bella Coola, British Columbia.

56. Frank Peebles, "Memorial Day for Tŝilhqot'in People Commemorated by All Modern Cultures," *Quesnel Cariboo Observer*, Nov. 3, 2023, https://www.quesnelobserver.com/news/photos-site-of-group-hanging-in-quesnel-now-reconciliation-hotspot-6831348; Cole Harris, *A Bounded Land: Reflections on Settler Colonialism in Canada* (University of British Columbia Press, 2020); Cole Harris, *Making Native Space: Colonialism, Resistance, and Reserves in*

British Columbia (University of British Columbia, Press, 2002); Peter Cook et al., *To Share, Not Surrender: Indigenous and Settler Visions of Vancouver Island and British Columbia* (University of British Columbia Press, 2021).

57. Bev Sellars, *They Called Me Number One: Secrets and Survival at an Indian Residential School* (Talonbooks, 2013), 26. See also Paulette Regan, *Unsettling the Settler Within: Indian Residential Schools, Truth Telling, and Reconciliation in Canada* (University of British Columbia Press, 2011); Celia Haig Brown, *Resistance and Renewal: Surviving the Indian Residential School* (Arsenal Pulp Press, 2006); Tricia E. Logan, *The Lost Generations: The Silent Métis of the Residential School System* (2001); John S. Milloy, *A National Crime: The Canadian Government and the Residential School System* (University of Manitoba Press, 1999); Marlene Brant Castellano, Linda Archibald, and Mike DeGagné, *From Truth to Reconciliation: Transforming the Legacy of Residential Schools* (Aboriginal Healing Foundation, 2008), https://ehprnh2mw03.exactdn.com/wp-content/uploads/2021/01/from-truth-to-reconciliation-transforming-the-legacy-of-residential-schools.pdf.

58. Ruth Lloyd, "Nuxalk Totem Pole Stuck in Limbo," *North Delta Reporter,* Jan. 20, 2022, https://www.northdeltareporter.com/news/nuxalk-totem-pole-stuck-in-limbo-no-clear-path-to-remove-it-from-royal-bc-museum-2744595; Kathryn Marlow, "Hugs, Smiles, and Tears Greet Nuxalk Totem Pole," *CBC News*, Feb. 13, 2023, https://www.cbc.ca/news/canada/british-columbia/nuxalk-nation-totem-pole-return-royal-bc-museum-1.6742581; Douglas Cole and Ira Chaikin, *An Iron Hand Upon the People: The Law Against the Potlatch on the Northwest Coast* (University of Washington Press, 1990), 1; Sergei Kan, *Symbolic Immortality: The Tlingit Potlatch of the Nineteenth Century* (Smithsonian, 1993). See also the documentary *Potlatch: A Strict Law Bids Us Dance* (U'mista Cultural Society of Alert Bay, 1975).

59. Jon Azpiri, "The Hill: The Story Behind One of BC's Most Treacherous Road and the Locals Who Built It," *Global News*, May 12, 2016, https://globalnews.ca/news/2696374/the-hill-the-story-behind-one-of-bcs-most-treacherous-roads-and-the-locals-who-built-it/.

60. Matt Simmons, "Nuxalk Nation Issues Eviction Notice," *The Narwhal*, Aug. 16, 2021, https://thenarwhal.ca/bc-mining-nuxalk-juggernaut-eviction/.

61. Rick Littlechild, "Why Native Women Go Missing, Part 2," *First Nations Drum*, Jan. 13, 2015, http://www.firstnationsdrum.com/2015/01/why-native-women-go-missing-part-2/; "Not Guilty Plea in Girl's Death," *Quesnel Cariboo Observer*, Sept. 14, 1967, A1–A2. On Helen Betty Osborne, see Lisa Priest, *Conspiracy of Silence* (McClelland & Stewart, 1989), and the documentary *Conspiracy of Silence*, dir. Francis Mankiewicz: Part 1 (1 hr., 31 mins.), YouTube, https://www.youtube.com/watch?v=jFGSiu9GoVc; Part 2 (1 hr., 27 mins.), https://www.youtube.com/watch?v=f77zZ5_YCoc. CBC screened the film on television in 1991, but the film was never released on DVD or VHS, nor was it ever digitized by CBC, which still owns the only physical copy of the film. Michael Mahonen, an actor who played one of the assailants in the film, recorded the film with a camcorder and uploaded this version to his YouTube channel, which is linked above. On Fred Quilt, see Lorne Brown

and Caroline Brown, *An Unauthorized History of the RCMP* (James Lewis & Samuel, 1973), 154–64.

62. Sterritt, *Unbroken*, 100.

63. Commissioner Anthony Sarich, *Report on the Cariboo-Chilcotin Justice Inquiry* (Cariboo-Chilcotin Justice Inquiry, 1993); Michael Nest et al., *Cold Case North: The Search for James Brady and Absolom Halkett* (University of Regina Press, 2020); Sterritt, *Unbroken*, passim.

64. "Police Budget, Officers Cut in Highway of Tears Probe," *Vancouver Sun*, Sept. 10, 2014, https://vancouversun.com/news/metro/police-budget-officers-cut-in-highway-of-tears-probe.

65. Brown and Brown, *An Unauthorized History of the RCMP*, 32, 165–81.

66. Lee Maracle, *My Conversations with Canadians* (Book Thug, 2017), 4.

67. *Marker of Change: The Story of the Women's Monument*, dir. Moira Simpson (Vancouver: Moving Images, 1998) documentary (Vimeo), https://vimeo.com/49609905 1; Christine Bold et al., *Remembering Women Murdered by Men: Memorials Across Canada* (Sumach Press, 2006); Robyn Bourgeois, "Generations of Genocide: The Historical and Sociological Context of Missing and Murdered Indigenous Women and Girls," in *Keetsahnak: Our Missing and Murdered Indigenous Sisters*, ed. Kim Anderson et al. (University of Alberta Press, 2018), 66; Butler, *Precarious Life*, 36.

68. Stevie Cameron, *On the Farm: Robert William Pickton and the Tragic Story of Vancouver's Missing Women* (Vintage Canada, 2010); Stevie Cameron, *The Pickton File* (Knopf Canada, 2007); *Taken*, TV Series, https://gem.cbc.ca/taken (CBC Gem, 2016–19); Hilary Beaumont, "The Unsolved Murder of Tanya Brooks," *Vice*, May 1, 2015, https://www.vice.com/en/article/4wba43/murdered-in-halifax-before-loretta-saunders-there-was-tanya-brooks; Kate Partridge, "Indigenous Woman Killed," *CBC News*, Aug. 12, 2021, https://www.cbc.ca/news/canada/british-columbia/murder-indigenous-women-rcmp-questions-1.6138214; "Douglas Hales Guilty," *CBC News*, Dec. 17, 2014, https://www.cbc.ca/news/canada/saskatoon/douglas-hales-guilty-of-2nd-degree-murder-of-daleen-bosse-1.2875884; Blair Rhodes, "Loretta Saunders Murder Was 'Despicable, Horrifying, and Cowardly,'" *CBC News*, Apr. 28, 2015, https://www.cbc.ca/news/canada/nova-scotia/loretta-saunders-murder-was-despicable-horrifying-and-cowardly-1.3052465; Leyland Cecco, "Dead Because She Was Indigenous," *The Guardian*, Oct. 6, 2021, https://www.theguardian.com/world/2021/oct/06/joyce-echaquan-coroner-indigenous-systemic-racism-death; Brandi Morin, "The Indigenous People Killed by Canada's Police," *Al Jazeera*, Mar. 24, 2021, https://www.aljazeera.com/features/2021/3/24/the-indigenous-people-killed-by-canadas-police; Assembly of Manitoba Chiefs, "Joint Statement," Jan. 29, 2021, https://manitobachiefs.com/press_releases/joint-statement-expresses-profound-disappointment-at-the-findings-of-the-independent-investigation-unit-report-into-the-wps-shooting-of-eishia-hudson/; Erica Belfi, "Native Solidarity with Black Lives Matter as Both Communities Confront Centuries-Long State Violence," *Cultural Survival*, July 2, 2020, https://www.culturalsurvival.org/news/native-solidarity-black-lives-matter-both-communities-confront-centuries-long-state-violence; BBC Staff, "Watchdog Clears Toronto Police in Korchinski-Paquet Death," *BBC News*,

Aug. 26, 2020, https://www.bbc.com/news/world-us-canada-53923362; Sherene Razack, *Dying from Improvement: Inquests and Inquiries into Indigenous Deaths in Custody* (University of Toronto Press, 2015), 5; Sherene Razack, "'It Happened More Than Once': Freezing Deaths in Saskatchewan," *Canadian Journal of Women and the Law* 26 (2014): 51–80; Brown, *Unauthorized History*, 145; Joanna Jolly, *Red River Girl: The Life and Death of Tina Fontaine* (Viking Canada, 2019); Caitlyn Gowriluk, "A Timeline," *CBC News,* Dec. 11, 2022, https://www.cbc.ca/news/canada/manitoba/jeremy-skibicki-winnipeg-alleged-serial-killer-timeline-1.6681433; Rachel Bergen, "Accused Killer's Allegedly Hate-Filled Online Presence," *CBC News,* June 7, 2022, https://www.cbc.ca/news/canada/manitoba/rebecca-contois-homicide-jeremy-skibicki-neo-nazi-holy-europe-1.6462730; Morgan Modjeski, "It's a Little Unsettling," *Winnipeg City News,* Dec. 2, 2022, https://winnipeg.citynews.ca/2022/12/02/neighbour-of-man-accused-of-killing/; Charles Lefebvre, "Alleged Serial Killer in Winnipeg," *Winnipeg CTV News*, Dec. 1, 2022, https://winnipeg.ctvnews.ca/alleged-serial-killer-in-winnipeg-accused-of-killing-3-more-women-1.6177003; Erin Brohman, "Alleged Serial Killer Went to Winnipeg Homeless Shelters," *CBC News*, Dec. 16, 2022, https://www.cbc.ca/news/canada/manitoba/jeremy-skibicki-alleged-killer-winnipeg-homeless-shelters-1.6687836; Canadian Press, "New Report on Landfill Search," *CBC News*, Jan. 17, 2024, https://www.cbc.ca/news/canada/manitoba/amc-delivers-second-landfill-report-1.7087149. Some of the reports resulting from inquiries and commissions include, in sequential order, *Royal Commission on the Donald Marshall Jr., Prosecution* (Nova Scotia, 1989); *Aboriginal Justice Inquiry of Manitoba: Final Report* (Aboriginal Justice Inquiry of Manitoba, 1991); *Report of the Aboriginal Justice Inquiry of Manitoba: The Deaths of Helen Betty Osborne and John Joseph Harper, Vol. 2* (Queen's Printer, 1991); *Report of the Task Force on the Criminal Justice System and Its Impact on the Indian and Métis People of Alberta, Chaired by Mr. Justice R. A. Cawsey* (Alberta, 1991); Sarich, *Report on the Cariboo-Chilcotin Justice Inquiry*; *Report of the Commission on Systemic Racism in the Ontario Criminal Justice System* (Queen's Printer for Ontario, 1995); *Report of the Royal Commission on Aboriginal Peoples*, 5 vols. (Canada Communications Group, 1996); *Report of the Aboriginal Justice Inquiry of Manitoba* (Aboriginal Justice Implementation Commission, 1999); *Final Report of the Aboriginal Justice Implementation Commission* (Aboriginal Justice Implementation Commission, 2001); *Report of the Commission of Inquiry Into Matters Relating to the Death of Neil Stonechild* (Government of Saskatchewan, 2004); Jeffrey Pfeifer, *Missing Persons in Saskatchewan: Police Policy and Practice* (University of Regina, 2006); *First Nations Representation on Ontario Juries: Report of the Independent Review Conducted by the Honourable Frank Iacobucci* (Ontario Ministry of the Attorney General, 2013); *Stolen Sisters: Discrimination and Violence Against Indigenous Women in Canada* (Amnesty International, 2004); *Missing Women Investigation Review* (Vancouver Police Department, 2010); *Forsaken: Report of the Missing Women Commission of Inquiry Executive Summary, the Honourable Wally T. Oppal* (Missing Women Commission of Inquiry, 2012); *Voices of the Families—Recommendations of the Families of the Missing and*

Murdered Women: A Consultation Report Prepared for the Missing Women (Missing Women Commission of Inquiry, 2012); Linda Locke, QC, *Standing Together and Moving Forward: The Northwest Consultations* (Missing Women Commission of Inquiry, 2012); *Final Report of the Truth and Reconciliation Commission of Canada* (McGill-Queen's University Press, 2015); Native Women's Association of Canada (L'Association des Femmes Autochtones du Canada), *Fact Sheet: Missing and Murdered Aboriginal Women and Girls* (NWAC, 2015), https://www.nwac.ca/assets-knowledge-centre/Fact_Sheet_Missing_and_Murdered_Aboriginal_Women_and_Girls.pdf; *Reclaiming Power and Place: The Final Report of the National Inquiry into Missing and Murdered Indigenous Women and Girls* (National Inquiry into Missing and Murdered Indigenous Women and Girls, 2019); Carol Muree Martin and Harsha Walia, *Red Women Rising: Indigenous Women Survivors in Vancouver's Downtown Eastside* (Downtown Eastside Women's Centre, 2019); *Forsaken: The Report of the Missing Women Commission of Inquiry 2020 Status Update* (Ministry of Public Safety and Solicitor General, 2020).

69. Glaim's sister, Delphine Nikal, went missing in 1995 from Highway 16. See "The Disappearance of Delphine Nikal," *Hue and Cry*, https://thehueandcry.com/delphine-nikal. See also Amber Dean, *Remembering Vancouver's Disappeared Women: Settler Colonialism and the Difficulty of Inheritance* (University of Toronto Press, 2015), 45; Adele Perry, *On the Edge of Empire: Gender, Race, and the Making of British Columbia, 1849–1871* (University of Toronto Press, 2001), 54; Sarah Carter, "Categories and Terrains of Exclusion: Constructing the 'Indian Woman' in the Early Settlement Era in Western Canada," in *In the Days of Our Grandmothers: A Reader in Aboriginal Women's History in Canada*, ed. Mary-Ellen Kelm and Lorna Townsend (University of Toronto Press, 2006), 147, 148. See also Sarah Carter, *Capturing Women: The Manipulation of Cultural Imagery in Canada's Prairie West* (McGill-Queen's University Press, 1997).

70. *Highway of Tears*, directed and reported by Sharmeen Obaid Chinoy, 2006, 24 min., aired on Al Jazeera International, https://socfilms.com/portfolio-item/highway-of-tears/, with permission of director; Sharmeen Obaid-Chinoy, *Canada: "Highway of Tears,"* video report, Frontline World, PBS, Aug. 18, 2006, https://www.pbs.org/frontlineworld/blog/2006/08/canada_highway.html; Lee Maracle, *I Am Woman: A Native Perspective on Sociology and Feminism* (Press Gang Publishers, 1996), 16, 49, 55; Janice Acoose-Miswonigeesikokwe, *Iskwewak Kah' Ki Yaw Ni Wahkomakanak: Neither Indian Princesses nor Easy Squaws*, 2nd ed. (Women's Press, 2016); Patricia Monture-Angus, "Standing Against Canadian Law: Naming Omissions of Race, Culture, and Gender," in *Locating Law: Race/Class/Gender Connections*, ed. Elizabeth Comack (Fernwood Publishing, 1999), 85–86. Now renamed Ramada, the hotel wants to eliminate its association with the murders of First Nations women. It still sits at 149th Street and Yellowhead Trail behind Shakers' Roadhouse, a trucker hangout. Sherene H. Razack, "Gendered Racial Violence and Spatialized Justice: The Murder of Pamela George," *Canadian Journal of Law and Society* 15 (2000): 125; Naomi Sayers, "#MMIW: A Critique of Sherene Razack's Piece Exploring the Trial of Pamela George's

Murder," *Kwe Today*, Dec. 26, 2014, https://kwetoday.com/2014/12/26/mmiw-a-critique-of-sherene-razacks-exploration-of-the-trial-of-the-murder-of-pamela-george/; Sherene H. Razack, "Gendering Disposability," *Canadian Journal of Women and the Law* 2 (2016): 289–90.

CHAPTER 3: FRED/FC/FREDRIKA/BEYONCÉ

1. Melanie Yazzie et al., *Red Nation Rising: From Bordertown Violence to Native Liberation* (PM Press, 2021).

2. Yazzie et al., *Red Nation Rising.*

3. *Two Spirits: Sexuality, Gender, and the Murder of Fred Martinez*, dir. Lydia Nibley (Say Yes Quickly, 2009), 65 mins.

4. *Two Spirits.*

5. Personal conversation with John R. Peters-Campbell, Feb. 17, 2023.

6. Prison Register, Colorado Department of Corrections; Aspen C. Emmett, "Mother, Son Have History of Trouble, Documents," *Cortez Journal*, Sept. 11, 2001; Aspen C. Emmett, "Martinez's Mother Releases Statement," *Cortez Journal*, July 19, 2001. The online articles from the *Cortez Journal* cited in this work were accessed throughout 2023 and early 2024 via the newspaper's publicly available internet archive at archive.cortezjournal.com. Subsequent to the completion of this research, the *Cortez Journal* has taken this archive offline, rendering the hyperlinks inactive. The citations retain the original URLs to document the precise source of the information.

7. Elyssa Ford, *Rodeo as Refuge, Rodeo as Rebellion: Gender, Race, and Identity in the American Rodeo* (University of Kansas Press, 2020).

8. "Ute Mountain Roundup PRCA Rodeo," https://www.utemountainroundup.org/.

9. July 4 Affidavit, Montezuma County Clerk Archives.

10. *Two Spirits*; Aspen C. Emmett, "Killing Raises Specter of Hate Crime," *Cortez Journal*, July 12, 2001; Jeremy Quittner, "Death of a Two Spirit," *The Advocate*, Aug. 28, 2001, https://www.thefreelibrary.com/Death+of+a+Two+Spirit.-a077660063.

11. Personal conversation with Peters-Campbell, Jan. 28, 2023; "Killing of Two Spirits," *Evil Lives Here: Shadows of Death*, season 5, ep. 4, aired May 9, 2023.

12. Personal conversation with Peters-Campbell, Jan. 28, 2023; July 4 Affidavit, Montezuma County Clerk Archives; Emmett, "Killing Raises Specter of Hate Crime"; Aspen C. Emmett, "Autopsy Report Provides Few New Facts," *Cortez Journal*, July 26, 2001; Quittner, "Death of a Two Spirit"; Sarah Lamble, "Retelling Racialized Violence, Remaking White Innocence: The Politics of Interlocking Oppressions in Transgender Day of Remembrance," *Sexuality Research & Social Policy* 5, no. 1 (2008): 33; Electra Draper, "Gay Cortez Teen Buried; N.M. Man, 18, Held," *Denver Post*, July 6, 2001, p. A-01.

13. Autopsy Report, Montezuma County Coroner, 2001. The July 4 affidavit said their backpack was still on, and bloody rocks were nearby. The autopsy report does not document this. The mirror was reported by Sheriff Joey Chavez: Aspen C. Emmet, "Suspects Questioned in Boy's Murder," *Cortez Journal*, June 28, 2001; Aspen C. Emmett, "Man's Body Found Near Park," *Cortez*

Journal, June 23, 2001; Aspen C. Emmett, "Murphy Appears in Court," *Cortez Journal*, July 10, 2001. On the trail of blood, see the documentary *Two Spirits*.

14. "GenderPAC Condemns Martinez Killing: Urges FBI to Investigate," GenderPAC, Aug. 27, 2001, https://web.archive.org/web/20080411081559/; http:/www.gpac.org/archive/news/notitle.html?cmd=view&archive=news&msgnum=0329; Emmett, "Martinez's Mother Releases Statement"; Emmett, "Man's Body Found Near Park"; July 4 Affidavit, Montezuma County Clerk Archives; Autopsy Report, Montezuma County Coroner.

15. Emmett, "Man's Body Found Near Park"; Autopsy Report, Montezuma County Coroner; Juan Camilo Márquez-Garcia et al., "Isolated Depressed Fracture of the Inner Table of the Skull," *Interdisciplinary Neurosurgery* 30 (2022): 101530.

16. Autopsy Report, Montezuma County Coroner; Emmett, "Man's Body Found Near Park"; Emmett, "Martinez's Mother Releases Statement"; July 4 Affidavit, Montezuma County Clerk Archives; GenderPAC, "Interview with the Mother of Fred Martinez," Sept. 4, 2001, https://web.archive.org/web/20090408174757/http:/www.gpac.org/archive/news/notitle.html?cmd=view&archive=news&msgnum=0338.

17. July 4 Affidavit. Montezuma County Clerk Archives; Emmett, "Suspects Questioned in Boy's Murder"; Emmett, "Martinez's Mother Releases Statement"; Prison Register, Colorado Department of Corrections. Shaun's prison record says he completed his adult education in Durango, but after extensive consultation with the current Adult Education Centers in both Durango and Cortez, I learned that neither existed in 2000. However, Unlimited Learning began in 2004 by Ann Miller. Prior to this, Southwest Board of Cooperative Services functioned in Cortez as the unit where students could study for their GED. Source: Aleita Sanders emails, Mar. 2–19, 2024.

18. July 4 Affidavit, Montezuma County Clerk Archives.

19. All references to interviews by police with Murphy and Sanchez come from Montezuma County Sheriff Records. 2001. Digitized copies obtained from Gina Watson, HBO Documentary Films. In author's possession.

20. July 4 Affidavit, Montezuma County Clerk Archives.

21. Aspen C. Emmett, "Former Cortez Resident Arrested in Murder," *Cortez Journal*, July 7, 2001; Associated Press (AP), "Teen Admits Fight with Dead Student," *Arizona Republic* July 7, 2001, A5.

22. Emmett, "Murphy Appears in Court"; Court Register of Actions, Montezuma County Clerk Archives; Emmett, "Killing Raises Specter of Hate Crime"; Aspen C. Emmett, "Charges Increased in Homicide," *Cortez Journal*, Aug. 11, 2001; People v. Christopher Daniel Leroi, https://www.coloradosupremecourt.com/pdj/Decisions/Leroi,%20Conditional%20Admission%20of%20Misconduct,%2014PDJ050,%206-27-14.pdf, accessed Mar. 20, 2024; Timothy J. Huthill, JD, University of Colorado. His crimes are documented in source A, https://www.coloradosupremecourt.com/pdj/Decisions/Tuthill,Conditional%20Admission,No.03PDJ111,6-7-04.pdf, and source B, https://caselaw.findlaw.com/court/co-supreme-court-disciplinary-judg/1155777.html. His social media presence is archived at Facebook: https://www.facebook.com/people/Tim-Tuthill/100011128958074/?paipv=0&eav=Afafmmy7eCQ

tndJ3iE9AcU5bWLOcZjQp8AHGlvGBCpKSJySyi_oAdiJyoDWQRJXC_NA&_rdr.

23. Court Register, Montezuma County Clerk Archives; Emmett, "Killing Raises Specter of Hate Crime"; "Mother Upset by Talk of Hate Crime," Indianz.com, July 9, 2001, https://www.indianz.com/News/show.asp?ID=tc/792001-4; Emmett, "Murphy Appears in Court"; Emmett, "Charges Increased in Homicide"; Aspen C. Emmett, "Don't Blame Cortez, Says Anti-Bias Group," *Cortez Journal*, July 14, 2001; Emmett, "Autopsy Report Provides Few New Facts."

24. July 4 Affidavit, Montezuma County Clerk Archives; Emmett, "Don't Blame Cortez, Says Anti-Bias Group"; Emmett, "Man's Body Found Near Park."

25. Court Register, Montezuma County Clerk Archives; Emmett, "Killing Raises Specter of Hate Crime"; Emmett, "Don't Blame Cortez, Says Anti-Bias Group"; Emmett, "Autopsy Report Provides Few New Facts"; Emmett, "Charges Increased in Homicide"; Aspen C. Emmett, "Murphy's Mother Arrested on Charges of Intimidating Witness," *Cortez Journal*, Sept. 8, 2001; Aspen C. Emmett, "Court Hears Motions in Murder Case," *Cortez Journal*, Feb. 2, 2002.

On August 11, the *Cortez Journal* repeated the story that Shaun "bragged about beating up a homosexual," without saying who said it, just as the affidavit had done. When Detective Harmon took the stand September 7, 2001, Harmon admitted Clint Sanchez heard Shaun make the utterance. By February 2, 2002, the *Cortez Journal* said the "beaten up a f—" statement was reported anonymously through Crimestoppers, suggesting Shaun said this to multiple people and one of them called Crimestoppers.

26. Court Register, Montezuma County Clerk Archives; Coroner Report, Montezuma County Coroner; "Martinez's Mother Releases Statement"; Aspen C. Emmett, "Martinez's Mother Says Olt Violating Victims' Rights," *Cortez Journal*, Aug. 9, 2001; "Police Defend Actions on Navajo Teen Case," Indianz.com, July 24, 2001, https://indianz.com/News/show.asp?ID=law/7242001-6; Electra Draper, "Cortez Mom Didn't Report Son Missing, Police Say," *Denver Post*, July 24, 2001, B-5; Emmett, "Autopsy Report Provides Few New Facts."

27. Court Register, Montezuma County Clerk Archives; Emmett, "Charges Increased in Homicide"; Aspen C. Emmett, "Slaying Prompts Vigil, Forums on Gay Issues," *Cortez Journal*, Aug. 6, 2001; Aspen C. Emmett, "Olt Seeks Help with Murder Case," *Cortez Journal*, Aug. 16, 2001; AP, "Chemical Used to Ignite Cortez Judge's Car," *Denver Post*, Dec. 9, 2008, https://www.denverpost.com/2008/12/09/chemical-used-to-ignite-cortez-judges-car/.

28. Court Register, Montezuma County Clerk Archives; Arrest Record of Angel Murphy Tacoronte, Sept. 7, 2001, Montezuma County Sheriff Archives; Emmett, "Murphy's Mother Arrested on Charges of Intimidating Witness"; Aspen C. Emmett, "Murphy Enters Plea of Not Guilty," *Cortez Journal*, Oct. 20, 2001.

29. Court Register, Montezuma County Clerk Archives; Emmett, "Murphy Enters Plea of Not Guilty"; Aspen C. Emmett, "Court Hears Motion in Murder Case," *Cortez Journal*, Feb. 2, 2002; Agent Brooks Bennett, LinkedIn, https://www.linkedin.com/in/brooks-bennett-a4293962.

30. The last known location of the shoes and belt was the Colorado Bureau of Investigation. These items were never entered as evidence in Montezuma County Court. "List of Exhibits," June 4, 2002 (Event ID 000153), Montezuma County Clerk Archives, shows a list of seventeen exhibits, including photos, two rocks, a videotape, and exhibits 12–14 as "skipped." "Order Returning Exhibits," Apr. 7, 2004 (Event ID 000183), shows a return of exhibits 1–17 to the Sheriff's Department. "Inventory of Exhibits and Receipt," May 4, 2004 (Event ID 000184), shows the court taking exhibits 15 and 16, two rocks with blood evidence, into their possession. "Notice/Receipt of Exhibit," Feb. 13, 2018 (Event ID 000200), shows the return of exhibit 17, a videotape provided by Mary Lobato, the ex-girlfriend of Shaun Murphy, to the attorney of record or to be destroyed within thirty-five days. My request for "Exhibits released or destroyed," Mar. 23, 2018 (Event ID 000201), could not be fulfilled. They confirmed by email that it was a system entry for which no physical document exists.

31. AP, "Farmington Teen Decides to Honor Plea," *The Daily Sentinel*, May 24, 2002, 3.

32. AP, "Farmington Teen Decides to Honor Plea," 3.

33. Court Register, Montezuma County Clerk Archives; AP, "Farmington Teen Decides to Honor Plea," 3.

34. Court Register, Montezuma County Clerk Archives. The court obtained a victim impact statement from their mother, Pauline Mitchell, on July 16 and one from their father, Fred Martinez Sr., on August 5, 2001, both of which could have been read aloud but were not. Her statement reads as follows: "The murder of my beloved precious & beautiful son, Fred C. Martinez, Jr. is so devastating a loss there are no words that would ever begin to describe my feelings. I believe Shaun Murphy be charged with first degree murder and as a hate crime. I also feel that Shaun Murphy deserves to be put to death just as he took the life from my child." Fred Sr. wrote: "The murder my son Fred C. Martinez Jr. There no words that would every [*sic*] begin to describe my feelings. I believe Shaun Murphy be charged with 1 degree murder and as a hate crime. I want Shaun Murphy to be put to death just as he took my Baby Life." Montezuma County Clerk Archives. The court holds a full trial transcript, and I requested a copy of the portion of the transcript of Murphy's statement. This request was denied. The court clerk allowed me to order a transcript. I ordered a portion of a transcript on October 16 and received it on December 11. Shaun Murphy claimed self-defense and inebriation in his statement to the court at his sentencing. His mother also made a statement at the sentencing claiming her son did not kill Martinez. Montezuma County Clerk Archives.

35. Personal conversation with Peters-Campbell, Jan. 28, 2023.

36. Court Register, Montezuma County Clerk Archives; Prison Record, Colorado Department of Corrections.

37. Colorado Judicial Department, *Records Management: Retention and Disposition Schedules & Imaging Procedures for Designated Records* (Office of the State Administrator, 2017). The manual is published by the Office of the State Court Administrator under the direction of the Colorado Supreme Court: "It reflects the continuing responsibility of the Chief Justice and

the Supreme Court to supervise and administer the court system under Article VI of the Colorado Constitution." According to the 2017 manual, for felony cases: "Destroy only if the case has not been bound up to district court." For criminal cases, the manual simply says "Permanent."

38. Personal interview, Pauline Martinez Mitchell, Apr. 17, 2024, Farmington, NM.

39. Jodi Byrd, "What's Normative Got to Do with It? Toward Indigenous Queer Relationality," *Social Text* 38, no. 4 (2020): 105–23; Kai Pyle, "'Women and 2Spirits': On the Marginalization of Transgender Indigenous People in Activist Rhetoric," *American Indian Culture and Research Journal* 43, no. 3 (2019): 85–94; Kimberly F. Balsam et al., "Culture, Trauma, and Wellness: A Comparison of Heterosexual, Lesbian, Gay, Bisexual, and Two-Spirit Americans," *Cultural Diversity and Ethnic Minority Psychology* 10, no. 3 (2004): 287–301; Dean Spade, *Normal Life: Administrative Violence, Critical Trans Politics, and the Limits of Law* (South End Press, 2011), 3, 4; Billy Ray Belcourt, "Can the Other of Native Studies Speak?" *Decolonization* (blog), Feb. 1, 2016, https://decolonization.wordpress.com/2016/02/01/can-the-other-of-native-studies-speak/.

40. Steve Pavlik, "Of Saints and Lamanites: An Analysis of Navajo Mormonism," *Wíčazo Ša Review* 8, no. 1 (1992): 21–30; Klara Kelley and Harry Francis, *A Diné History of Navajoland* (University of Arizona Press, 2019); Peter Guardino, *The Dead March: A History of the Mexican-American War* (Harvard University Press, 2020); Matt Fitzsimmons, *The Counterfeiters of Bosque Redondo: Slavery, Silver, and the U.S. War Against the Navajo Nation* (History Press, 2022); Hampton Sides, *Blood and Thunder: The Epic Story of Kit Carson and the Conquest of the American West* (Vintage, 2007); Jennifer Nez Denetdale, *Reclaiming Diné History: The Legacies of Navajo Chief Manuelito and Juanita* (University of Arizona Press, 2007); Erica Cottam, *Hubbell Trading Post: Trade, Tourism, and the Navajo Southwest* (University of Oklahoma Press, 2015); Krista Allen, "Virus Strikes at Rally," *Navajo Times*, Mar. 25, 2020, https://navajotimes.com/coronavirus-updates/two-deaths-in-western-may-have-been-covid-virus-spread-at-church-rally/; Marsha Weisiger, *Dreaming of Sheep in Navajo Country* (University of Washington Press, 2011); Richard White, *Roots of Dependency: Subsistence, Environment, and Social Change Among the Choctaws, Pawnees, and Navajos* (University of Nebraska Press, 1988); Broderick Johnson and Ruth Roessel, *Navajo Livestock Reduction: A National Disgrace* (Navajo Community College Press, 1974); Tommy Rock and Jani C. Ingram, "Traditional Ecological Knowledge Policy Considerations for Abandoned Uranium Mines on Navajo Nation," *Human Biology* 92, no. 1 (2020): 19–26.

41. Colleen O'Neill, *Working the Navajo Way: Labor and Culture in the Twentieth Century* (University Press of Kansas, 2005); Jennifer Nez Denetdale, "'No Explanation, No Resolution, and No Answers': Border Town Violence and Navajo Resistance to Settler Colonialism," *Wíčazo Ša Review* 31, no. 1 (2016): 111–31.

42. Rodney Barker, *The Broken Circle: A True Story of Murder and Magic in Indian Country* (Simon & Schuster, 1992), 14, 15.

43. Denetdale, "No Explanation, No Resolution, and No Answers"; Barker, *Broken Circle*, 27, 28.

44. New Mexico Advisory Committee to the US Commission on Civil Rights, *The Farmington Report: A Conflict of Cultures*, July 1975, https://permanent.fdlp.gov/www.usccr.gov/pubs/122705_FarmingtonReport.pdf; United States Commission on Civil Rights, *The Farmington Report: Civil Rights for Native Americans 30 Years Later*, New Mexico Advisory Committee (Washington, DC: US Commission on Civil Rights, November 2005).

45. Susy Buchanan, "Violence Against American Indians Is a Pervasive Problem," *Intelligence Report*, Jan. 16, 2007, Southern Poverty Law Center, https://www.splcenter.org/fighting-hate/intelligence-report/2007/violence-against-american-indians-pervasive-problem; Shannon Mullane, "After 45 Years, Have Race Relations Improved in Farmington?" *Cortez Journal*, Oct. 16, 2020, https://www.the-journal.com/articles/after-45-years-have-race-relations-improved-in-farmington/; Marley Shebala, "Not Guilty," *Navajo Times*, June 11, 2009, https://navajotimes.com/news/2009/0609/061109clintjohn.php.

46. Denetdale, "'No Explanation, No Resolution, and No Answers,'" 123.

47. Sam Stecklow, "Colorado Punishes Sergeant Who Killed a Man in Utah," *Salt Lake Tribune*, Sept. 27, 2021, https://www.sltrib.com/news/2021/09/27/colorado-punishes/.

CHAPTER 4: ERNESTINA

1. Norma Trujillo Báez, "Felipe Calderón y Fidel Herrera ocultaron la violación a Ernestina Ascencio: Perito," *Pie de Pagina*, Feb. 25, 2020, https://piedepagina.mx/felipe-calderon-y-fidel-herrera-ocultaron-la-violacion-a-ernestina-ascencio-perito/; Lawyers for Justice and Human Rights A. C.; Center for Municipal Services, Heriberto Jara, A. C. (CESEM); Kalli Luz Marina A. C., National Coordinator of Indigenous Women (CONAMI), and Robert F. Kennedy Human Rights, 2023; *Ernestina Ascencio Rosario and Another v. Mexico*, brief of requests, arguments and evidence, Inter-American Court of Human Rights.

2. Amnesty International, *Amnesty International Report 1998-Mexico*, Refworld, 1998, https://www.refworld.org/reference/annualreport/amnesty/1998/en/92552.

3. Gualberto Díaz González, *La matanza de Tehuipango: movimiento social y represión en la Sierra de Zongolica, 1966–1982* (Universidad Veracruzana, 2023); Carolina Sánchez, coord., *Territorio y conocimientos tradicionales en el Totonacapan* (Programa Universitario de Estudios de la Diversidad Cultural y la Interculturalidad, PUIC–UNAM, 2021); Carlos A. Casas Mendoza, "Escritores nahuas, utopías comunitarias y futuros posibles en la Sierra de Zongolica, Veracruz," *Encartes* 7, no. 14 (Sept. 2024–Feb. 2025): 47–73.

4. Erich Adolfo Moncada Cota, "Mexico's Military and the Murder at Zongolica," *Banderas News*, Parts I and II, Mar. 2007, https://www.banderasnews.com/0703/eded-mexmilitary.htm.

5. Author interview with Norma Trujillo, assisted by translator, Apr. 5, 2024, Mexico City.

6. Professor Octavio Rodríguez Araujo, National Autonomous University of Mexico, "El Misterio de Zongolica," *Memoria* 221 (July–Aug. 2007), http://www.rodriguezaraujo.unam.mx/graficos/pdfs/zongolica1.pdf.

7. Blanche Petrich Sent, "El ataque a Ernestina Ascención, posible 'mensaje de escarmiento,'" *La Jornada*, Apr. 9, 2007, https://www.jornada.com.mx/2007/04/09/index.php?section=politica&article=010n1pol.

8. "Gobierno Entrampado en last Contradicciones del Ejército por Casi Ernestina Ascencio," *Notiver*, Feb. 1, 2025, https://www.notiver.com/nacionales/gobierno-entrampado-en-las-contradicciones-del-ejercito-por-caso-ernestina-ascencio/; Laura Castro Medina, "Soldados violaron y mataron a anciana, acusan indígenas nahuas," *Cimacnews*, Feb. 28, 2007, https://cimacnoticias.com.mx/2007/02/28/soldados-violaron-y-mataron-a-anciana-acusan-indigenas-nahuas/.

9. Blanche Petrich, "Dictamen de Ginecóloga Señala Agresión Sexual en Contra de Ernestina Ascensión," *La Jornada*, Apr. 24, 2007, https://www.jornada.com.mx/2007/04/24/index.php?section=politica&article=010n1pol.

10. Blanche Petrich Sent, "Todo apunta hacia el Ejército', decían visitadores de la CNDH: líder indígena," *La Jornada*, Apr. 10, 2007, https://www.jornada.com.mx/2007/04/10/index.php?section=politica&article=011n1pol; Cota, "Mexico's Military and the Murder at Zongolica." Veracruz state officials interviewed Dr. Gante on February 27, 2007, and surely collected his medical documentation of her injuries. See Comisión Nacional de los Derechos Humanos (CNDH), *Informe sobre la Recomendación 34/2007: Memoria, Verdad, Justicia y Reparación* (CNDH, 2021), https://www.cndh.org.mx/sites/default/files/documentos/2021-11/Informe_Ernestina_Ascencio_Recomendacion_342007_0.pdf.

11. Comisión Nacional de los Derechos Humanos, *Informe sobre la Recomendación 34/2007: Memoria, Verdad, Justicia y Reparación* (CNDH, 2021), https://www.cndh.org.mx/sites/default/files/documentos/2021-11/Informe_Ernestina_Ascencio_Recomendacion_342007_0.pdf; Editorial Staff, "Se Deslindarán Responsabilidades en el Caso de la Sra. Ernestina Ascensio," *Orizaba En Red*, Mar. 30, 2007, http://www.orizabaenred.com.mx/cgi-bin/web2?b=VERNOTICIA&%7bnum%7d=52030; "Hubo Anomalías en la Autopsia de Ernestina Ascencio: CNDH," *Proceso*, Mar. 15, 2007, https://www.proceso.com.mx/nacional/2007/3/15/hubo-anomalias-en-la-autopsia-de-ernestina ascencio-cndh-32371.html.

12. Comisión Nacional de los Derechos Humanos, *Informe sobre la Recomendación 34/2007: Memoria, Verdad, Justicia y Reparación* (CNDH, 2021), https://www.cndh.org.mx/sites/default/files/documentos/2021-11/Informe_Ernestina_Ascencio_Recomendacion_342007_0.pdf.

13. Medina, "Soldados violaron y mataron a anciana, acusan indígenas nahuas."

14. Andres T. Morales, "Exhuman Restos de Anciana que Murió tras Violación en Zongolica," *La Jornada*, Mar. 10, 2007, https://www.jornada.com.mx/2007/03/10/index.php?section=estados&article=032n1est.

15. Cota, "Mexico's Military and the Murder at Zongolica," citing *Proceso* 1587 (Apr. 1, 2007), "¡Tenemos valor!" (article no longer accessible);

Blanche Petrich, "Autoridades de Veracruz, Sedena y CNDH Enturbian Más el Casto Ascensión Rosario," *La Jornada*, Apr. 11, 2007, https://www.jornada.com.mx/2007/04/11/index.php?article=008n1pol&section=politica; Blanche Petrich Enviada, "El Ataque a Ernestina Ascención, Posible 'Mensaje de Escarmiento': Autoridades," *La Jornada*, Apr. 9, 2007, https://www.jornada.com.mx/2007/04/09/index.php?section=politica&article=010n1pol.

16. Comisión Nacional de los Derechos Humanos, *Informe sobre la Recomendación 34/2007: Memoria, Verdad, Justicia y Reparación* (CNDH, 2021), https://www.cndh.org.mx/sites/default/files/documentos/2021-11/Informe_Ernestina_Ascencio_Recomendacion_342007_0.pdf.

17. Cota, "Mexico's Military and the Murder at Zongolica"; Petrich, "Autoridades de Veracruz, Sedena y CNDH Enturbian Más el Casto Ascensión Rosario."

18. Cota, "Mexico's Military and the Murder at Zongolica."

19. Cota, "Mexico's Military and the Murder at Zongolica"; Por La Redacción, "Hubo anomalías en la autopsia de Ernestina Ascencio: CNDH," *Proceso*, Mar. 15, 2007, https://www.proceso.com.mx/nacional/2007/3/15/hubo-anomalias-en-la-autopsia-de-ernestina-ascencio-cndh-32371.html; Por La Redaccíon, "CNDH pide a Fiscalía de Veracruz reabrir caso de Ernestina Ascencio Rosario," *Contralínea*, Apr. 25, 2021, https://contralinea.com.mx/noticias/cndh-pide-a-fiscalia-de-veracruz-reabrir-caso-de-ernestina-ascencio-rosario/.

20. Morales, "Exhuman restos de anciana que murió tras violación en Zongolica."

21. Andres T. Morales, "Investigan a peritos por el caso Ascencio Rosario," *La Jornada*, Mar. 30, 2007, https://www.jornada.com.mx/2007/03/30/index.php?article=010n1pol&section=politica; *Por La Redacción*, "Los peritos del caso Ernestina Ascencio, suspendidos," *Proceso*, Mar. 30, 2007, https://www.proceso.com.mx/nacional/2007/3/30/los-peritos-del-caso-ernestina-ascencio-suspendidos-32789.html; Petrich, "Dictamen de ginecóloga señala agresión sexual en contra de Ernestina Ascensión"; Norma Trujillo Baez, "Suspenden a los tres peritos de la procuraduría que dictaminaron violación en caso de Ernestina," *Al Color Politico*, Mar. 29, 2007, https://www.alcalorpolitico.com/informacion/suspenden-a-los-tres-peritos-de-la-procuradur-a-que-dictaminaron-violaci-n-en-caso-de-ernestina-9599.html.

22. Comisión Nacional de los Derechos Humanos, *Informe sobre la Recomendación 34/2007: Memoria, Verdad, Justicia y Reparación* (CNDH, 2021), https://www.cndh.org.mx/sites/default/files/documentos/2021-11/Informe_Ernestina_Ascencio_Recomendacion_342007_0.pdf; *Diario de Xalapa*, Apr. 13 and 28, 2007, cited in Octavio Rodriguez Araujo, "The Mystery of Zongolica," July–Aug. 2007, no. 221, archived at Universad Nacional Autónoma de México, http://www.rodriguezaraujo.unam.mx/graficos/pdfs/zongolica1.pdf. *Diario de Xalapa* is no longer in publication.

23. Sistema de Información Legislativa, "Iniciativa con proyecto de decreto por el que se reforman los artículos 13" (July 4, 2007), http://sil.gobernacion.gob.mx/Archivos/Documentos/2007/07/asun_2348961_20070704_1183576329.pdf; Comisión Nacional de los Derechos Humanos, *Informe sobre la Recomendación 34/2007: Memoria, Verdad, Justicia y Reparación* (CNDH,

2021), https://www.cndh.org.mx/sites/default/files/documentos/2021-11/Informe_Ernestina_Ascencio_Recomendacion_342007_0.pdf.

24. Cota, "Mexico's Military and the Murder at Zongolica"; Gral. Brig. DEM Mario Lucio González Cortés, director general de Comunicación Social, "Aclaración de la Secretaría de la Defensa Nacional," *La Jornada*, Apr. 6, 2007, https://www.jornada.com.mx/2007/04/06/index.php?section=opinion&article=002a2cor; Comisión Nacional de los Derechos Humanos, *Informe sobre la Recomendación 34/2007: Memoria, Verdad, Justicia y Reparación* (CNDH, 2021), https://www.cndh.org.mx/sites/default/files/documentos/2021-11/Informe_Ernestina_Ascencio_Recomendacion_342007_0.pdf; Juan Santos Carrera, "Acusa CNDH a Gobierno de Veracruz de Desvirtuar Caso de Ernestina Ascencio," *Orizaba en Red*, Apr. 20, 2007, http://www.orizabaenred.com.mx/cgi-bin/web2?b=VERNOTICIA&%7Bnum%7D=52515; Estephanye Reyes Aguiñaga, "Recuento del caso de violación de Ernestina Ascencio," *CimacNoticias*, Mar. 18, 2010, https://cimacnoticias.com.mx/2010/03/18/recuento-del-caso-de-violacion-de-ernestina-ascencio/.

25. Báez, "Felipe Calderón y Fidel Herrera Ocultaron la Violación a Ernestina Ascencio"; author interview, Norma Trujillo, assisted by translator, Apr. 5, 2024, Mexico City.

26. Comisión Nacional de los Derechos Humanos, 2021, *Informe sobre la Recomendación 34/2007: Memoria, Verdad, Justicia y Reparación* (CNDH), 2021. https://www.cndh.org.mx/sites/default/files/documentos/2021-11/Informe_Ernestina_Ascencio_Recomendacion_342007_0.pdf.

27. Comisión Nacional de los Derechos Humanos, *Informe sobre la Recomendación 34/2007: Memoria, Verdad, Justicia y Reparación* (CNDH, 2021), https://www.cndh.org.mx/sites/default/files/documentos/2021-11/Informe_Ernestina_Ascencio_Recomendacion_342007_0.pdf; Andres T. Morales, "Dan carpetazo al caso Ascensión: 'no fue violada ni asesinada,'" *La Jornada*, May 2, 2007.

28. Author interview with Barbara Yllán Rondero, assisted by translator, Apr. 4, 2024, Mexico City.

29. El Sol de Orizaba, Apr. 5, 2007, cited in Octavio Rodríguez Araujo, "El misterio de Zongolica," *Memoria* 221 (July–Aug. 2007); Miryam Rodriguez Hernandez, "Denocen a René Huerta de la CROISZ; Sospechan que se vendió," *Al Color Politico*, Apr. 24, 2007, https://www.alcalorpolitico.com/informacion/deconocen-a-ren-huerta-de-la-croisz-sospechan-que-se-vendi--10268.html; Petrich, "Dictamen de ginecóloga señala agresión sexual en contra de Ernestina Ascensión"; Elena Gallegos and Claudia Herrera, "Mexico asumirá liderazgo, sin importar lo que diga EU," *La Jornada*, Mar. 13, 2007, https://www.jornada.com.mx/2007/03/13/index.php?article=008e1pol&section=politica.

30. Inés Ascensio Family, "No Vendimos a Nuestra Madre; Responden Hijos de Ernestina," ed. Juan Santos Carrera, *Orizaba en Red*, Apr. 26, 2007.

31. Author interview with Norma Trujillo, assisted by translator, Apr. 5, 2024, Mexico City.

32. Laura Castro Medina, "Operativo de aislamiento a familia de Ernestina Ascencio," *Proceso*, May 15, 2007, archived by UNAM, https://catedraunescodh

.unam.mx/catedra/mujeres/menu_superior/Feminicidio/4_Noticias/Mayo 2007/15_Mayo/01.pdf; Elizabeth C. Velasco, "La familia Inés Ascensión calla sobre caso Ernestina," *La Jornada*, May 9, 2007; Andrés Timoteo Morales, "Manto de silencio al cumplirse un año de la muerte de Ernestina Ascensión," *La Jornada*, Feb. 24, 2008.

33. Morales, "Dan carpetazo al caso Ascensión"; Blanche Petrich, "Tras 18 años, hija de Ernestina Ascensión pudo dar testimonio," *Política*, Jan. 31, 2025, https://www.jornada.com.mx/2025/01/31/politica/007n1pol.

34. Comisión Nacional de los Derechos Humanos, *Informe sobre la Recomendación 34/2007: Memoria, Verdad, Justicia y Reparación* (CNDH, 2021), https://www.cndh.org.mx/sites/default/files/documentos/2021-11/Informe_Ernestina_Ascencio_Recomendacion_342007_0.pdf.

35. Author interview with Lucia Melgar, Apr. 5, 2024, Mexico City.

36. In July 2007, federal deputy Valentina Valia Batres Guadarrama, a member of the Parliamentary Group of the Party of the Democratic Revolution, introduced a decree to reform the constitution of Mexico in response to the gang rape and assassination of Ernestina Ascencio Rosario and the 2006 attack on women in Coahuila by soldiers, and the 2007 case of the military attacking four teenagers from Michoacán. See Valentina Valia Batres Guadarrama, *Iniciativa con proyecto de decreto por el que se reforman los artículos 13 de la Constitución Política de los Estados Unidos Mexicanos, y 37, 57 y 435 del Código de Justicia Militar, en relación con la responsabilidad exclusiva de la autoridad civil en los delitos cometidos por militares contra civiles* (Sistema de Información Legislativa, Secretaría de Gobernación, July 4, 2007), sil.gobernacion.gob.mx; Comisión Nacional de los Derechos Humanos (CNDH), Dirección General de Comunicación, "Posicionamiento de la CNDH en el Caso de Ernestina Ascencio Rosario," comunicado de prensa DGC/061/2021, https://www.cndh.org.mx/sites/default/files/documentos/2021-03/COM_2021_061.pdf (CNDH, Mar. 12, 2021).

37. Comisión Intramericana de Derechos Humanos (CIDH), Case No 13.425, Ernestina Ascensio Rosario y Julia Marcela Suárez Cabrera v. México (June 11, 2023), https://www.oas.org/es/cidh/decisiones/corte/2023/mx_13.425_nderes.pdf.

38. Lawyers for Justice and Human Rights A. C., Center for Municipal Services Heriberto Jara, A.C. (CESEM), Kalli Luz Marina A. C., National Coordinator of Indigenous Women (CONAMI), and Robert F. Kennedy Human Rights. 2023. *Ernestina Ascencio Rosario and Another v. Mexico*, brief of requests, arguments and evidence, Inter-American Court of Human Rights.

39. Unidad Fiscal Especializada en Violencia contra las Mujeres (UFEM), *Resumen oficial: Caso Ascencio Rosario y Otros vs. México, Sentencia de 30 de septiembre de 2025* (Ministerio Público Fiscal de la Nación, Dec. 2025), https://www.mpf.gob.ar/ufem/files/2025/12/resumen_567_esp.pdf; Robert & Ethel Kennedy Human Rights Center, "Ascencio Rosario et al. v. Mexico: Indigenous Woman Victim of Sexual Violence, Tortured by the Mexican Army," https://kennedyhumanrights.org/litigation/indigenous-women-victims-of-sexual-violence-tortured-by-mexican-army/; International Institute on Race, Equality and Human Rights, "Case of Ernestina Ascencio Rosario:

Compliance with the Sentence of the Inter-American Court of Human Rights," Feb. 25, 2026, https://raceandequality.org/resources/case-ernestina-ascencio-rosario-compliance-sentence-inter-american-court-human-rights/.

40. Francisco-José Quintana, "The (Latin) American Dream? Human Rights and the Construction of Inter-American Regional Organisation (1945–1948)," *Journal of the History of International Law* 25, no. 4 (2024): 560–91; Justina Uriburu, "Organizing Peace in the Americas: Collective Security versus International Adjudication," *Journal of the History of International Law* 25, no. 4 (2024): 592–618.

41. Álvaro Paúl, *Los trabajos preparatorios de la Declaración Americana de los Derechos y Deberes del Hombre y el origen remoto de la Corte Interamericana* (Instituto de Investigaciones Jurídicas, UNAM, 2017); Nicolás M. Perrone, "Locating the 1948 Economic Agreement of Bogotá: The Rise and Fall of Latin America's International Economic Law Project," *Journal of the History of International Law* 25, no. 4 (Apr. 2024): 529–59, https://doi.org/10.1163/15718050-bja10099; Bogdan Ghidirmic, "The American Declaration of the Rights and Duties of Man: An Underrated Gem of International Human Rights Law," *Journal of Law and Public Administration* 4, no. 7 (2018): 50–60.

42. Lizbeth Diaz, "Mexican Armed Forces Knew About Attack on 43 Students, Report Says," Reuters, Mar. 28, 2022, https://www.reuters.com/world/americas/mexican-armed-forces-knew-about-attack-43-students-report-says-2022-03-28/; Tommaso Gravante, "Forced Disappearance as a Collective Cultural Trauma in the Ayotzinapa Movement," *Latin American Perspectives* 47 (2020): 87–102.

43. C. Matthew Snipp, "What Does Data Sovereignty Imply: What Does it Look Like?" in *Indigenous Data Sovereignty: Toward an Agenda*, ed. Tahu Kukutai and John Taylor (Australian University Press, 2016), 39–56. This chapter does not address deportation and detention as Ernestina never left her Nahua community, but Shannon Speed addresses deportation and detention in *Incarcerated Stories: Indigenous Women Migrants and Violence in the Settler-Capitalist State* (University of North Carolina Press, 2019); "Mexico's Constitution, Indigenous Rights and the Future," *IACL-AIDC Blog*, Oct. 7, 2021, https://blog-iacl-aidc.org/2021-posts/2021/10/7/mexicos-constitution-indigenous-rights-and-the-future-l9894; Katherine Marino, *Feminism for the Americas: The Making of an International Human Rights Movement* (University of North Carolina Press, 2019).

44. James Baldwin, *Nobody Knows My Name* (Dial Press, 1961), 62.

45. Rachel Sieder, ed., *Demanding Justice and Security: Indigenous Women and Legal Pluralities in Latin America* (Rutgers University Press, 2017). On Indigenous communities other than Nahua, such as Zapotec, see Anya Royce, *Becoming an Ancestor: The Isthmus Zapotec Way of Death* (SUNY, 2011). On Zapatistas, see Subcomandante Marcos, *Our Word Is Our Weapon: Selected Writings* (Anarchist Library, 2002); Beth E. Jörgensen, "Making History: Subcomandante Marcos in the Mexican Chronicle," *South Central Review* 21 (2004): 85–106; Bill Weinberg. *Homage to Chiapas: The New Indigenous Struggles in Mexico* (Verso, 2002); Tom Hayden,

The Zapatista Reader (Hachette Book Group, 2002); Hilary Klein, *Compañeras: Zapatista Women's Stories* (Seven Stories Press, 2015); Gloria Muñoz Ramírez, *The Fire and the Word: A History of the Zapatista Movement* (City Lights, 2008); Bob Clifford, *The Marketing of Rebellion: Insurgents, Media, and International Activism* (Cambridge University Press, 2010); Dawn Paley, *Drug War Capitalism* (AK Press, 2014); Rachel Dolan, "A Translation Crisis at the Border," *New Yorker*, Jan. 6, 2020, https://www.newyorker.com/magazine/2020
/01/06/a-translation-crisis-at-the-border.

46. Emil Keme, "For Abiayala to Live, the Americas Must Die: Toward a Transhemispheric Indigeneity," *Native American and Indigenous Studies* 5, no. 1 (2018): 43, 46; Victoria Bomberry, "The Struggle for Indigenous Autonomy in Twentieth-First-Century Bolivia," in *Comparative Indigeneities of the Americas: Toward a Hemispheric Approach*, ed. Bianet Castellanos, Lourdes Gutierrez, and Arturo Aldama (University of Arizona Press, 2012), 213.

47. Marcela Lagarde, "Preface: Feminist Keys for Understanding Feminicide: Theoretical, Political, and Legal Construction," in *Terrorizing Women: Feminicide in the Américas*, ed. Rosa-Linda Fregoso and Cynthia Bejarano (Duke University Press, 2010), xxi, xxiii, xv; Marcela Lagarde, "Aculturación feminista," in *Género en el Estado: Estado del género*, ed. Eliana Largo, Ediciones de las Mujeres, no. 27 (Isis Intrenacional, 1998), 140, 152, 153.

48. Rita Segato, *Las estructuras elementales de la violencia: Ensayos sobre género entre la antropología, el psicoanálisis y los derechos humanos* (Prometeo/Universidad Nacional de Quilmes, 2003); Rita Segato, *La Guerra Contra las Mujeres* (Tinta Limón/Traficantes de sueños, 2017), 35; Rita Segato, "Territory, Sovereignty, and Crimes of the Second State: The Writing on the Body of Murdered Women," in Fregoso and Bejarano, *Terrorizing Women.*

49. Marcela Lagarde, "Presentación a la edición en espanol," in *Feminicidio: Una Perspectiva Global*, ed. Diana E. H. Russell and Roberta A. Harmes (UNAM-CEICH, 2006), 12; Rossana Reguillo Cruz, "La turbulencia en el paisaje: de jóvenes, necropolítica y 43 esperanzas," in *Juvenicidio: Ayotzinapa y las vidas precarias en América Latina y España* (NED Ediciones/ITESO/El Colef, 2015), 63, 65, 68, 69; Michel Foucault, "The Archaeology of Knowledge," *Social Science Information* 9, no. 1 (1970): 175–85; Achille Mbembe, *Necropolítica seguido de sobre el gobierno privado indirecto*, trans. and ed. Elisabeth Falomir Archambault (Melusina, 2011); Susan Sontag, *Sobre la Fotografía* (Alfaguara, 2006); José Manual Valenzuela Arce, *Sed de mal: feminicidio, jóvenes, y exclusión social* (El Colegio de la Frontera Norte, 2012); Rossana Reguillo Cruz, *Culturas Juveniles: Formas Políticas del Desencanto* (Siglo XXI, 2012); Rossana Reguillo Cruz, *Paisajes Insurrectos: Jóvenes, Redes y Revueltas en el Otoño Civilizatorio* (NED Ediciones, 2017); Rossana Reguillo Cruz, *Necromáquina: Cuando Morir no es Suficiente* (NED Ediciones, 2021).

50. *Killer's Paradise*, dir. Giselle Portenier (National Film Board of Canada; BBC co-production, 2007), documentary.

51. Anthropologist Irma Alicia Velásquez Nimatuj, the first Maya-K'iche' woman to earn a doctorate in social anthropology, was one of the expert witnesses in the Sepur Zarco trial. She interviewed the women victims extensively

and presented her findings to the court. See Nimatuj, *Pueblos Indígenas, Estado y Lucha po Tierra en Guatemala* (AVANSCO, 2008) and *La Pequeña Burguesía Indígena Comercial de Guatemala Desigualdades de Clase, Raza y Género* (AVANCSO_SERJUS, 2002). Rita Segato also appeared as an expert witness, largely because of her books *Las Nuevas Formas de la Guerra y el Cuerpo de las Mujeres* (Pez en el Árbol, 2014) and *La Escritura en el Cuerpo de las Mujeres Asesinadas en Ciudad Juárez* (Tinta Limón, 2013). Segato was writing *La Guerra Contra las Mujeres* (Tinta Limón/Traficantes de sueños, 2017) when she testified in 2016.

52. Irina Popescu documents the use of social media and performance art within Ni una Menos in Argentina in "Memorialization and Esraches: Ni una Menos and the Documentation of Feminicidio in Argentina," *Latin Americanist* 65, no. 3 (2021): 367–92.

53. Sarah Cline, "Native Peoples of Colonial Central Mexico," in *The Cambridge History of the Native Peoples of the Americas, Volume II: Mesoamerica*, part 2, ed. Richard E. W. Adams and Murdo J. MacLeod (Cambridge University Press, 2000), 216–17.

54. Javier LaFuente and Lucía Abellán, "España rechaza con firmeza la exigencia de México de pedir perdón po los abusos de la Conquista," *El País*, Mar. 26, 2019, https://elpais.com/internacional/2019/03/25/mexico/1553539019_249884.html.

CHAPTER 5: SAVANNA

1. Many thanks to Norberta Greywind for reading this chapter and correcting the record: Savanna moved in with her parents when she moved to Fargo, and she was looking into enrolling at Rasmussen College. Personal correspondence with Norberta Greywind, Mar. 19, 2022.

2. Margaret later refused to return the deposit to the family.

3. Blake Gumprecht, "'Something's Wrong': Disappearance of Pregnant Fargo Woman Still a Mystery," *InForum*, Aug. 23, 2017, https://www.inforum.com/newsmd/somethings-wrong-disappearance-of-pregnant-fargo-woman-still-a-mystery.

4. *Me Hereafter*, season 1, ep. 1, "First She Stole My Baby," Hulu, Feb. 29, 2024.

5. Wendy Reuer, "Family Seeks Help in Search for Pregnant Fargo Woman," *InForum*, Aug. 20, 2017, https://www.inforum.com/news/family-seeks-help-in-search-for-pregnant-fargo-woman. In response to my 2024 request for the 911 calls from Savanna's parent's apartment building that weekend, Cass County State Attorney's Office fulfilled the request in 2026. What they provided were not the calls I sought. Based on my extensive requests for records from all North Dakota agencies, no agency saved the 911 calls from the Greywind apartment building, including those from apartment 5 that weekend. Personal correspondence with Jean Syverson at City of Fargo and with Jill Shafer, Kimberlee Hegvik, and Kara Olson at Cass County.

6. David Olson, "Family Urges Prayers, More Police Resources in Search for Missing Pregnant Fargo Woman," *InForum*, Aug. 23, 2017, https://www.inforum.com/newsmd/family-urges-prayers-more-police-resources-in-search

-for-missing-pregnant-fargo-woman; Helmut Schmidt, "'We Are Treating It as a Criminal Investigation,' Fargo Police Say About Missing Pregnant Woman," *InForum*, Aug. 23, 2017, https://www.inforum.com/newsmd/we-are-treating-it-as-a-criminal-investigation-fargo-police-say-about-missing-pregnant-woman.

7. Much of the narrative about Saturday comes from Mona Gable, *Searching for Savanna: The Murder of One Native American Woman and the Violence Against the Many* (Simon & Schuster, 2023), chaps. 1–2.

8. Forum Staff reports, "Fargo Police Chasing Leads as Searches for Pregnant Woman Unsuccessful," *InForum*, Aug. 24, 2017, https://www.inforum.com/newsmd/fargo-police-chasing-leads-as-searches-for-pregnant-woman-unsuccessful; Mike McFeely, "Hoping for the Best, Fearing the Worst in Case of Missing Woman," *InForum*, Aug. 24, 2017, https://www.inforum.com/newsmd/mcfeely-hoping-for-the-best-fearing-the-worst-in-case-of-missing-woman; Mona Gable, "Searching for Savanna," *Pacific Standard*, July 30, 2019, https://psmag.com/social-justice/searching-for-indigenous-woman-savanna-lafontaine-greywind/.

9. City of Fargo Police Records, audio recording of Brooke Crews, Aug. 20, 2017.

10. *Lies, Crimes & Video*, season 2, ep. 4, "Nightmare in Fargo," HLN, Feb. 28, 2021; City of Fargo Police Records, audio recordings of police officers, Aug. 20, 2017.

11. City of Fargo Police Records, audio recording of Brooke Crews, Aug. 20, 2017.

12. City of Fargo Police Records, audio recording of Brooke Crews, Aug. 20, 2017.

13. Christopher S. Hagen, "Savanna's 24 Steps," *High Plains Reader*, Aug. 28, 2017, https://hpr1.com/index.php/feature/news/savannas-16-steps; *Me Hereafter*, "First She Stole My Baby"; City of Fargo Police Records, video of William Hoehn, Aug. 24, 2017.

14. Blake Gumprecht, "What Happened in Apartment 5?" *Dickinson Press*, Sept. 18, 2017, https://www.thedickinsonpress.com/news/what-happened-in-apartment-5-everything-we-know-and-dont-know-about-savanna-lafontaine-greywinds-death.

15. Fargo Police, Facebook post, Aug. 24, 2017, https://www.facebook.com/fargopolicedepartment/videos/message-from-chief-david-todd-with-an-update-to-the-savanna-greywind-investigati/10155586713228334/; Gumprecht, "What Happened in Apartment 5?"

16. City of Fargo Police Records, video of Ashton Matheny, Aug. 22, 2017.

17. City of Fargo Police Records, video of Brooke Crews, Dec. 7, 2017.

18. *Me Hereafter*, "First She Stole My Baby."

19. City of Fargo Police Records, video of William Hoehn, Aug. 23, 2017; video of Brooke Crews, Aug. 24, 2017; video of William Hoehn, Aug. 24, 2017.

20. City of Fargo Police Records, Walmart receipt, Walmart parking lot footage, Walmart cash register footage, Aug. 22, 2017.

21. City of Fargo Police Records, video of Ashton Matheny, Aug. 23, 2017.

22. City of Fargo Police Records, video of Ashton Matheny, Aug. 23, 2017.

23. City of Fargo Police Records, search warrant for apartment #5, storage units, the Jeep Grand Cherokee, and the Oldsmobile 98, signed at 10:37 a.m., Aug. 24, 2017.

24. City of Fargo Police Records, search warrant for apartment #5, storage units, the Jeep Grand Cherokee, and the Oldsmobile 98, signed at 10:37 a.m., Aug. 24, 2017.

25. Blake Gumprecht, unpublished photo of Norberta LaFontaine-Greywind and Joe Greywind speaking with Detective Jason Nelson, https://www.flickr.com/photos/gumprecht/28058661559.

26. Gumprecht, photo of Greywinds speaking with Detective Jason Nelson; Blake Gumprecht, "'She's Mine': DNA Results Confirm the Parents of the Baby Found in Suspects' Apartment," *WRAL News*, Sept. 12, 2017, https://www.wral.com/archive/16943402/.

27. City of Fargo Police Records, video of William Hoehn, Aug. 24, 2017.

28. Cass County Court Records, video of Brooke Crews, Aug. 24, 2017.

29. Cass County Court Records, video of Brooke Crews, Aug. 24, 2017.

30. Cass County Court Records, video of Brooke Crews, Aug. 24, 2017.

31. Christopher S. Hagen, "Search for Savanna Continues," *High Plains Reader*, Aug. 25, 2017, https://hpr1.com/index.php/feature/news/search-for-savanna-continues; Christopher S. Hagen, "Savanna's 24 Steps," *High Plains Reader*, Aug. 28, 2017, https://hpr1.com/index.php/feature/news/savannas-16-steps.

32. C. S. Hagen, "Savanna's 24 Steps," *High Plains Reader*, Aug. 28, 2017, https://hpr1.com/index.php/feature/news/savannas-16-steps.

33. C. S. Hagen, "Search for Savanna Continues," *High Plains Reader*, Aug. 25, 2017, https://hpr1.com/index.php/feature/news/search-for-savanna-continues/.

34. *State of North Dakota v. William Henry Hoehn*, No. 20180400, 2019 ND 222 (filed Aug. 22, 2019, by Clerk of the North Dakota Supreme Court).

35. Blake Gumprecht, "Reporter's Discovery of Murder Suspect's Apparent Belongings in Dumpster Prompts Police Response," *InForum*, Dec. 7, 2017; "Our Opinion: *InForum*'s History of Shoddy Journalism Repeats Itself," *High Plains Reader*, Dec. 8, 2017, https://hpr1.com/index.php/opinion/editorial/our-opinion-the-forums-history-of-shoddy-journalism-repeats-itself; C. S. Hagen, "In the Mind of Brooke Lynn Crews," *High Plains Reader*, Dec. 7, 2017, https://hpr1.com/index.php/feature/news/in-the-mind-of-brooke-lynn-crews.

36. City of Fargo Police Records, video of Brooke Crews, Dec. 7, 2017.

37. City of Fargo Police Records, Walmart receipt, Aug. 22, 2017.

38. *Forum* Staff Reports, "North Dakota Woman Charged in Adoption Scam with Purported Link to Case of Slain Pregnant Fargo Mother," *Dickinson Press*, Apr. 9, 2018, https://www.thedickinsonpress.com/news/north-dakota-woman-charged-with-adoption-scam; Mike McFeely, "Anatomy of Alleged Adoption Scam Is Tale of Deep Deception, Lies," *InForum*, Apr. 12, 2018, https://www.inforum.com/opinion/mcfeely-anatomy-of-alleged-adoption-scam-is-tale-of-deep-deception-lies.

39. Audra Simpson, "The State Is a Man: Theresa Spence, Loretta Saunders, and the Gender of Settler Sovereignty," *Theory and Event* 19, no. 4 (2016), https://muse.jhu.edu/article/633280.

40. "Trial Begins for Greywind's Second Alleged Murderer," *High Plains Reader*, Sept. 18, 2018, https://hpr1.com/index.php/feature/news/trial-begins-forgreywinds-second-alleged-murderer; Raju Chaduvula and Dave Olson, "Jury Acquits William Hoehn of Murder Conspiracy in Savanna LaFontaine-Greywind's Killing," *InForum*, Sept. 28, 2018, https://www.inforum.com/newsmd/jury-acquits-william-hoehn-of-murder-conspiracy-in-savanna-lafontaine-greywinds-killing.

41. Editorial, "Part 1 of 2: Lt. Jason Nelson Discusses the Timeline Leading up to Finding Savanna Greywind's Body," *Valley News Live*, Aug. 30, 2017, https://www.valleynewslive.com/content/misc/Part-1-of-2-Lt-Jason-Nelson-discusses-the-timeline-leading-up-to-finding-Savanna-Greywinds-body-442297803.html.

42. Raju Chaduvula, "Judge Reluctantly Cuts Sentence for Fargo Man Convicted of Kidnapping Savanna's Baby," *InForum*, Oct. 7, 2019, https://www.inforum.com/news/local/judge-reluctantly-cuts-sentence-for-fargo-man-convicted-of-kidnapping-savannas-baby.

43. Rayna Green, "The Pocahontas Perplex: The Image of Indian Women in American Culture," *Massachusetts Review* 16 (1975): 698–714.

44. Robert M. Alison, "Dakotas in Canada Before 1850," *Chitty's Law Journal and Family Law Review* 48, no. 2 (2000): 18–20.

45. Taylor Spence, "Naming Violence in United States Colonialism," *Journal of Social History* 53, no. 1 (2019): 157–93.

46. Gwen Westerman, *Mni Sota Makoce: The Land of the Dakota* (Minnesota Historical Society Press, 2012); Sarah Deer, *The Beginning and End of Rape: Confronting Sexual Violence in Native America* (University of Minnesota Press, 2015), 33.

47. North Dakota Department of Public Instruction, *The History and Culture of the Turtle Mountain Band of Chippewa* (NDDPI, 1997).

48. Beth H. Piatote, *Domestic Subjects: Gender, Citizenship, and Law in Native American Literature* (Yale University Press, 2013), 52.

49. Margaret D. Jacobs, *A Generation Removed: The Fostering and Adoption of Indigenous Children in the Postwar World* (University of Nebraska Press, 2014), chaps. 3–4.

50. Norberta referenced Hoehn's declaration in her victim impact statement on October 29, 2018. See Bailey Hurley, "William Hoehn Plans on Appealing Life Sentencing," *Valley News Live*, Oct. 29, 2018, https://www.valleynewslive.com/content/news/William-Hoehn-has-been-sentenced-to-life-in-prison--498915341.html.

51. Connie Walker, "Missing and Murdered: Finding Cleo," *CBC Radio*, Apr. 1, 2018, https://www.cbc.ca/radio/findingcleo.

52. Leah Litman and Matthew L. M. Fletcher, "The Necessity of the Indian Child Welfare Act," *The Atlantic*, Jan. 22, 2020, https://www.theatlantic.com/ideas/archive/2020/01/ffth-circuit-icwa/605167/.

53. "Native Adoption Scammer Guilty, Behind Bars," *High Plains Reader*, Jan. 28, 2019, https://hpr1.com/index.php/feature/news/native-adoption-scammer-guilty-behind-bars/.

54. Captain R. H. Pratt, "The Advantages of Mingling Indians with Whites," in *Proceedings of the National Conference of Charities and Correction at the Nineteenth Annual Session Held in Denver, Col., June 23–29, 1892*, ed. Isabel C. Barrows (Press of Geo. H. Ellis, 1892), 46.

55. Thomas Jefferson, *Notes on the State of Virginia*, ed. William Peden (1787; Chapel Hill: University of North Carolina Press, 1982); Robert Aquinas McNally, "Four More Heads for the Indian Trophy Room," *ICT News*, June 15, 2016, https://ictnews.org/archive/four-more-heads-for-the-indian-trophy-room/; Margaret M. Bruchac, "Colonizing the Indigenous Dead," *History of Anthropology Review*, February 19, 2021, https://histanthro.org/news/observations/colonizing-the-indigenous-dead/; Megan J. Highet, "Body Snatching & Grave Robbing: Bodies for Science," *History and Anthropology* 16, no. 4 (2005): 415–40; Kenn Harper, *Give Me My Father's Body: The Life of Minik, the New York Eskimo* (Profile Books, 1986), 145.

56. Samuel J. Redman, *Bone Rooms: From Scientific Racism to Human Prehistory in Museums* (Harvard University Press, 2016); David H. Thomas, *Skull Wars: Kennewick Man, Archaeology, and the Battle for Native American Identity* (Basic Books, 2000); Ronald P. Rohner, *The Ethnography of Franz Boas: Letters and Diaries of Franz Boas Written on the Northwest Coast from 1886–1931* (University of Chicago Press, 1969); Devon A. Mihesuah, "American Indians, Anthropologists, Pothunters, and Repatriation: Ethical, Religious, and Political Differences," *American Indian Culture and Research Journal*, 20, no. 2 (1996): 95–105; and James Riding In, "Without Ethics and Morality: A Historical Overview of Imperial Archaeology and American Indians," *Arizona State Law Journal* 24, no. 3 (1992): 11–34.

57. Loren Dean Boutin, *Cut Nose: Who Stands on a Cloud* (North Star Press, 2006); Judith Hartzell, *I Started All This: The Life of Dr. William Worrall Mayo* (Arvi Books, 2004); Charles W. Mayo, *Mayo: The Story of My Family and My Career* (Hodder and Stoughton, 1968); Helen Clapesattle, *The Doctors Mayo* (Mayo Foundation, 1960).

58. City of Fargo Police Records, video of William Hoehn, Aug. 24, 2017.

59. Keith R. Richotte Jr., *Claiming Turtle Mountain's Constitution: The History, Legacy, and Future of a Tribal Nation's Founding Documents* (University of North Carolina Press, 2017).

60. Gwen Ifill, "User Clip: Gwen Ifill Coins the Term 'Missing White Woman Syndrome,'" C-SPAN, Aug. 5, 2004, https://www.c-span.org/video/?c4666788/user-clip-gwen-ifill-coins-term-missing-white-woman-syndrome; Jennifer Nez Denetdale, "Loreal: The Ordinariness of Being," *Navajo Times*, Oct. 26, 2017, 2.

EPILOGUE

1. Interview with Hamilton Hall occupier, WKCR, May 2, 2024, 1 p.m. ET, https://x.com/WKCRFM/status/1786071886004191571.

INDEX